THE CORRUPTION OF
AMERICAN
POLITICS

OTHER BOOKS BY ELIZABETH DREW

Washington Journal: The Events of 1973–74
American Journal: The Events of 1976
Senator
Portrait of an Election: The 1980 Presidential Campaign
Politics and Money: The New Road to Corruption
Campaign Journal: The Political Events of 1983–1984
Election Journal: The Political Events of 1987–1988
On the Edge: The Clinton Presidency
*Showdown: The Struggle Between the Gingrich Congress and the
    Clinton Whitehouse*
Whatever It Takes: The Real Struggle for Political Power in America

THE CORRUPTION OF
AMERICAN
POLITICS

WHAT WENT WRONG AND WHY

Elizabeth Drew

A BIRCH LANE PRESS BOOK
Published by Carol Publishing Group

A Birch Lane Press Book
Published by Carol Publishing Group
Birch Lane Press is a registered trademark of Carol Communications, Inc.

Editorial, sales and distribution, rights and permissions inquiries should be
addressed to Carol Publishing Group, 120 Enterprise Avenue, Secaucus, N.J.
07094.

In Canada: Canadian Manda Group, One Atlantic Avenue, Suite 105,
Toronto, Ontario M6K 3E7

Carol Publishing Group books may be purchased in bulk at special discounts
for sales promotion, fund-raising, or educational purposes. Special editions
can be created to specifications. For details, contact: Special Sales
Department, Carol Publishing Group, 120 Enterprise Avenue, Secaucus, N.J.
07094.

Manufactured in the United States of America
10 9 8 7 6 5 4 3 2 1

Library of Congress Cataloging-in-Publication Data

Drew, Elizabeth.
    The corruption of American politics : what went wrong and why /
Elizabeth Drew.
        p.   cm.
    "Birch Lane Press book".
    ISBN 1–55972–520–6 (hard)
    1. Political corruption—United States. 2. Campaign funds—United
States. I. Title.
JK2249.D72 1999
364.1'3230973—dc21   99–28684
                                                                CIP

CONTENTS

AUTHOR TO READER

This is a book about the debasement of American politics over the past twenty-five years. It is about the decline in statesmanship and leadership, civility and quality, and the growth of partisanship. And it is about corruption: the expanding corruption of money in all its pervasive ways, some of them novel, and including the corruption of the Washington culture—and the inability of the system to reform itself.

The dramatic and strange impeachment proceedings of the Congress against President Clinton had their roots in those changes, in fact, seemed (but for the reckless behavior of the President that set the whole thing off) almost their natural outgrowth. The differences between the impeachment proceedings in 1974 and 1998–1999 reflected much of what had happened to our politics within that period.

Similarly, and inevitably, the public's attitude toward our political system underwent a profound transformation over that span of time.

IN 1974, Americans had found fresh confidence in their government. Richard Nixon, who had run a criminal conspiracy from the Oval Office and caused a constitutional crisis, was forced to leave office on the verge of being impeached by the House of Representatives. Nixon's departure caused a great many Americans to believe that "the system worked." (But since the end had actually come about because Nixon was caught on his taping system ordering an obstruction of justice, which led Republican Party elders to tell him to go, it was a closer call than people realized.)

Then, spurred by some of what were then seen as horrors in the collecting and spending of money and rewarding of contributors in the Nixon 1972 re-election campaign, the Congress in 1974 passed the first comprehensive campaign finance reform law, a surprisingly broad document that placed important new restrictions on the gathering and spending of money in federal elections.

That November, in reaction to Watergate, seventy-five new Democrats, known as the "Watergate Babies," were elected to the House of Representatives. Several were elected from longtime Republican districts. They had run on a reform platform, and they tended to be young and idealistic. They were intent on shaking up the musty, seniority-bound institution they had just entered.

Nixon's successor, Gerald Ford, was a bland, calming figure, just what the country needed at that moment.

Now, TWENTY-FIVE years later, public confidence in government and in those who govern us is dangerously low. The 1996 presidential election saw the lowest turnout since 1924. And despite great efforts by both political parties to turn out their allied groups in the 1998 congressional elections, overall turnout was only thirty-six percent, lower than that for any midterm elections since 1942.

A study by Andrew Kohut for the Pew Charitable Trusts, released in March 1998, in the midst of an economic boom, showed that only thirty-four percent of the public basically trusted the government. "Disillusionment with political leaders is essentially as important a factor in distrust of government as is criticism of the way government performs its duties," Kohut wrote.

I use the words "dangerously low" not out of any overblown hysteria but because such low trust during good economic times suggests that something serious has been at work on the public's attitude. Lack of trust creates the risk of susceptibility to demagoguery, or of abuses of the democratic process.

So, WHAT have I seen, from my up-close perch in Washington over that period, that justifies this negative public view? What, actually, was behind the decline in the way Washington works? How, exactly, did those changes come about?

THE ENORMOUS and ever-growing role of money in our political campaigns—with corruption now outpacing even that of the Nixon era—was a major factor. The abuses of the campaign finance system, as practiced by both parties in 1996, but to a greater extent by the Democrats—perhaps only because they controlled the presidency and therefore had more levers—destroyed what was left of this country's campaign finance laws. There were now effectively no limits on how much money could be raised and spent in a campaign, and the limits on how it could be raised were rendered meaningless. Powerful people had undermined the law in order to retain power, or to gain it. The hope of many people was that the finance scandals of the 1996 elections would provide a boost for new reforms, but in the end, no reforms were enacted.

More of the public wanted the system fixed than was commonly assumed. Opponents of reform of the laws kept asserting that the public wasn't interested, but that, as usual, depended on how the poll question was put. And there was concrete evidence that when the public's attention was focused on the question, it did react in favor of reform.

I WILL demonstrate how, in several respects, Washington, and our politics, have changed over the past twenty-five years: the alterations in the nature of our major institutions; the decline in the quality of the politicians themselves; the erosion of trust; and the effects of too much polling and too little leadership. It will be seen that seemingly disparate events formed a pattern.

I will also show how those changes played out in the much-misunderstood hearings on campaign finance headed by Senator Fred Thompson, Republican of Tennessee. What took place in the hearing room, but even more so behind the scenes, was a direct reflection of the changes in our political system in the period since Nixon was driven from office—with Thompson having played a key role then. What happened to Thompson was a metaphor for what had happened to Washington. As was the difficulty in getting reform of the campaign finance system.

So, how has our system of government changed over the past twenty-five years, and why has it done so?

I will also offer suggestions on what citizens can do to make that system better.

Elizabeth Drew
March 1999

THE CORRUPTION OF
AMERICAN
POLITICS

1

Setup

Dressed dapperly as usual, in a gray pin-stripe suit, a white shirt with French cuffs, and a maroon tie, Fred Thompson looked older, more sophisticated than when he first became famous as minority counsel to the Ervin committee hearings on Watergate in 1973. The then-unknown thirty-year-old Nashville attorney had grown up in a small, rural Tennessee town. The son of a used-car dealer, he had worked his way through college and law school. Sporting fashionable long sideburns, Thompson looked then more rough-hewn than he was. He had been selected by Howard Baker, the Tennessee senator and ranking Republican on the Ervin committee, over legal lions who considered themselves far better qualified for the job. But as the gruff but alert young attorney questioned witnesses, he established himself as no one to be fooled with.

On July 16, 1973, Thompson, in his deep, sonorous voice, asked Alexander Butterfield, who had been in charge of day-to-day operations of the Nixon White House, "Mr. Butterfield, are you aware of the installation of any listening devices in the Oval Office of the President?" The large crowd of people who had managed to obtain seats in the Senate Caucus Room fell silent.

Butterfield replied, "I was aware of listening devices, yes, sir." Thompson became a national hero. (Thompson knew the answer,

3

having been briefed by the committee staff member who had inter-
viewed Butterfield.) When the Ervin hearings ended, they were
considered a great success—and so was Thompson.

Now, twenty-four years later, on October 23, 1997, after twelve
weeks of hearings by his own Senate committee into another presidential election scandal—and of attacks from the Democrats on
his committee, and of delays and obfuscation by the White House,
and of sabotage from within his own party—Thompson had had
enough.

Quietly, reflectively, he said to the committee room something
that had been building within him. It wasn't the sort of thing that
senators say, at least in public.

Speaking slowly, Thompson, who had come to the Senate in
late 1994, said, "I haven't been here a long time. Maybe things have
changed....Maybe it is more partisan. Maybe it is the times that
we live in."

Thompson added, "You didn't hear Howard Baker spending all
of his time trying to dredge up something on Democrats."

Unintentionally, Thompson had put his finger on what had
happened to the country, and what had happened to him as he
tried to conduct his hearings.

WHEN HE accepted the invitation by Trent Lott, the Senate majority leader, to conduct the hearings on the Clinton financial scandals
in the 1996 elections—a position several senators had sought—
Thompson thought he was taking on a familiar role, a logical
extension of the part he had played in the Ervin hearings. But he
was stepping into a new, far more partisan, far more poisonous
state of politics than he had experienced then.

Lott was pleased with his selection. Thad Cochran, Lott's fellow
Mississippi senator, said, "Trent especially was very excited that
Thompson was eligible to be chairman of the Governmental Affairs
Committee and run the hearings. He thought Thompson would be
an excellent choice, because of his manner and because he would
bring back memories of Watergate. At first, Trent had what
appeared to be total confidence in the ability and judgment of Fred
Thompson to handle his job."

THOMPSON, who had sought the role of conducting the hearings,
was confident as well. The Ervin hearings had gone smoothly

enough. So, Thompson had noticed, had the Iran-Contra hearings of 1987, on the bizarre dealings in which the Reagan administration secretly sold arms to Iran in exchange for release of American hostages in Lebanon and diverted some of the profits from the sales to clandestinely aid the Nicaraguan Contras. Those hearings, jointly conducted by a Democratic chairman and a Republican vice chairman (an unusual arrangement), stopped short, by prior agreement of the chairs, of taking the issue to Reagan. They thought the country couldn't go through another impeachment.

THOMPSON, six-foot-five, with a baritone voice and a craggy, mobile face, had tremendous presence. Not conventionally handsome, he dominated a room with his height, his voice, his charisma. He was also, though this was little understood by people who didn't know him well, a very funny man—a quick wit, a searing mimic—and he had a big, belly-shaking laugh. He particularly enjoyed the company of people who made him laugh.

One day during the hearings, when he and John Glenn, the ranking Democrat, were going after each other with particular bitterness, Dick Durbin, Democrat of Illinois, uncharacteristically praised Thompson. Thompson shot back, "Now, don't ruin the spirit of the morning, Senator Durbin."

Thompson's origins showed through in the colloquialisms that popped out on occasion. At a press conference one day, Thompson said, "My daddy once said of an investigator, 'He couldn't find a blackbird in a bowl of milk.'"

After the Ervin hearings, Thompson played character roles in his fourteen-year movie career, and he made eighteen films; a couple of them, such as *The Hunt for Red October*, were famous. His acting range wasn't extensive; he was the heavy, or the good guy—a CIA director, an admiral, usually the one in command. The movie career intersected with a lucrative law practice, in which he was of counsel to a major Washington law firm, commuting between Washington and Nashville. He was mainly a trial lawyer and thought of himself that way. (He played one in his first movie, *Marie*, based on a case in Tennessee he had tried and won.) Fifty-six years old, divorced, and the father of three children (he had married quite young), Thompson squired beautiful women and had had a major romance with country singer Lorrie Morgan. When he pondered a presidential candidacy, he considered whether life as a bachelor President would be tolerable in this age of scrutiny. (In March of 1999, Thompson, who had made no real move to run for the 2000 presidential election, let it be known that he wouldn't do so.)

In 1994, in his first try, to fill out the remaining two years in Al Gore's Senate term, Thompson started out behind an incumbent Democratic congressman with Harvard credentials. He ran as a folksy man of the people, utilizing a gimmicky red pickup truck. Aided by the anti-incumbent wave in 1994, he whooshed past his opponent in the last two months of the election. In 1996, he won a full six-year term by another large margin. Thompson retained the lesson that he could start behind and still win. In 1994, shortly after he had been first elected to the Senate, Thompson was already considered such a political star that in December of that year then-Senate Majority Leader Bob Dole selected him to give the Republicans' official response to a speech by President Clinton on his economic program.

ON TUESDAY, March 11, 1997, the Senate Republicans gathered for their weekly lunch in Room S 207, the Mansfield Room, which the majority party uses, on the second floor of the Capitol. The Republican leaders sat at a long table beneath a portrait of George Washington, the other senators at round tables. The atmosphere was unusually tense. Three important senators—including Lott—had already become upset with Thompson for wanting to broaden the scope of the inquiry beyond just the activities of the Clinton campaign in 1996, for supporting campaign finance reform (Thompson had cosponsored a major campaign finance reform bill since 1995), and for telling the Democrats on the committee that he wanted to be "fair" and "bipartisan." Another Republican said, of Thompson's early dealings, before the hearings began, with the Democrats on his committee, "Fred showed an awful lot of patience, and Trent and others thought Fred had leaned over too far to try to accommodate the Democrats."

The other two Republican senators who were particularly down on Thompson were Mitch McConnell, of Kentucky, the Senate's leading opponent of campaign finance reform, a man who had great influence on—virtually amounting to control over—Lott on this subject; and Richard Santorum, a brash freshman from Pennsylvania, a strong ally of the religious right, who had a way of inserting himself into all sorts of policy matters before the Senate Republican leaders. A Republican senator said, "Mitch McConnell started telling Trent, You're going to create a monster here. Thompson is going to be beyond control and influence. He doesn't care about the Republican Party. He's not loyal; he's not a team player; he wants to be President."

Unlike the overwhelming majority of his own party, including its Senate leaders, Thompson believed that consideration of new reforms had to be a part of examining what had gone wrong. To McConnell, Thompson, by signing on as a cosponsor of a broad campaign finance reform bill, was threatening the majority's status by seeking to change the rules by which it had been elected.

As it happened, McConnell was chairman of the National Republican Senatorial Committee in 1997–98, a role he had long sought; since the committee raises and dispenses campaign funds, it gives whoever fills it substantial power over his colleagues. McConnell's goal was to maintain and preferably expand the Republican majority in the Senate. Lott said in February 1997 that unlimited campaign spending—which Republicans felt gave them the advantage—was "the American way."

But at the moment, Thompson's greatest sin in the eyes of these three Republican senators was that he agreed with the Senate Democrats that the hearings shouldn't cover just "illegal" acts—the Clinton campaign's apparent acceptance of contributions from foreign nationals—but also "improper" ones. In fact, some of the controversial activities in 1996 were arguably legal (taking advantage of a loophole) or on the margin. The expanded definition, backed by the Democrats, meant that the committee's inquiry wouldn't be limited simply to fund-raising by the Clinton campaign in 1996. Some Democratic strategists wanted to press the issue of the scope of the inquiry because they figured the Republicans would have a hard time explaining to the public why they wanted to restrict it.

Under the broader definition, the committee could explore not just the Clinton scandals but also the abundant evidence from the 1996 election of fundamental changes, and not for the better, in our election system. The most significant development was that both parties had made egregious and unprecedented use of funds known as "soft money."

Soft money is funds that, through a loophole, are outside the fund-raising laws for federal campaigns. Those laws prohibit unions and corporations from making direct contributions to such campaigns, and they limit the amount that individuals can give to federal candidates and to a political party. The limits for such "hard money"—so called because, unlike soft money, it comes under the limits of the law—are $1,000 per individual per election (a primary, the general election, and any runoff) and $5,000 per election by political action committees, or PACs, maintained by labor or business or other interest groups. Hard money goes directly to individual candidates and the political parties. Under the law, individuals' overall donations to a party are limited to $20,000 per year.

Through the soft money loophole, corporations and labor unions can make direct contributions to the political parties, and individuals can make unlimited contributions. Soft money could be given to the parties for the purpose of "party-building activities"— such as registration and get-out-the-vote drives. But the definition of such activities had been stretched over the years, and in 1996 it snapped. Though soft money can only go to the political parties, the parties have found ways to spend it to help individual candidates. The distinction between hard and soft money has become a fiction. Outside groups and the political parties themselves used soft money to pay for ads that they deemed "issue ads," by claiming falsely that the ads were for the purpose of discussing an issue and weren't for the purpose of electing or defeating a candidate.

"Issue ads," paid for mainly with soft money, are attractive to the parties and outside groups as campaign tools because the soft money can be raised in large amounts. Unions, corporations, wealthy donors, and the political parties could merrily evade the legal limits established in the 1974 campaign reform law.

"Issue ads" paid for with soft money had been utilized sporadically before 1996, but their unprecedented use in 1996 by the political parties and outside groups transformed our politics.

IN ANOTHER BIG breakthrough, of sorts, in 1996, in legally questionable acts, groups running the phony "issue ads" had actually collaborated with party committees and the candidates' campaigns in targeting races and running the ads.

"Issue ads" were a handy way of making indirect contributions, of circumventing the contirbution limits in the 1974 campaign reform law, and, just as important, the long-standing bans on direct contributions by corporations and unions. In numerous races in 1996, the outside ads drowned out the voices of the candidates themselves and determined the issues in the race.

An inquiry into "improper" acts, being urged by the Democrats, was dangerous to Republicans because it could examine activities in 1996 by the Republican campaign committees and their outside allies such as the Christian Coalition, the National Right to Life Committee, and the National Rifle Association. Democratic committees and allies, such as the AFL-CIO, would be subject to examination as well. In the Thompson committee's organizing meetings early in 1997, another influential Republican, Majority Whip Don Nickles, of Oklahoma, who acted as Lott's representative on the committee, had warned Thompson against allowing the Democrats to call in groups allied with the Republicans. Thompson was also being warned by Republicans not to be generous with the Democrats in their requests for subpoenas.

Lott, McConnell, and Santorum had taken it upon themselves to preempt the resolution authorizing the inquiry that came out of Thompson's committee, which they considered too broad, and to write their own resolution. Their resolution covered only "illegal" activities, and this was the one that was now before the Senate. The Democrats had threatened to filibuster unless the investigation was broadened. That morning, Lott put off further consideration of the resolution until the Republicans could talk the matter over at their weekly lunch.

Lott was taken by surprise at the lunch. More Republican senators than he had anticipated spoke for broadening the Thompson committee's mandate.

Arlen Specter, a moderate from Pennsylvania and a committee member, argued that the public would respond badly if the hearings didn't cover soft money. He and others also argued that if the resolution was limited to simply "illegal" matters, the President's people could maintain that they didn't have to produce documents on a given subject because no illegality was involved. This might rule out, he said, such subjects as the sleep-overs in the Lincoln bedroom for big contributors and the hundred-some White House coffees for donors.

Susan Collins, a freshman from Maine who had formerly served on the Senate staff of William Cohen, now the Defense Secretary, made her first statement as a senator at such a meeting. She told her Republican colleagues, "I can't vote against an amendment that adds 'improper.' I don't know how I could explain a vote like that. It would be politically and substantively a mistake." Collins was already suspect in the eyes of her more conservative colleagues: She was from the Northeast, a moderate, and had worked for the independent-minded and moderate Cohen.

John McCain, of Arizona, who was sponsoring a major campaign finance reform bill, told his fellow Republicans that it would be "very difficult for us to vote against [broadening the hearings] because the American people expect us to investigate not only illegal but also improper actions."

Dan Coats, a conservative from Indiana and respected in the Senate as an honest and decent man, spoke in even stronger terms against limiting the scope of the hearings. McCain had been in touch with him and Collins the day before. Lott had asked Thompson, in effect, not to lobby against him; Thompson agreed to that, but left no doubt as to what position he'd take.

The lunch went on unusually long and became unusually tense. At one point, Lott instructed staff members to leave the room.

Santorum spoke against broadening the scope, arguing that the Senate's responsibility was to investigate illegal matters only. Santorum suggested using as a precedent the resolution for the Watergate committee; he looked pleased with himself, thinking he had scored one against Thompson. Someone suggested that Thompson explain what was in that mandate, and Thompson replied that the Watergate resolution called for an investigation of "illegal, improper, or unethical activities" in the 1972 presidential election. Santorum was crushed: He had been trying to help Lott and he ended up strengthening Thompson's position.

Thompson also told his fellow Republican senators, "It's important for the American people that we have a broad charter, and that they think we're being evenhanded."

Two unexpected senators, Ted Stevens, of Alaska, and Pete Domenici, of New Mexico—both tough-minded and right-of-center—also spoke for a broader scope. That brought the group of Republican senators calling for widening the hearings to ten—enough, when combined with the united Democrats, for it to pass the Senate by a comfortable margin.

Lott, seeing that he was outnumbered, ended up cosponsoring

the amendment to expand the jurisdiction of the committee, which that afternoon passed the Senate unanimously.

When the vote was taken, Lott joined with the rest of the senators for a vote of 99–0. Afterward, Lott looked like a man who had been mugged—which, in a way, he had been.

As a part of the price for letting the hearings go forward at all, rather than conducting a filibuster, the Democrats scored one of their deadliest hits by forcing a cutoff date of December 31, 1997. Minority Leader Tom Daschle, of South Dakota, had insisted on this point, in the face of arguments from some Democrats that they would look like lackeys of the White House. Daschle finally told his colleagues, "I'll take the public hit if people are behind me."

The cutoff date would end the hearings before the 1998 election year and impose on the committee a finite period of time in which to gather material, depose possible witnesses, hold hearings, and, if necessary, compel the cooperation of those under investigation. The Democrats didn't want the hearings to spill over into the 1998 election year. The deadline was to have a significance not foreseen at the time.

LOTT, A PRICKLY man, had a sort of jumpiness about him. He had been an effective whip under Bob Dole, an energetic vote counter and rounder-up. Lott was upbeat (when he wasn't in a bad mood), peppy; he rallied his troops with lines like "We've got to all stick together"—a throwback perhaps to his days as cheerleader at "Ole Miss." He had come to the Senate from the House in 1989 and though he had been close to Newt Gingrich, who had become the House Speaker, there were now strains between the two men, based largely on the different pulls on them from within their institutions. But while Gingrich liked to think of himself as a man of ideas (even if they were sometimes inconsistent and shallow), Lott had no such pretensions. He was a mechanic; his bent was on making the place work. He was far more interested in process than substance. He lacked the polish and the patience to deal well with Republican senators who were of different viewpoints and style. He often had a glint in his eye that suggested that he thought he was very clever. And he took defeats personally.

Now Lott was in his ninth month as majority leader, having taken over from Dole in June 1996, and was still proving himself.

Lott was in a very bad mood when he lost out on the scope of the hearings. When asked by the press afterward if the Republican moderates had staged a coup against him, he snapped, "No, they did not."

Washington is full of quickly changing wisdom, and the wisdom in late 1996, after the Republicans had picked up two Senate seats, for a 56–44 ratio, was that Lott would be the king of Washington. By early March, Lott had already lost a battle on a Constitutional Amendment requiring a balanced budget, which he favored. So his loss over the scope of the campaign finance reform hearings led to a new wisdom that questioned his effectiveness.

Lott never forgave Thompson for beating him at this early point.

IN JULY 1995 two House committees were to hold joint hearings— a sign of how rewarding the Republicans thought the hearings would be—on the Clinton administration's horrendous blunder on April 19, 1993, in Waco, Texas. Eighty-six men, women, and children were killed when the building housing the Branch Davidians, headed by cult leader David Koresh, was accidentally set on fire during a raid conducted by the Bureau of Alcohol, Tobacco, and Firearms. The nation had watched in horror as flames engulfed the large compound. The President at first ducked responsibility, hid out. He was upstaged by Attorney General Janet Reno, who went from network to network that night taking responsibility and was praised as a hero, even though her judgment regarding the attack was to be questioned.

The two committee chairmen had every reason to feel that the hearings would embarrass the Clinton White House. Then, on the first day of the hearings, a fourteen-year-old named Kiri Jewel appeared. Her mother had been killed in the fire. Holding her father's hand, she told the rapt congressmen that Koresh had raped young women in the compound, including herself when she was ten years old.

Don Goldberg, a White House aide assigned to protect the Clinton administration during the Thompson hearings, told me later, "They couldn't restore Koresh." At the time of the Waco hearings, Goldberg was the chief Democratic staff member of the House Government Reform and Oversight Committee, and in the course of that and other threatening hearings for the Clinton White

House—the firing of the seven travel office employees, the mysterious accumulation of over four hundred FBI files, mainly on former Republican officials, in the White House office of a political hack—he had worked closely with the White House. The Clinton people were sufficiently impressed with his talents that he was hired in late 1996 specifically to handle difficult congressional hearings.

Goldberg, a lanky, bearded thirty-eight-year-old, candidly explained to me the White House strategy for adversarial hearings by the Republican Congress. "It's an obvious strategy," he said. "On the Hill, if you don't have much to go on, you decry the partisanship, and the print reporters will write in the first or second paragraph, and the TV stories will begin, 'In a hearing mired in partisanship,' and then they get to the subject of the hearing and you've won. That's Damage Control 101."

Goldberg further explained, "In a hearing if you're playing defense, the goal is not to get your message out, the goal is to keep the other side from getting their message out. Then you've won. The 'partisan bickering' is standard fare. If you get your message out, that's a bonus."

THUS, BY THE TIME the Thompson hearings got under way, the Clinton White House had changed the rules of the game on congressional hearings. It had perfected the art of wrecking potentially troublesome hearings—by offering as little information as possible, as slowly as possible, and by casting the hearings as "partisan." To the Clinton White House, there was no such thing as a legitimate hearing into their activities; it therefore set forth to delegitimize any inquiry it considered adversarial. Every hearing was a war zone. This approach hadn't been taken ever before in such a systematic way.

On top of that, Thompson was facing a decline, if not abandonment, of the media's interest in covering hearings, and a shortened attention span on the part of the public, which made it all the harder for the real story of the hearings to get through.

The many avowals of cooperation from the White House notwithstanding—"I think we have a vested interest in making sure the facts come out, that we continue to cooperate," said White House spokesman Michael McCurry on June 6, 1997—the White House had no intention of cooperating with the Thompson hearings.

JOHN PODESTA, then deputy chief of staff to the President and manager of the White House strategy for the Thompson hearings, and Goldberg urged the "partisan" strategy on the Thompson committee Democrats. A wiry man of forty-nine, with a keen political intuition and, unlike some of his colleagues, a sense of right and wrong, Podesta had taken charge after a worried emissary from Vice President Gore's office asked him to do so. The Gore people felt that the White House management of the campaign finance scandal needed to be more focused. Podesta's importance in the Clinton White House was ironic. He had left in 1995 largely because he had fallen into disfavor with Mrs. Clinton for having written a report on the travel office that attributed to her a role in the firings.*

Though some of the Democrats on the committee worried at first about appearing to be tools of the White House, most of them and their staff followed the "partisan" strategy: not only in the hearings themselves but in the hallways and in phone conversations as well. One couldn't get down the corridors outside the hearing room, in the Hart Senate Office Building, without being approached by one Democratic staff member or another, or a representative of the Democratic National Committee, or a White House aide, who said, "Isn't it awful how partisan these hearings are?" or variations thereof. The strategy was as obvious as it was successful.

The White House aides were particularly worried about John Glenn. Glenn was one of the nicest people in the Senate, but not the brightest; he had an equable temperament, a straightforward Ohio friendliness, and though a national hero for his participating in the first American space flight to orbit the earth, in February 1962, he had no airs.† But Glenn turned uncharacteristically partisan in the course of the hearings, and a lot of people wondered why. The answer began at the White House. His niceness worried the President's strategists. Glenn's initial instinct was, in fact, to be cooperative with Thompson and to keep his distance from the White House. The White House and its closest allies on the committee made sure that this didn't happen.

* Podesta was named chief of staff to President Clinton in a Rose Garden ceremony on October 20, 1998.
†Glenn was to become a hero once again when he rode back into space on a nine-day mission in October 1998.

A White House aide said, "The concern was that Thompson would start with charges against the Democrats, and Glenn would say, 'Thank you very much for these important hearings. We hope they'll be fair.' It was a joke among us." He added, "There was a lot of pressure on John Glenn to step up his partisanship in the first three months."

The White House counted on Minority Leader Tom Daschle, of South Dakota, to help. Daschle's mild manner, his prairie-preacher aspect, masked a tough, smart partisan; his fierce legislative tactics were in large part behind Bob Dole's decision in 1996 that staying in the Senate was hurting his presidential candidacy. Don Goldberg was in constant touch with Daschle's chief counsel, Glenn Ivey, a smart, smooth attorney who had been the chief strategist for the Democrats in the Senate hearings in the Clintons' unfortunate 1978 Whitewater land deal. Ivey became one of the major strategists for the Democrats throughout the hearings, and was the principal conduit between the Democratic leadership and the White House.

From the outset, two new Democratic senators, Robert Torricelli, of New Jersey, and Richard Durbin, of Illinois, were particularly forceful in pushing Glenn to be more partisan. Torricelli and Durbin had just come from the House of Representatives, where partisanship and rough tactics had been more prevalent than in the Senate. Glenn didn't appreciate their efforts, but then higher authority weighed in. The White House was working with Torricelli and Durbin, and also with Daschle, who in turn went to work on Glenn.

At an early meeting of the committee Democrats, Glenn set forth his own position that none of them should be in touch with the White House, that their approach should be bipartisan. Durbin and Torricelli objected. On one occasion, Torricelli and Durbin were so concerned that Glenn was being too deferential to Thompson that they went to Daschle and asked for help. According to one participant, they told Daschle, "We love John Glenn, but this isn't working." For some time after that, in meetings in Daschle's suite of offices in the Capitol, Daschle himself urged Glenn to be more partisan.

Carl Levin, a four-term senator from Michigan, also felt that Glenn should be tougher. Levin's top aide, Linda Gustitus, a veteran of many hearings, was also in close touch with Goldberg at the White House.

Glenn was also pushed to be more confrontational by two of his closest advisors: Leonard Weiss, his longtime aide, and Mark Mellman, his pollster. Weiss spoke frequently with Goldberg. The White House called on Mellman for help in getting Glenn to be more partisan. Mellman, a stocky man with a short, black beard and thick, dark hair, played an almost unnoticed role in shaping the Democrats' strategy. The White House aide said, "Mellman was responsible for the Democrats' overall message, 'partisanship,' as opposed to defending the White House. He was able to line them all up." Mellman also counseled Glenn to follow a strategy of saying that there had been wrongs on both sides and that therefore there should be campaign finance reform (which most Republicans were likely to oppose). Glenn followed that advice.

Torricelli also conferred with the President himself from time to time to keep him informed about what was going on in the committee and to listen to Clinton's complaint, which he made often and elsewhere as well, that he was being picked on unfairly. Clinton, whose capacity for self-pity seemed boundless, complained to Daschle (once in a postmidnight call) and to his own staff. A Clinton aide said to me, "He's quite rightly feeling that everybody does do it, and he got outspent by two hundred million."

Clinton, mixing two different points, maintained to his listeners that it was unfair for the media to conclude that there was a one-sided campaign finance problem when the Republicans actually raised more money than the Democrats (as they always did) in 1996. Torricelli told me in the course of the hearings, "He feels it's extraordinary that the media has come to the conclusion that there was a partisan campaign finance problem, especially when, after all, the Democrats lost the race for funds to the Republicans."

A White House aide bragged to me that at one point during the hearings, when Don Nickles attacked fund-raising coffees at the White House, a response was in Durbin's hands within five minutes of Nickles's charge. (When Nickles was the chairman of the Senate Republican campaign committee, he wrote a letter inviting people to then-Vice President Dan Quayle's home for a fund-raiser on September 23, 1990.)

A White House team, working under Podesta and the White House counsel's office, monitored the hearings from their offices, while Goldberg and others—depending on how big a day they expected—patrolled the situation on the Hill, sometimes in the committee room, sometimes in the corridors just outside it, and sometimes (though this was kept secret) from Vice President Gore's seldom-used office in the Dirksen Building.

Lanny Breuer, the White House special counsel, spoke with the committee's Democratic counsels every day. Sometimes the White House monitors got advance word of what the Republicans planned the next day from the press, who had been briefed by Michael Madigan, the chief majority counsel, and called the White House for a response. Or the White House would learn of reporters working on a story based on leaks from Capitol Hill. Podesta told me in an interview, "There was always a possibility to detonate an incoming story."

The White House team met every morning in Podesta's spacious office, on the main floor of the West Wing, a short walk from the Oval Office, to review what would happen that day, and how to react to it. They would discuss, Podesta told me, "Did we have a story to tell? Are there holes in their story? What's our story? Which committee members could we deal with?" Don Goldberg said, "All the decisions are message: What's our first spin?"

At first, the White House team leaned toward detonation through a "document dump"—dumping on several members of the press a bunch of documents on a story White House aides knew the committee Republicans were about to break, so as to reduce its impact. Then, finding that this maneuver created a big news story of its own, drawing attention to something they would rather not draw attention to, they moved to leaking a prior response to selected reporters.

Thus the White House itself, knowing what was coming in the press and on the Hill, put out the story of Roger Tamraz, a naturalized American and shady international financier and big donor who had received appointments with high-level officials over the objections of a member of the National Security Council staff. During a break in the hearings, Goldberg told me that the White House had been tipped off the night before by reporters that a certain matter would be raised in the hearings that day. He said, "We have more people working reporters today, to get the counterstory line out."

The young Turks on the committee, working with Daschle, managed to get Glenn's first choice as minority counsel as well as his own spokesman replaced by people with more partisan instincts, more edge. All of these goings-on were motivated by one controlling fear. As Durbin said to me, "It was clear from the outset that this wasn't just another investigation. It concerned the future of the Democratic Party." Durbin's concern was that if the party took too much of a beating in the hearings, contributors might turn away, or that the campaign finance rules would be changed to the Democrats' disadvantage.

By June, even before the hearings had begun, the effects of the pressures, on the chairman and the ranking Democrat, led to some very ugly scenes. After a meeting of the committee Democrats with Daschle, Glenn, at a press conference, threatened a boycott of the hearings by Democrats over the number of subpoenas the Republicans would allow them. The next day, at another press conference, Torricelli questioned whether Thompson had the "personal integrity" to handle the investigation. This was a bit much for Thompson, especially given that Torricelli had a somewhat unsavory reputation. (He had, among other things, held a fund-raiser in the home of a convicted felon.)

THUS, THOMPSON, caught between his own party leaders and the White House, was in a vise even before the hearings began.

2

———— ∎ ————

What's Happened to Washington?

As I look around this floor, I see as many
Daffy Ducks as I see James Madisons.
—Representative David Obey, in House debate,
August 6, 1998

The sharp-edged partisanship that confronted Fred Thompson from the outset of his hearings on the campaign finance scandals reflected one of the significant ways in which Washington had changed since 1974.

Perhaps the most important change is that the quality of the politicians in Washington has declined during the past twenty-five years, and that the rate of decline has accelerated. The country has paid a big price for that—in ways that are largely invisible to the citizens. In general, the newer politicians are less grounded on issues, and many have scant interest in governing. A growing number have had no experience in government, which in this anti-government era is supposed to be an advantage, but it leads many of them to be at sea—or simply destructive—when they reach Washington.

Representative Peter King, a Republican from New York, talking to me about the seventy-three (two short of the "Watergate Babies") Republican freshmen elected in 1994 when the Republicans retook the House after forty years, said, "The extent of their knowledge was listening to Newt's GOPAC [Gingrich's PAC to develop and support Republicans for Congress] tapes and to Rush Limbaugh. Not being part of the political system, they really didn't hear the other side. They felt they were totally right and the other side was totally wrong."

THE CLASS OF 1994, which came in under Gingrich's guidance—the takeover was due more to him than anyone else—contained a large proportion of inexperienced ideologues. Nearly a third of the Republican freshmen had no political background at all. Their overreaching in the famed Hundred Days, passing radical legislation and indulging their ideological impulses, ultimately did them in as a force. In the end, they didn't accomplish a great deal, both because of the more moderate Republican Senate, under Majority Leader Bob Dole, and because in several instances President Clinton outfoxed them. (As of the two elections since 1994, twenty-three of the original seventy-three members of the class of 1994 no longer held congressional office: fourteen were defeated, five lost bids for other offices, one died, two retired, and one went to the Senate.)

A FAIR AMOUNT of the cultural change in the Congress in recent years can be attributed to Newt Gingrich. When Gingrich was a backbencher, he thought nothing of taking on, very combatively, not only the opposition's leaders, but his own as well. Gingrich changed the way Members of Congress thought about their role. During the speakership of Massachusetts Democrat Tip O'Neill, Gingrich led a pack of fellow-thinkers in giving one-minute speeches, which would appear on C-SPAN, against government itself. They worked themselves into a frenzy attacking the Congress. It's no surprise, then, that graduates of that school, or disciples of it elected later, have had little respect for the institution itself or for making it work.

There has been a lot of talk of how much those of the class of 1994 who remain have mellowed. But there were occasions when the '94 class made it difficult for even Gingrich to compromise.

Several of its members were part of the failed coup against him in the summer of 1997, and played a role in his dethronement after the 1998 elections. The issue was that Gingrich seemed too eager to compromise with the Democrats on such matters as the budget and taxes.

The same objections were raised about the result of Gingrich's negotiations on the 1998 budget. The ideologues thought Gingrich had yielded too much, but he did so to avoid another government shutdown, which in 1995 Gingrich had thought a great idea, but which had redounded to the Republicans' misfortune. The negotiations on a $500 billion budget, which was carved up by only three people—Lott, Gingrich, and then-White House chief of staff Erskine Bowles—at the very end of the session, were so frenzied that there was no way to make considered decisions that affected, in toto, virtually all Americans. It represented a total collapse of the budget process, adopted into law, as it happens, also in 1974. Referring to this debacle, Daniel Patrick Moynihan, Democratic senator from New York, observed in October 1998, "There has been a breakdown of all our legislative procedures." (In November 1998, Moynihan, seventy-one, who had the most reflective mind in the Senate, announced that he wouldn't seek a fifth term; one of his reasons was the heightened meanness of our politics.)

Nick Calio, a Republican lobbyist, says that the class of '94 has mellowed "somewhat," but "it needs to go further." He added, "By and large the class of ninety-four needs to have a more practical understanding of how far its leadership can go within the confines of a constitutional system. And directly related to that, the class of 'ninety-four needs to understand what constitutes a victory in legislative and principled terms. There's a point of view that if you just stake out your position and say it loud enough and long enough things will come your way."

IN RECENT years, the overriding concern of an ever-increasing proportion of Members of Congress has been advancing their careers. One political consultant says, "We've always had lunkheads, and we had exotica—but they were talented. They used to have ideas. Now you have a whole set of politicians whose guiding idea is 'Where's my pollster?'" He added, "In the old days, to run for office you had to have some convictions, weather some storms, get to know people. Today we have 'hyper democracy' based on polling and PAC money. If you can get the money, it propels you into the House, and then, whether you've achieved anything in the House, whether or not you have anything to recommend you, you go to the Senate. It's the next step." Then, of course, some of them want to run for president.

A midseniority senator, complaining about the decline in the quality of his colleagues, told me, "One senator has said, 'I sometimes can't get out of bed in the morning and deal with all these graniteheads.'"

A former Democratic Senate aide agreed that careerism was taking the Congress downward. (Like many others, this person became a lawyer-lobbyist after leaving Capitol Hill, and he declined to speak on the record about people on whose goodwill he was dependent for his livelihood.) He said, "I have the impression that everyone in government is now polishing their credentials for the next job. When I was there [until the late seventies] we had nineteen or twenty senators on our side who felt that the Senate was the ultimate career role. And they also had great respect for the institution as a whole. That provided a baseline of conduct."

Some people within the institution attribute the decline of quality of senators in part to the increasing rate by which they come from the House. A middle-aged Democrat who had served more than two Senate terms said to me, with exasperation, "There are too many former House members around here."

The former House members who have entered the Senate in recent years are more aggressive, more partisan, less interested in issues, and more tactical, than the average senator used to be. This same phenomenon has affected the style of the Senate leadership—Trent Lott, the majority leader, and Tom Daschle, the minority leader, both of came from the House. Lott is all tactics and transactions. A Democratic senator describes Daschle as "a great tactician, but not necessarily a great strategist."

And then this senator made a larger point about Washington in these times. "We're reacting too much—to daily, weekly events. Part of it is that there's so much media now. People rattle around the D.C. room."

A Republican lobbyist said to me, "House members move more quickly to the Senate than historically they used to. They're brash enough to do this. Some of the people that have moved to the Senate in the past few years have been schooled in the polarization of the House. The effect is that they move to the point of confrontation more quickly."

But there has been an even larger change. Taken as a whole, the Members of Congress today are less rounded, less reflective than before. In part, this is by default, as other people who might be more thoughtful decide not to run, because of the amount of money they have to raise, the loss of privacy in the age of more intrusive reporting, and the quality of their lives if they do get there. Not only has the rate of retirements from Congress increased but it has become increasingly difficult for the parties to recruit able candidates to run for the House or Senate. A man here who has had significant political experience asked, "Are we facing, through what's happened to our campaign finance system and the quality of the candidates, the delegitimization of government?"

A HOUSE MEMBER who had come in as an idealist about two decades earlier said at lunch one day in 1998, "I wouldn't tell my son to go into politics. I had a notion that this was a worthy job, a public service. I still believe that, but people don't view it as a worthy endeavor. Politics has become particularly difficult and nasty.

"When people want to run for office, the first thing they're asked is, How much money can you raise? The candidate comes to Washington to talk to the leadership and the campaign committees. It's the first thing they're asked. If they talk to other officeholders from the area, it's the first thing they're asked.

"I still get encouraged that you can legislate, make policy changes. But I still feel discouraged, too. A large part of being in Congress is the never-ending chase for money for the next election."

TWO SENATORS who were elected in 1996, one an incumbent, the other a former House member, told me that the 1996 election had changed them.

Dick Durbin, the Democratic former House member, said, "I have been radicalized by this, after spending all my time raising millions of dollars to give to my television stations. As the British move toward our system, we should move closer to theirs. We should shorten campaigns, and give candidates free airtime. I wasn't there before, but I'm there now."

Durbin continued, spelling out the pain and problems of fundraising. "It was eighteen months of my life as a beggar. I'd get up every morning—it was like Camus's book about the myth of Sisyphus. We would push that rock up to the top of the mountain and it would roll down again. It's what I had to do every morning. I wasn't focusing on the issues. We made a point of having cheerful young women with the best personalities to sit next to me every day while I made the phone calls. When I got the rejections—and they were ninety percent—I'd tend to get depressed otherwise. I knew I had to do it—I'm not naive. I'm not wealthy. Every step of the way, I ask myself, 'Could I emerge with any dignity?'

"I had mixed feelings about my donors. Was I giving them the impression they would have more access to me, or that I was now on board for their agenda, whatever it happened to be? It was a moral dilemma all the time.

"I continue to vote my conscience, but I realize that each vote affects your fund-raising. If the system isn't corrupt, it's corrupting. It forces you into compromising yourself.

"The current system is designed to increase the level of skepticism on the part of the voters. As I said in my opening statement [in the Thompson hearings], 'Isn't it odd that every election we spend more money and fewer people vote?'"

A SENATE AIDE said, "We don't have policy debates any more. Instead of voting on 'the great issues of the day'—whatever they may be—we haven't framed them very well. We go from skirmish to skirmish until the next election. So much time is wasted on petty issues instead of big ones."

David Cohen, one of Washington's wise people and a liberal activist, said to me in 1998, "You don't have convenors any more, people who throw out ideas and then convene people to flesh them out. Now the political institutions are simply reactive. The reason you have a decline in civility is that you have fewer people who think about the whole. It's seriously distressing. Even in a time of tremendous prosperity there is no sense of public purpose—in the presidency or the Congress." Cohen pointed to past senators, liberals and conservatives—Paul Douglas, Democrat of Illinois, James Pearson and Frank Carlson, Republicans of Kansas, Barry Goldwater—who had a sense of purpose, of the institutions, and believed in governing.

There are only a few great legislators anymore. Senator Edward M. Kennedy is one of them. Kennedy loves issues and creating coalitions to get things done. Even before the Republicans took over the Senate in 1994, he was careful to find a Republican cosponsor for most of his initiatives—often the conservative Orrin Hatch of Utah. Even in a Senate under Republican control, he was able to get through a health-care reform bill (Kennedy-Kassebaum), an increase in the minimum wage, and the first major expansion of health care coverage—in this instance, to children.

SOME DEMOCRATS argue that the era of "wedge issues" began with the late Lee Atwater, the knuckleball South Carolinian, Reagan White House political aide, Bush campaign manager, and Republican Party chairman, who devised ways to divide the Democratic Party and cause blue-collar workers and others to vote for Republicans. (It was Atwater who sanctioned the use of the famous "Willie Horton" ad in 1988, which suggested that Michael Dukakis was soft on black rapists.) Such inflammatory social issues as abortion, race, crime, flag-burning, and school prayer—also designed to get Democrats on record on these divisive questions—became a major feature of our politics beginning in the eighties. Democrats used the Brady bill, to control the ownership of handguns, as a wedge issue. A Senate aide said, "Now everything is like that."

The level of courage in the face of these challenges to vote with popular sentiment has dropped. Former Democratic Senator John Culver, of Iowa, was often in a small minority voting against purposely inflammatory proposals—he was one of four senators who voted against an amendment offered by Republican Senator Jesse Helms, who specialized in this sort of thing—to prohibit any foreign aid or transfer of any goods to Vietnam, Uganda (then headed by the butcher Idi Amin), or Cuba. He was one of twenty-two senators who voted against a five percent cut in the unpopular foreign aid program. He was defeated in 1980, when five liberal Democratic senators were caught in the tide as Ronald Reagan rolled to victory over Jimmy Carter. Some senators have drawn the wrong conclusion from Culver's defeat, saying that they wish he hadn't been so stubborn (that is, principled) in his voting.

The full-time campaign at the presidential level—the elected President does not stop running, even as Clinton has demonstrated, after he has been reelected to a second term—has now been taken up by senators and representatives. They do everything they can do to avoid displeasing a constituent or casting a controversial vote. They think in terms of message rather than policy. The result isn't leadership.

To TALK of flaws in our political system isn't to engage in nostalgia, or fall into the "the-high-school-teachers-are-getting-younger" syndrome. And it's not unprecedented for people to think that the politicians were better before. "The Senate is no longer a place for any decent man," Henry Clay wrote in 1836 to his wife back in Kentucky. "It is rapidly filling up with blackguards." But the current complaints about the overall quality of our politicians are an accurate reflection of reality.

Not everything about the prior era was wonderful, of course: In some ways it was too cozy; the system is more open now; there are more women and minorities in politics; and this country's diversity is better represented in its political institutions.

But some of the politicians of the past were more rounded, more interesting, and more capable legislators. Among the "exotica" to whom the consultant referred were a few men of tremendous legislative talent, if eccentric or flawed in some conspicuous way.

Russell Long was the bulbous-nosed descendent of the colorful Longs of Louisiana, a man who told wonderful stories, especially about his father, Huey, and his uncle Earl. He could be drunk on the Senate floor, and was hard to understand even when sober, as his words seemed to go down his gullet. But he was a highly effective legislator and chairman of the Senate Finance Committee, which handles such big issues as taxes and trade. (Long, who retired in 1985, was reformed by his wife, Caroline, and has drunk very little in recent years.)

Long had what Robert Strauss, the perceptive Democratic elder, called "a pure political mind." Once, in front of a visitor, Long told an assistant to put a hold on a bill that was moving quickly through his committee. Smelling that someone was trying to sneak something through the Senate, Long said, "That bill's moved so fast there must be something in it—if I hold it someone will come squealing."

Wilbur Mills, the former chairman of the House Ways and Means Committee, may have kept open company with the stripper Fanne Foxe, who ended up in the Tidal Basin during one of their late-night excursions, but he also had a deep understanding of the big issues before his committee—medical care, Social Security, taxes—and of how to move them. The late Everett McKinley Dirksen, of Illinois, the Senate minority leader from 1959 to 1969, with the corduroy face and hound-dog eyes, entertained the galleries with his odes to the marigold. But when it came to serious legislating, he was quite capable, and led his party into accepting the 1964 civil rights bill.

There are almost no great debates in the Senate any more. When Hubert Humphrey and Dirksen debated, people came to listen. There's virtually no one who people come to the Senate chamber to listen to when word spreads that a certain senator is about to speak. There are no oratorical descendants of Daniel Webster. Arkansas Democrat Dale Bumpers, who retired in 1998, was one of the last of the great orators. But as a liberal and a man weary of the place and discouraged by the changes that had occurred, he had become a somewhat isolated figure.

When Bumpers announced his retirement from the Senate, Fred Thompson told him he'd miss him, because he was one of the few who stood on principle no matter what, and because he spoke "like a master musician."

Bumpers's eloquence caused Clinton to call on him to sum up his case in the Senate impeachment trial. As he began his speech, Bumpers remarked, "It is especially pleasant to see an audience which represents about the size of the cumulative audience I had over a period of twenty-four years."

Television—the requirement that candidates be smooth and telegenic—has just about rid us of eccentrics, particularly in the Senate. The blanding of our politicians robs our politics of texture, of interest, of creativity.

INCIVILITY in the Congress isn't entirely new, of course. In 1856, a House member, Preston Brooks of South Carolina, caned Senator Charles Sumner of Massachusetts, beating him insensate, over an abolitionist speech Sumner had given, naming names, including that of Brooks's uncle, of senators who supported slavery.

But the marked decline in civility in both chambers in the past few years has had an adverse effect on the job of doing the people's business. Civility abetted the formation of coalitions for large purposes. "There was a point to decorum," the former Democratic Senate aide said. "It describes a level of interpersonal contact." The higher level of interpersonal contact helped the Congress address serious issues and work them out.

The former Democratic Senate aide said, "So often when I was there members would fight like cats and dogs on an issue, and when the debate was over, they'd go out together and have a drink in someone's cubbyhole"—some senior Senator's private offices in the Capitol.

He added, "They understood that an opponent in debate was equally honorable. Now it's 'Are you with me or against me?' The current process doesn't permit the spectrum of views that was tolerated before. People's positions on issues are personalized by other members. It's a significant change."

Nick Calio, who headed the Legislative Liaison Office in the Bush White House and set up his own lobbying firm the day after Clinton took office, made much the same point. "The biggest changes in Washington are fundamental in the way business is done here. Certain Members of Congress don't know that people could fight all day and go have drinks together at night. People liked each other more, they trusted each other more, and, frankly, they were able to get more done." He said that some of the Republican members "are surprised that I have Democratic friends, which is really absurd."

It was not uncommon, until sometime in the late eighties, for senators and representatives to socialize across the aisle, go to each other's homes. But now, serving in the Senate or the House is an atomizing experience, what with the constant fund-raising demands and the constituent demands. Because the level of public trust is lower, the politician must show up at home more often. There's little time for socializing at all. Roll-call votes, which can go on until all hours, committee meetings, subcommittee meetings, greeting visiting constituents, all get crammed into a three-day workweek. For most of them, the rest of the time is spent in their states or districts—or elsewhere—to cultivate grass roots and raise money.

And the relatively recent development of a twenty-four-hour news cycle on cable news channels and the Internet contributes to the frenzy on Capitol Hill as well as at the White House. Policy makers and politicians have little time, or no time, to reflect before having to—or wanting to—respond to events or answer press queries.

The wife of a senator who retired in the early nineties was asked at a small farewell dinner what she would remember most about being in Washington. A woman of considerable intelligence, and interests of her own, she replied, "Loneliness."

The large number of Senate retirees in 1996—thirteen, plus the resignations of Bob Dole and Bob Packwood (because he couldn't control himself around women and he kept a diary of it all to boot)—created a big hole in the center, and a major hemorrhage of experience. Some of the retirements were less than heroic. Several Democrats left because they couldn't see their returning to committee chairmanship any time soon. But getting another life after Congress can be a healthy thing.

Still, the exodus in 1996 bespoke the deteriorating work conditions there. The collective departures of, among others, Alan Simpson, William Cohen, Nancy Kassebaum, Sam Nunn, David Pryor, Paul Simon, Mark Hatfield, and Bob Dole removed a substantial body of experience and judgment. A Republican Senate aide said, "The soul went out of the place with the last bunch of retirements." A crucial core who understood the point of compromising for the good of the whole was gone. The pressures to raise money, the obsessive reliance on polls, and, frankly, a diminution of the character level of the politicians in Washington, have led to a decline in leadership.

People tend to think that the politicians in Washington are "out of touch" with their constituents, but if they were any more in touch their ears would never leave the ground. The politicians of today are, on the whole, a highly reactive breed. They would consider passé, and even a bit weird, Edmund Burke, who said, in 1777, that a representative "is in Parliament to support his opinion of the public good and does not form his opinion in order to get into Parliament, or to continue in it." Now, with few exceptions, the representative reflects the momentary mood of the public.[*]

IN THE SPRING of 1998, I went to call on Bob Michel, the former leader of the House Republican minority, and now a "senior advisor" at a major Washington law firm. Michel was tan, his white hair receding, and he had developed a bit of a paunch and was

---

[*]The House's impeachment of President Clinton was, of course, an exception (see chapter 13).

cheerful as ever as he sat in his regal office in downtown Washington. Speaking euphemistically, he said, "When Jim Wright was having his troubles"—that is, when Gingrich took on Speaker Wright, in 1987, and eventually drove him from office—"then it really began to get partisan." (Michel retired in 1994 because he knew that Gingrich would challenge him for leadership of the House Republicans, and might well succeed.)

Michel did point out, correctly, that Wright, a Democrat, had been pretty partisan himself. Several Republicans—with some reason—complained that the longtime Democratic majority had abused power.

When I spoke with him, Michel made no such complaint, and reminisced about when O'Neill was Speaker and Michel was minority leader. Michel said, "We both accepted that we had to be out there for our parties, and we both knew that it ended at the end of the day. Some of my colleagues couldn't take it as well as I could. Tip and I played golf a lot of times."

Referring to Wright's Democratic successor, Michel said, "Tom Foley and I were the best of friends. Tom even wanted to alternate our weekly meetings between our offices." (Gingrich had tried, but failed, to drive Foley from office as well.) After Gingrich became Speaker in 1995, he and Minority Leader Dick Gephardt met only a half-dozen times.

Michel, who came from central Illinois, and Dan Rostenkowski, the Chicago Democrat who headed the Ways and Means Committee (he later went to jail for misusing government funds), would drive to Illinois together on weekends. Ray LaHood, Michel's then chief of staff and now his successor in representing the same Illinois district, told me, "That drive, and their playing golf together, endeared them to one another and enabled them to work together for the good of not just Illinois but the country. They had differences, but they knew you had to get something done around here." He added, "And as you know, that era's gone."

A number of the newer Senate Republicans are Gingrichites from the House. In 1995, Gingrich proudly claimed to me that he had at least twenty-six ideological descendants in the Senate, "which give[s] us a pretty big bloc over there." He added, "All the activists and all the grass-roots pressures that helped us in the House are all going to come to bear in the Senate." He was right.

The 1994 Republican takeover of the House after forty years

wrought other cultural changes. Vin Weber, a former Republican congressman from Minnesota, recalls that after he was elected to Congress in 1980, party leaders urged the newly elected Republicans to move their families to Washington. Weber recalls, "They were told, 'First of all, it's going to be one of the most exciting experiences of your life and your family should share in it.'" But now, Weber said, "No one talks about coming to Washington for the excitement, they talk about coming to Washington to tear it down."

The freshmen elected in 1994 were told to leave their families at home, and some of them simply slept in their offices, or on a cot in the House gym, to spare themselves rent money or the cost of owning two homes. The problem with keeping the family in the district, Weber said, is that "when you go back home you can't have a family life. You're on call twenty-four hours a day"—meeting constituents and donors, attending local events.

Weber added, "You can't be a normal guy. In conservative circles," Weber, himself a conservative, said, "it's politically incorrect to say that Washington is a nice place to live."

One upshot perhaps was the six divorces among the seventy-three members of the class of 1994 during its first two years.

MEMBERS OF Congress have also been atomized through following their own polls, gathering their own information, forming their own relationships with donors and interest groups. This has had a distinct impact on the Senate in particular.

Charlie Ferris, who was general counsel to the Senate Democratic majority from 1963 to 1977, said, "They've lost the interdependence senators had on each other. In foreign policy you followed William Fulbright, or John Sparkman. You had umbrellas, on every issue. There would be a connection of values among senators. They knew they couldn't follow everything going on in all the committees; there was an interdependence that was good for the institution. Senators used to talk to each other; now they only talk to their staffs. The communications are predominantly vertical in their offices; the senators used to rely on the horizontal communications amongst one another to be informed. Now every senator seems to zero-base everything in his office. The computer made this possible. Everyone can get information about anything they wish. Their notions are set primarily by their staff. And every member now has a perceived expertise on every issue."

A senator said, "It's less fun being a senator now." He continued, "Because of advances in communications technology, everybody's an expert. Leaders aren't trusted as much. You can get your own information."

THE NEW, higher degree of partisanship stems from the fact that both parties have become increasingly the captive of their fringes. Clinton's partially successful effort to move the Democratic Party to the center moderated the Democrats' behavior and image somewhat, but no one could know whether Clintonism would succeed Clinton, and the partial transformation affected the Democrats'— that is, Clinton's—presidential politics far more than it did the congressional wing of the Democratic Party, which was still dominated by liberals. (This caused considerable strain between Clinton and the congressional Democrats throughout most of his presidency.) The Republicans, especially in the House, lived in fear of the Christian right because they needed its foot soldiers in elections. This dependence forced them into extreme positions on abortion, school prayer, and other matters they saw as moral questions— including the impeachment of President Clinton.

THE TRANSFORMATION of the Republican Party from an establishment-dominated, center-conservative organization with most of its power located in the East, to more of a grass-roots party with its power located mostly in the West and South, began with the Barry Goldwater movement in 1964. It was given new strength during Ronald Reagan's ascendancy. The two movements both reflected and were aided by population growth in the West and the South.

But the Goldwater movement was essentially about economic and foreign policy—drastically reducing the size and power of the federal government and hawkishness. ("Extremism in the defense of liberty is no vice.")

At about the same time, but apart from the Republican Party, there arose the concept of a movement on the right (or the "New Right") that would use computers and direct mail to focus on particular issues and seek the defeat of specified liberal candidates, and to raise money. This first took shape in the form of the National Conservative Political Action Committee (called "Nicpac"), formed in 1975. NCPAC focused on single issues and targeted for defeat specific liberal candidates, through television ads paid for as "independent expenditures." Such use of "independent expenditures" was a new development in American politics and can be considered the inspiration for much that followed. NCPAC was deemed a major factor in the defeat of three liberal Democratic senators in 1980. Ironically, the rise of Ronald Reagan helped finish off NCPAC, as conservatives chose to contribute to Reagan's cause rather than to outside groups.

But the 1973 Supreme Court decision *Roe v. Wade* that struck down state laws banning abortion in the first two trimesters had provided conservatives with a new organizing principle. So, at the same time that NCPAC was phasing out, the concept of organizing around "Christian values" took form in the Moral Majority, founded by the Reverend Jerry Falwell in the 1970s. The founders felt that they had to work outside the Republican Party of that time, that Richard Nixon was too much the pragmatic centrist. The idea was to organize around evangelical and fundamentalist Protestant churches. The issues were not just abortion but also homosexuality and creationism. (The sensational Scopes monkey trial of 1925 settled nothing.) But the Moral Majority imploded from its own extremism and in 1989 went out of business.

Some of the same conservative political operators who were behind the formation of the Moral Majority, working with the Reverend Pat Robertson, picked up the pieces from the Moral Majority and went on to found the Christian Coalition, in 1989. Robertson was shrewd enough to recognize that he himself might be a scary figure, so he brought in the bright, fresh-faced young Republican strategist Ralph Reed to front for him and help build the coalition as a political force. (Reed's background had been in political organizing, not Christian politics.) Under Reed's influence the Christian Coalition became a far larger and more powerful movement than the Moral Majority had been, and as a result of some polling, and Reed's pragmatism, its concerns broadened beyond social and religiously based ones to include economic issues as well.

But the church-centered organizing was crucial. On Sundays just before elections the Christian Coalition's "voter guides"—which told worshipers how the candidates for President, Congress, and state offices stood on issues such as abortion, school prayer, and tax cuts for the middle class—were distributed at churches. The

Christian Coalition is a corporation, and under the law it isn't supposed to spend its funds "for the purpose of influencing any election for federal office." But the supposedly neutral guides varied from district to district or state to state in the issues they raised, enabling the preferred candidates to win high scores. In 1996 the Federal Election Commission charged the Christian Coalition with illegally "coordinating" its activities with certain Republican campaigns.*

The Christian Coalition also used phone banks and get-out-the-vote drives in specified congressional districts. ("We can really bump turnout in the primary," Ralph Reed told me in 1996.) By getting its people out, the Christian Coalition played a major role in helping the Republicans recapture the House in 1994, and therefore had an honored seat at the table. So, by the time Newt Gingrich became Speaker of the House, the religious right and the Republican Party had effectively merged. "Rockefeller Republicans"—liberal to moderate Republicans, backed by Wall Street rather than ideological footsoldiers—were nearly extinct.

A COUPLE OF Democrats I spoke to suggested that it was their own party that had started a bitter chain of action-reaction over nominations when, in 1987, Senate Democrats, backed by some of the party's major interest groups, fought and defeated the Supreme Court nomination of Robert Bork. Liberal Democrats went at Bork on the combined grounds of his conservative views and his aggressive temperament. Though this wasn't the first defeat of a Supreme Court nomination—two Nixon appointees had been rejected by the Senate—it left such a bitter aftertaste that it contributed a new transitive verb, to "bork" someone. Ever since, Republicans have been bent on "borking" liberal court nominees, even at lower levels than the Supreme Court. Nomination struggles became more rancorous, more personal, and meaner after the Bork fight.

A Democratic Senate aide says, "During the eighties, we did a real series of nasty stuff." He mentioned, in addition to the Bork episode, the fracases over the nominations of Clarence Thomas, in 1991, to the Supreme Court and of John Tower, in 1989, as George Bush's first Secretary of Defense. The Tower case was particularly ugly, this person said, resting as it did on objections to his personal behavior—drinking and womanizing—and the leaking of

*The matter is still pending in the courts.

supposedly secret items, corroborated or not, in his FBI file. Tower was defeated.

Democrats would of course say that all of these fights were on the merits, but they couldn't expect Republicans to see it that way.

In recent years, Republican retaliation has led to a sort of "preborking" conservative Republican circles, having got wind of a possible nomination by Clinton of a liberal, would go to work on that person, mainly through columns by allies, and, in several cases, got Clinton to back off. From Bork on, nomination fights became not only nasty but highly intrusive into nominees' personal lives.

A Washington lawyer, a Democrat who had served on the Senate staff, who also asked not to be named, said, "Everything is much more personal, much more partisan, and much more confrontational—and ideological." He offered as reasons the need for money, the role of television—the more partisan and inflammatory statement is more likely to get you on the air—and the increasing resort to the advice of political consultants. He described the Bork and Clarence Thomas hearings as "watersheds" and said that "the Bork event was a mistake on the part of Democrats." He explained, "That was a highly politicized process that clearly sent a message to the right wing that everything goes. Bork was being attacked for purely ideological reasons."

The insistent tit-for-tatting reflected the immaturity, even infantilization, of politics in recent years. The Republicans, if they were grownups, would have got over it.

THE GROWING ROLE of political consultants in the maneuvering on Capitol Hill has had a big impact on the tone and substance of our national political life. The Democratic lawyer who had served on a senator's staff said, "Over the last twenty years people are hired and paid to foment these things, which go well beyond campaigns. They're brought into meetings on the Hill for policy discussions all the time, and of course the White House has them virtually on staff. Consultants will always focus on the short-term advantage."

He pointed out that Joseph Biden, Democratic Senator from Delaware, was the leader of the anti-Bork attack just before he ran for president. "It raised the stakes," he said. "Bork opponents saw this solely as an issue to stop Bork. But it's had much wider ramifications. If you politicize judicial nominations, what's left?"

A senator complains that Senate staff members have become at least as partisan as their bosses. Ordinarily, many of the coalitions are formed and much of the legislation is shaped by staff. The senator says that in the past few years it's become much more difficult to get staffs of the opposite party to work together this way.

On occasion, partisanship becomes an end in itself, killing off legislation of great interest to the public. A dramatic example of this was the demise in October 1998 of a bill to impose new standards on managed-care companies, an issue that rated very high in the polls. As the 1998 midterm elections approached, it became more important to the parties to stick to their respective positions than to resolve a matter causing millions of Americans great difficulty.

A TELLING EXAMPLE of what it has all come to can be found in the person of Rick Santorum, the junior Republican senator from Pennsylvania. Elected to the House in 1990 and then the Senate in 1994, Santorum, forty, is the apotheosis of the brash newer member who imposes himself on the working order of the Senate, demonstrates little respect for the institution, becomes a one-man ideological enforcer, and brings down the level of civility. Toothy, with a shock of dark hair, Santorum looks the perfect pol for the television age. Unburdened by brilliance, he makes his impact through pestiferousness.

A senior Republican senator said to me of Santorum, "He's busy, busy, busy. He hangs around in the cloakroom and kibitzes conversations between the majority leader and minority leader. Anytime anybody is trying to work things out, there he is."

Santorum had been a troublemaker from the moment he arrived. Shortly after the 1994 election, the newly elected Santorum and some other younger senators, most of them graduates of the Gingrich School of Government, pushed for stripping of their chairmanships both Mark Hatfield, of Oregon, who headed the Appropriations Committee; and John Chafee, of Rhode Island, chairman of the Environment and Public Works Committee, an environmentalist and one of the shrinking group of moderate Republicans remaining in the Senate, because they didn't reflect the view of the Republican Conference. (In 1990 Chafee was ousted as chairman of the Republican Conference because of his views.)

This move by conservative Republican senators failed, but when, in 1995, Hatfield, a fifth-term senator from Oregon, a serious, religious, man, refused, on principle, to vote for a constitutional amendment to balance the budget, Santorum once again sought to strip him of his chairmanship.

But these Cromwellian instincts were cooled by more senior Republicans who may not have loved Hatfield but could see the chaotic consequences—and threats to their own seniority—that might ensue. The idea of punishing Hatfield received scant support even within the Republican Conference.

But as a result of the Hatfield experience the Senate Republicans changed their rules to require that committee chairmen be approved, not by their own committee members, but by the Senate Republican Conference as a whole—by secret ballot.

This unnerved several senior Republicans. One Republican committee chairman told me after that, "Each of us operates on the graces of our colleagues now. Nobody has to be told there's a penalty to be paid, but you can also find yourself separated on a particular issue." He cited Arizona Senator John McCain's pushing a campaign finance reform bill, which the majority of his party opposed.

The committee chairman said, "The fear is if you get too far out of line and are not carrying out the requirements of the leadership, if you're not voting right, you can be replaced as chairman." (The "Watergate babies" had forced a similar rule on House Democrats, but though a couple of committee chairmen were deposed—on grounds of a pattern of arbitrary and abusive actions—the Democratic leaders didn't use it to impose their will on the committees.)

Following the Hatfield episode, the administration of the traditionally independent committees came under virtually daily supervision from the Senate Republican Conference and the Republican leadership. A Republican senator says, "Trent doesn't go along with the traditional prerogatives of committee chairs. He comes in and tells them what to do. His staff communicates with the chief staff of the subcommittees of the Appropriations Committee about what he wants funded. He's become more aggressive in telling committees in detail what he wants."

The word had gone forth that if committee chairmen wanted to keep their seats, they had to behave according to the dictates of the leadership and the Conference, with the balance of power increasingly on the right.

SANTORUM brought a new low to Senate decorum—and respect for the presidency—in 1996, when he regularly came to the Senate floor with a large poster saying "Where's Bill?" and referring to the number of days that had passed without Clinton's offering a budget plan. Even Republicans were made uncomfortable by this behavior.

The other contender for worst decorum would be Al D'Amato, Republican of New York, who, in 1995, brought to the Senate floor a large drawing of a pig, with a veto pen stuck in it, to protest "pork" spending, and, on the floor of the U.S. Senate, sang his version of "Old MacDonald Had a Farm."*

IN RECENT YEARS, the House of Representatives has gone beyond the traditional raucousness to a new level. The House debate on welfare reform in 1995 was the ugliest anyone could remember. Partly this stemmed from the open disrespect each party in the House now showed for the other; partly it was the tension over this particular issue, with Democrats charging that Republicans were trying to punish the poor in order to provide "tax cuts for the rich."

Worried that the charge might stick, the Republicans fought back hard. The anger in the debate reached the point where even the normally gentle John Lewis, one of the saints of the civil rights movement, evoked the specter of Nazi Germany. The Republicans booed Florida Democrat Sam Gibbons when he charged that the bill was "mean." Gibbons shouted back, "Boo if you want to—make asses of yourselves." Booing had been quite rare in the House. Even Majority Leader Dick Armey, not one of the more dainty members of the House, waved his arms to try to calm the Republicans. Both sides knew that they were creating a spectacle that would be featured in television reports of the debate. It was.

At another point during the welfare-reform debate, a red-faced Gibbons shouted to his colleagues, "You all sit down and shut up. Sit down and shut up."

Also in 1995, the first year of the Republican takeover, George Miller, Democrat of California, a hot-tempered remnant of the Watergate Babies (there were four left in the House), called a

---

*D'Amato was defeated for reelection in 1998.

Republican move to curb lobbying by nonprofit groups "fascist" and refused to stop speaking when his allotted time had elapsed. Rep. Bob Walker, a Gingrich ally whom Gingrich had put in the chair for what promised to be a tough situation, gaveled Miller down so hard that the gavel flew apart.

In June 1996, J. D. Hayworth, a heavyset Republican freshman from Arizona, a former sportscaster seated in the House, laughed aloud at David Obey as he spoke about a procedural motion. This was the second time Hayworth had done this.

The Wisconsin Democrat could be barbed, as in his suggestion that the House contained more Daffy Ducks than James Madisons. Addressing Hayworth, Obey said, "Every time somebody says something you don't like, you open your mouth and start shouting from your seat. You are one of the most impolite members I have ever seen in my service in this House."

Upon an objection, Obey's last sentence was stricken from the record. Then a long argument ensued over who should apologize first. After intervention by Henry Hyde, Republican of Illinois, Hayworth, like a chastened schoolboy, offered an apology of sorts, and Obey accepted and apologized in turn.

At another point, in 1997, Obey and House Majority Whip Tom DeLay got into a pushing match on the House floor, over Obey's charge that DeLay had used foul language, which he had.

DAVID SKAGGS, a fifty-five-year-old six-term Democratic congressman from Colorado, retired from politics in 1998. He had had enough of the House, frustrated with how little he could accomplish there. He considered running for the Senate but found that he couldn't raise enough money to be competitive.

A serious, thoughtful man with dark hair and dark eyes and an almost old-fashioned courtliness, Skaggs said in an interview in early 1998, "I'm worried that if we don't regenerate people's belief in democracy, if people don't feel they need to stay involved, we'll become weaker in the rest of the world."

He talked about the changes in politics in recent years. "People running for office now, as compared to ten, twenty years ago, are trained to a manipulative view of their constituents. It's been gradual. The people who come here have to some extent been trained not to be candid with the people who sent them. But there are nonverbal cues, and the public picks up the fact that they're being manipulated. They see, at the nonverbal level, that we're trying to fool them, no matter what we're saying.

"We all spend proportionately more money on polling and TV ads than twenty years ago. That's all packaging, and I think people have figured that out. The legislators are less and less willing to be educators, to cast the tough vote and go back home and explain it. They don't have enough rapport with people to talk with them about it. There was always some of that, but now there's more of it. It goes to public cynicism. There isn't enough understanding between us of what the job description is—that we've been hired to understand the issues and vote as we see best, as opposed to being driven by public opinion polls. If we and they don't understand this, then we get to the manipulation and cynicism."

Then Skaggs talked about the negative things that Members of Congress have done to try to try to fend off criticism by the public. One is a reduced amount of foreign travel. Fearful of taking trips that might be characterized in the press as "junkets," fewer members go abroad. To be sure, some of the trips have been pure junkets, but some also broaden the members' understanding of the world. The fear of junketing has contributed to the decline in the understanding of foreign policy questions.

Skaggs said, "You have fewer members willing to take trips because they can't explain it to their constituents. We're a world power and the world's a complicated place and we need to understand it, but we don't talk to our constituents about it."

Michael Berman, a major Democratic lawyer-lobbyist, said, "One of the big losses is junkets. The end of the junket could be the greatest contributor to the end of across-the-aisle dealings. They could leave everything else behind. They went off and bonded."

After the House Judiciary Committee had voted the Articles of Impeachment against Richard Nixon in 1974, I was startled to learn that it was one of the great junketeering committees. And then I realized that that was one of the reasons the committee was able to deal with such a politically loaded subject in a civil way. There's always an international judicial conference to attend. Following the conclusion of the Nixon impeachment proceedings, James Mann, a conservative Democrat from South Carolina who had acquired, in many minds, Madisonian dimensions, told me in graphic detail about the trips and who took girlfriends, and who made a move on whose girlfriend and other such disconcerting goings-on. Later, I realized that there wasn't as great a distance between the junketeers and the statesmen as I had thought.

Skaggs also mentioned the gift ban, passed by the House in 1995, which prohibited members from accepting anything but items of nominal value, such as T-shirts and caps, and banned the acceptance of meals. The Senate put a limit of fifty dollars on gifts and meals.* The idea that a member could be corrupted over a meal was silly, Skaggs said, and the ban lessened the amount of free-floating discussion that just might be educational.

In March 1998, a very unusual event occurred on Capitol Hill. The Senate paused and listened to a thoughtful speech. It was given in the Old Senate Chamber, just off the Capitol Rotunda, a room that originally held the Senate until 1859, and later was used for cots during Senate filibusters. It has been restored with rich vermilion carpets and gold-leaf decor.

Looking not a minute older than when he retired from the Senate in 1976, the ninety-five-year-old Mike Mansfield, in a clear, strong voice, made a speech he had intended to deliver in the third of his sixteen years as majority leader, but the date for the speech was November 22, 1963, the day that John F. Kennedy was assassinated. Instead he quietly inserted it in the *Congressional Record*, explaining later that he had "no heart" for delivering it after that. Now he was giving the first in a lecture series established by Trent Lott.

The former Montana Democratic senator and ambassador to Japan evoked an era almost unknown to the current Senate (only four of the current senators were there when he retired): one of civility, of seriousness of purpose about big questions. Mansfield, always a laconic, modest, unflashy man, did, as he acknowledged, enjoy a majority of sixty-five Democrats to thirty-five Republicans. "Think of it!" he said, in a rare moment of impishness.

As the senators sat at the restored desks like attentive students, Mansfield mentioned great names from the past—Daniel Webster, Henry Clay, John Calhoun—and, eerily, in a thirty-five-year-old speech, landed on the great flaws of current politics. His

---

*In January 1999 the House altered its gift ban so that it matched the Senate's rules.

speech was intended to respond to criticisms at the time of what many saw as his passive leadership of the Senate, especially after the hyperbolic Lyndon Johnson. But, compared to their current proportions, the problems he addressed were mere specks in the year the speech was intended for delivery.

"We need no cloakroom commandos," Mansfield said, but "respect for one another and mutual restraint." He warned of election-time "concern with our own individual performance and not with the Senate as a whole."

Mansfield's speech was powerful in its own terms, but it was like a pebble tossed into the Niagara of the self-centered, short-sighted, limited-vision, reactive politics of today.

3

———■———

The First Amendment

"The First Amendment," Mitch McConnell said. "We can kill this bill with the First Amendment." He was speaking in March 1997 to the representatives of about twenty-five interest groups that he had convened for a series of meetings in his office, Room 120 of the Russell Senate Office Building, to discuss how to defeat the pending campaign finance reform legislation. McConnell was hopeful that he could kill the bill by arguing—speciously, as we will see—that it violated the First Amendment's guarantee of free speech.

McConnell and his allies were worried. The new Congress had convened amid much public criticism of the way the 1996 elections had been financed; there were to be congressional hearings. The scandals of the 1996 campaign could lead to a new and stronger push for reform.

The people gathered in McConnell's office formed an unlikely coalition that included the liberal National Education Association, the antiabortion National Right to Life Committee, the National Rifle Association, the National Association of Business PACs, the American Civil Liberties Union, and three unions: the National Association of Letter Carriers, the National Rural Letter Carriers, and the International Association of Firefighters.

The National Association of Broadcasters joined the group as time went on. The NAB had usually been able to cut a deal with key Members of Congress that broadcasters wouldn't be forced to give up free time for political broadcasts, and had managed to keep any such proposal out of the basic campaign finance bill that was to come before the Senate in 1997. But though the broadcasters faced no immediate threat, they were concerned that reformers might get out of hand.

The combined power of the groups in the coalition that McConnell had put together was considerable. In the meetings, they were given the strategy for defeating the bill and the names of senators who "need more work."

While it may seem odd that a representative of the ACLU, often branded by Republicans as a left-wing organization, was sitting in McConnell's office, it had opposed most campaign finance reform over the years. And it was a useful ally for the forces against reform. A participant in the McConnell meetings said the ACLU "have been stalwart allies of the coalition from the start. They give people who don't agree with the ACLU on many things cover."

The role of the ACLU was to keep out of campaign finance reform proposals anything that, in their view, infringed on the "free speech" of the citizens guaranteed in the First Amendment to the Constitution. Actually, the ACLU had been divided internally for some time between absolutist civil libertarians who opposed any restrictions on "speech" posed, or perceived to be posed, by campaign finance regulation, and liberals who believed in such reform and thought that reform legislation could be written that didn't violate the right of free speech. This tension was to lead to a major split in the organization in 1998.

IN 1976, the Supreme Court, in the landmark decision *Buckley v. Valeo*, struck down major parts of the broad campaign finance reform law passed in 1974. For years, McConnell's most powerful and effective weapon against campaign finance reform has been his insistence that the Supreme Court ruled in that decision that spending money on campaigns was the equivalent of exercising one's First Amendment right to free speech. The shorthand for McConnell and his allies was that the Court said "money equals speech." But it did not.

McConnell's argument went that any new limits on money donated or spent in the federal election process would be an unconstitutional invasion of the citizens' rights of free speech. It's a bogus argument, one that McConnell had employed increasingly in Senate debate on campaign finance bills. For, as will be shown, the Court didn't rule that way.

When the owlish-looking, jowly senator from Kentucky, a man of serious mien, with graying hair, a somewhat nasal voice, and thin lips, giving him a parsonlike appearance, holds forth professorially on the Senate floor about the First Amendment, few senators take him on. They haven't done their homework, or they think the counterargument is too hard to make. The countermessage to the bumper-sticker slogan of "money equals speech" is more complicated, and complexity is out of fashion in American politics, made obsolete by the era of sound bites and glibness. Daniel Webster would have had no trouble debating such a proposition, but Daniel Webster wouldn't make it onto television today unless he learned how to keep it short and snappy. He might not even get elected.

Thus, while McConnell's reputation as a "constitutional scholar" rests on shaky ground, it is self-perpetuating.

There are some people, including some Republicans who fear McConnel's power—his hand on a campaign funds spigot, his closeness to the Senate leadership—and therefore decline to be named, who question whether he truly believes his First Amendment argument, or simply finds it convenient. A key Republican strategist I talked to said, "I don't have any doubt that McConnell doesn't believe that money is speech, but it fits his political position."

This person pointed out that McConnell does take a similar stand on other First Amendment issues, such as opposing a Constitutional Amendment, strongly backed by many Republicans, to make it a crime to burn the American flag. "That gives him standing here," the strategist said. Therefore, if McConnell is seen as sincere about some First Amendment issues, he can assert authority about others.

But McConnell's passion for protecting the First Amendment on the flag-burning issue hasn't been burdened with consistency. In 1989, and again in 1990, McConnell voted *for* an anti-flag-burning amendment. His turnabout came in 1995, when, having been chided for his inconsistency, he voted against it.

But Senate Republicans have another motive for blocking reform: They often talk among themselves about the power the "liberal media" would have in elections if the Republicans weren't able to outspend the Democrats. In a Senate speech in 1997, Lott said that when he first ran for the House in 1972, he needed money to get past Mississippi's Democratic establishment. He said, "If I hadn't been able to get the money to get my message across, how could a conservative Republican be elected in the State of Mississippi, where the courthouses were all owned and operated by Democrats almost entirely? So I had to fight the so-called courthouse gang fighting me and the biggest newspaper in the state bashing me regularly in its editorials and in its news stories."

McConnell's assault on campaign finance reform in the name of the First Amendment reached its full glory in the 1997–98 session of Congress. For the first time, in reaction to the 1996 elections, reformers tried to place curbs on phony "issue ads"—ads by outside groups or the political parties that were supposedly simply for the purpose of discussion of an issue but were obviously aimed at the defeat or election of a specific candidate. McConnell insisted that any such curbs were a direct violation of the *Buckley* ruling that the spending of money on elections was a constitutionally protected form of speech. This was his weapon for killing the new bill.

THE DECISION in *Buckley v. Valeo* grew out of a challenge to the Federal Election Campaign Act, passed in 1974 on a wave of reform sentiment.

There had been such waves before. In the nineteenth century big interests such as steel and the railroads considered it only sound business practice to buy legislators and influence the election of presidents. Theodore Roosevelt rose to power as a "trustbuster" after disclosures about the power of the "trusts" and the activities of Mark Hanna, an Ohio mining magnate and the first of the modern big-time fixers. Under Hanna, the Republican Party systematically assessed banks and corporations in exchange for a sympathetic ear—or more.

This innovation in governing led to the reform movement of Robert La Follette, and after Theodore Roosevelt became President in 1901, he proposed the banning of all corporate contributions for the election of any candidate for federal office. Roosevelt even proposed public financing of campaigns in exchange for limits on contributions from any individual. But, in espousing such a broad-range reform, Roosevelt was far ahead of his time.

In 1907, Congress banned contributions to federal campaigns from corporations and banks. After that, two laws were enacted. One of them, the Federal Corrupt Practices Act of 1925, enacted in the wake of the Teapot Dome scandal of the Harding Administration, imposed contribution and spending limits and disclosure requirements, but the two new laws were so ridden with loopholes that they couldn't be enforced.

The Taft-Hartley Act of 1947 placed the same ban on donations by labor unions in federal elections as had been placed on corporations in 1907.

In 1971, as the costs of campaigns began to get out of hand (for those days), a number of issues were raised—such as wealthy candidates spending large sums on their own races, the cost of television campaigns, how to pay for presidential campaigns (not only had Nixon spent much more than Hubert Humphrey in 1968, but Humphrey had run out of money), and the disclosure of new information about political contributions and spending; a Democratic Congress enacted the checkoff on tax forms, to be used to finance presidential campaigns. But this was not implemented until the 1976 election.

In the meantime, the laws had been interpreted to allow unions and trade associations and corporations, barred from making direct contributions to federal candidates, to raise dues and corporate funds to form committees that would contribute to federal candidates—thus introducing the world of political action committees, or PACs. There were no aggregate limits on how much these groups could give to federal candidates. The money race was on, only to be accelerated in future years as each side vied to outraise and outspend the other in a never-ending cycle.

The Watergate scandals revealed large contributions by individuals—of $50,000 or more, a shocking amount at the time—in 1972 to the infamous Nixon Committee for the Re-Election of the President. Secret slush funds maintained by corporations were discovered. It was also disclosed that over $1.7 million had been donated by people who were subsequently given ambassadorships by the Nixon administration. All this was considered so scandalous as to cry out for reform.

THE FEDERAL ELECTION CAMPAIGN ACT, signed into law by the new President, Gerald Ford, in October 1974 (Nixon had announced his resignation on August 8 and departed Washington the next day), was the most sweeping campaign finance reform law ever enacted. It placed the toughest-ever limits on spending and contributions to federal campaigns and strengthened the requirements for reporting contributions and expenditures.

The 1974 act provided for a voluntary system of public financing for presidential elections, to be paid for by a checkoff on income-tax returns. A presidential candidate who accepted the public money had to agree, by law, to spend only $50,000 of his own funds in the primary and general election. If a presidential candidate wanted to exceed the limits on the amounts his campaign could spend, he had to turn down the public financing. Limits were placed on what could be spent on campaigns for the Senate and House, but public financing wasn't provided for these campaigns, because House members were loath to make funds available to potential challengers.

Limits were placed on what individuals and PACs could contribute to federal candidates and to the political parties—$1,000 for individuals, and $5,000 for PACs, per candidate in any primary, general, or run-off election. And limits were supposedly placed on the amounts that the parties could spend on federal candidates. Independent expenditures—moneys spent on ads to help a candidate, independently of that candidate's campaign—were limited to $1,000. Individuals could give no more than an aggregate of $25,000 to all federal candidates and political parties and PACs. Cash contributions of over $100 were prohibited. This largely overlooked provision eliminated the brown bags—or black satchels—of cash that had been passed around to the candidates of both parties during recent federal elections. The Federal Election Commission was established to enforce the law, but Congress made sure it would be toothless by stocking it with three members from each of the two major political parties, giving Members of Congress a large say over the appointments, and providing it with an inadequate budget for the job.

Virtually all of the meaning behind the 1974 law has been obliterated over time.

THE FIRST BLOW to this law came in the *Buckley* decision. The suit to overturn key parts of the 1974 act—the public financing of presidential campaigns, because it put limits on both spending and contributions; the limits on what candidates for the Senate and House could spend; the limits on individual contributions to campaigns, as well as the limits on independent expenditures—was brought on January 2, 1975, by a coalition of people on the left and the right who had objections to the new law. They included James Buckley (brother of William), then a Conservative Party senator from New York; former senator and presidential candidate Eugene McCarthy, who opposed the entire law on First Amendment grounds; the liberal activist financier Stewart Mott; the conservative periodical *Human Events;* the ACLU, the New York Conservative Party, and the American Conservative Union. The coalition was put together by David Keene, then an assistant to James Buckley, who realized that these various people and groups shared the same objections to the law and could pool their resources to bring the suit.

The Court decision, handed down January 30, 1976, a per curiam decision (in the name of the Court, rather than signed by any particular justice), reflected a Court divided all over the place, and was very odd. It indicated little understanding of the real world of politics. It failed to foresee the actual impact of its decisions. It was reviewing the 1974 law on its face, because there had been no actual experience under it. The Court's frame of reference was Watergate.

The Court did not say that the right to exercise free speech through spending on campaigns was absolute. It said that there were two competing values: the right of free speech in donating or spending money for elections, and preventing corruption in elections. It said that in some instances the interest in preventing corruption justified restrictions on the donation of money.

In weighing the two values of free speech and clean elections, the Court said that expenditures made independently of campaigns are a highly protected form of speech and that contributions to a campaign are less protected, because they are an indirect form of speech and because they can lead to corruption or "the appearance" of corruption. With the 1972 Nixon campaign in mind, the Court offered that "the primary purpose" of the 1974 act was "to limit the *actuality and appearance of* corruption [italics the author's], resulting from large individual financial contributions." That, it said, was "a sufficient justification for the intrusion on freedom of political association" posed by the limits on contributions.

BUT THE COURT'S tortured distinction between expenditures and contributions didn't reflect the real world. Making a contribution is as much a political statement as making an independent expenditure. Someone who gives $1,000 to a candidate is likely to feel that that is as much an expression of his view as if he spent $1,000 helping to finance an ad on behalf of candidate. And there's as great a potential for corruption through "independent" expenditures as through making a contribution. Moreover, it's shortsighted to say that preventing corruption is the only legitimate reason for restricting campaign contributions and expenditures. Putting the candidates on an even, or a relatively even, playing field would be another (the Court rejected that concept). Under the current system, incumbents have a tremendous advantage over challengers—unless the challenger happens to be very wealthy.

The Court also struck down limits in the 1974 act on what candidates could contribute to their own campaigns. They can't corrupt themselves, after all. One result is that an estimated 39 percent of the one hundred current senators are millionaires—sixteen of them millionaires several times over.

Fred Wertheimer, of Democracy 21, which agitates for campaign finance reform, and a former president of Common Cause, says, of *Buckley*, "It undermines the concept of one-person, one-vote, in that it gives much greater influence to people who have money in the process once the politician is elected than it does to the average voter." Another reason for limiting contributions and expenditures could be to spare candidates from having to spend a large percentage of their time raising money. To run a successful Senate race, candidates must now raise an average of $16,000 a week, every week, for six years. A House candidate has to raise $7,100 a week for two years.

The Court's thinking led to a hodgepodge ruling in which the spending limits of the presidential public financing system were upheld, because the system was voluntary, but spending limits for congressional races were rejected because they weren't paired with public funds and therefore weren't voluntary. But at the same time, the limits on contributions to congressional campaigns were upheld (as preventing corruption). This led to the current situation wherein Members of Congress can spend unlimited amounts on their campaigns, but the money has to be raised in limited amounts.

In affirming the concept of "independent expenditures"—expenditures on behalf of a candidate made independently of the campaign (or ostensibly so)—the Court approved a whole new way of spending money on behalf of a candidate without regard to the contribution limits. It said that spending by individuals and PACs could be unlimited so long as there was no coordination with the candidate's campaign. The theory was that in the case of independent spenders there was no danger of a quid pro quo and therefore no danger of corruption.

When the Court made this finding, over twenty years ago, there was no problem of expenditures by independent groups because there were virtually no independent groups spending money to help campaigns. The independent expenditure decision opened the way for advocacy groups—from the National Rifle Association to the Sierra Club—to spend money to help campaigns "independently," outside the limits.

THE COURT IN the *Buckley* decision created the rationale for what has become a major circumvention of the law, the running of "issue ads" to help or hurt a candidate. It did this through a strange interpretation of what constituted advocacy on behalf of or against a certain candidate—"express advocacy"—as opposed to simply a discussion of issues. The Court spelled out the definition of "express" advocacy in one of the most shortsighted, and most exploited, footnotes in the history of such addenda.

Footnote 52, which was to deal a major blow to the 1974 campaign law, set forth a list of words that, if used in an ad, would constitute "express advocacy" of the election or defeat of a candidate. They were, said the footnote, words "such as": "vote for," "elect," "support," "cast your ballot for," "Smith for Congress," "vote against," "defeat," "reject." This list left a lot of possibilities.

The footnote led to a long-running debate, and conflicting lower court decisions, over its intent. People who wanted the widest possible leeway to run "issue ads" that were actually—and obviously—for the purpose of electing or defeating a candidate argued that anything went that didn't use the specifically forbidden words in the footnote. This interpretation allowed corporations and unions to use treasury money or union dues otherwise barred from being spent to influence a federal election to air "issue ads" that didn't use those words but were clearly intended to help or hurt a candidate.

People who wanted to rein in this new way of spending money on behalf of a candidate argued that the "such as" in the footnote meant that the words listed therein were simply for illustrative purposes and that the Court left room for Congress to define—or redefine—what constituted "express advocacy."

The dean of the first school was McConnell. He argued that the decision, and the footnote, were sacred text and that they left no room for any other interpretation. In a Senate debate on reform in 1998, McConnell said, misleadingly, "Issue advocacy is criticism of *us*....The Court has said it is impermissible for us to decide how much political speech is enough."

And right along with McConnell, and bolstering his cause as he was bolstering theirs, were advocacy groups that, for their various purposes, shared this position and met in his office. The ACLU argued that there could be no further infringements of "free speech," and, like other groups—the Christian Coalition, the NRA—contended that nothing should stand in the way of their "communicating with our members." This was a bogus argument, because communicating with members, through faxes, newsletters, mailings, etc., which weren't affected, and taking an ad to affect the wider electorate's opinion are very different things.

The Court actually recognized that "it would naively underestimate the ingenuity and resourcefulness of persons and groups desiring to buy influence to believe that they would have much difficulty devising expenditures that skirted the restriction on express advocacy of election or defeat, but nevertheless benefited the candidate's campaign." Having recognized this danger, the Court unleashed it anyway.

McConnell was crafty in his use of the *Buckley* decision to buttress his arguments against reform. For example, in a September 1997 debate on campaign finance reform, he said: "The Supreme Court said it was constitutionally impermissible for the government to try to level the playing field." In fact, the Court said, "The concept that government may restrict the speech of some elements of our society in order to enhance the relative voice of others is wholly foreign to the First Amendment."

McConnell went on, sonorously, "[E]ven if it were possible somehow for the government to figure out how to micromanage and level the playing field, it is truly, constitutionally impermissible for the government to try to do that."

But this definitive-sounding argument was based on taking what the Court said about one specific provision of the 1974 act, the part of the decision that struck down mandatory spending limits for congressional campaigns, and applying it to totally different kinds of provisions in the pending legislation.

At another point in that debate, McConnell told the Senate: "The Court has made it perfectly clear that the ability to speak and to influence the course of events in any way that is constitutionally permissible is going to be protected."

But this, of course is a tautology—a perfectly circular statement.

IN 1996, a group called Citizens for Reform ran an "issue ad" against Rep. Cal Dooley, Democrat of California, that said: "Congressman Cal Dooley makes choices for you and your family. Cal Dooley said no to increased money for federal prisons. Instead, Dooley gave the money to lawyers. Lawyers that used taxpayer's money to sue on behalf of prison inmates and illegal aliens. Cal Dooley said no to increased money for drug enforcement. Instead, Dooley gave your money to radical lawyers who represented drug dealers. Is Cal Dooley making the right choices for you?" (Dooley won reelection.)

Only after the election was it learned that Citizens for Reform was funded by Triad Management Services, Inc., an organization that steered conservative money into contributions and ads. According to the *Wall Street Journal*, Triad was backed by the highly conservative Koch brothers, owners of Koch Industries, a company specializing in chemical, oil, and energy services, and one of the country's largest privately held firms. Triad was believed to have taken ads in at least twenty-six congressional races in 1996. Many of these and other mysteriously sponsored ads came into the campaigns in the closing days.

Also in 1996, the League of Conservation Voters ran an "issue ad" against Rep. Greg Ganske, a moderate Republican from Iowa. It said: "It's our land; our water. America's environment must be protected. But in just eighteen months, Congressman Ganske has voted twelve out of twelve times to weaken environmental protections. Congressman Ganske even voted to let corporations continue releasing cancer-causing pollutants into our air. Congressman Ganske voted for the big corporations who lobbied these bills and gave him thousands of dollars in contributions. Call Congressman Ganske. Tell him to protect America's environment. For our families. For our future." (Ganske won.)

These sorts of ads proliferated like crazy in 1996, as more groups, including ad hoc groups, sponsorship and membership unknown, and the political parties, found new ways of getting around what limits there were on spending in campaigns.

THE OTHER death blow to the reforms of 1974 was the opening of the soft money loophole. Written by the Federal Election Commission in 1978, at the behest of the two parties, the regulation said that some party activities could be paid for by funds outside limits established by the act. That opened the way for corporate and union funds as well as unlimited amounts from individuals to be used for certain federal election activities. (The FEC, though largely ineffective, can be responsive when the two parties ask for the same thing.) The rationale for such soft money was that it would go to nice, benign, "party-building" activities, such as get-out-the-vote drives and paying for banners and balloons. But it has been used for purposes well beyond that—for hundreds of millions of dollars in "issue ads" by the parties and by interest groups. That a political party could run an ad to help their candidates and still call it an "issue ad" is absurd, but absurdity was the legacy of the *Buckley* decision.

THE IDEA that corporate and union money that cannot be contributed directly to federal candidates is completely acceptable when it is contributed, even in large amounts, to the parties to indirectly help the candidates fails any test of logic. The FEC said that the spending of soft money had to be paired in certain ratios with hard money expenditures, and further gummed up the works by ruling that state parties could spend a greater percentage of soft money than the national parties could.

This led to all manner of inventive schemes to funnel soft money through state parties: the national parties suggesting to large donors that they contribute to this state or that, swapping soft money among the states, or trading soft money for hard. James Riady, the President's Indonesia-based great friend and benefactor, gave $420,000 to seven state Democratic parties, including those of Louisiana, California, and North Carolina, in the 1992 election. It is fair to wonder what great interest James Riady had in the makeup of the Louisiana state legislature.

A lobbyist for a major trade association told me, "You find a lawyer who tells you what can you do to get this result, not what you can't do." A Senate Democrat said, "The role of the campaign lawyer is not to tell you how to violate the law but how to carry out an end run around the purpose of the law."

AFTER THE 1996 election, candidates on both sides complained that the ads by outside groups that came into their districts—not just the ones that attacked them, but even the ads taken on their behalf—were an unwelcome distraction. Even friendly ads could have a message that differed from their own, and the politicians felt that they lost control of their own campaigns.

A senator who said that the 1996 election had "radicalized" him explained, "In previous races, I could more or less control it—how much I raised, what my issues would be, and I'd have some sense what my opponent would raise and of his issues. Nineteen ninety-six was very different. A great deal of money was spent by groups ostensibly independent of the campaign, many of them at the last minute against me." Though he likes his job, he also said, "The last race was so bad that if there isn't reform I might not run again."

During the 1998 Senate debate on campaign finance reform, McConnell mocked the idea that "the campaigns belong to the candidate." He said, "The election is not the property of the candidates, and if people want to criticize us early or late, the courts are not going to allow us to interfere with that."

But there was reason to question whether McConnell actually meant this, either. One of his allies didn't think so. "Mitch doesn't believe it," said a major figure in moving business money into campaigns. "Mitch is the veteran of some very successful campaigns in Kentucky, and he's chairing the Senate campaign committee this year. I really don't think he wants people taking control of the campaign away from the candidates. But it's a very effective statement."

A foretaste of what was to come in congressional elections was presented in a special election in Santa Barbara, in March 1998, in which outside groups bombarded the populace with ads favoring term limits and opposing partial-birth abortions that had little to do with their real concerns. The business money man said, "You had outside groups with the resources to come in and take control of the campaign away from the candidates. That's a fact of life, and you're going to see a lot of it this year. I think it's deplorable, but I think it's inevitable."

THE FIRST AMENDMENT is a mobile missile, and in the past couple of years McConnell has also deployed it against proposals to ban soft money. His argument has been that such a ban constitutes a prohibition on spending, and therefore "speech." A prominent business lobbyist who deals with McConnell frequently told me, "The First Amendment is used. For the business community, if there's no soft money, they're at a disadvantage to labor. But when the subject of soft money comes up, they can't say 'We need it to survive.' So they say 'To ban it is infringement of free speech.' Of course, they use that argument almost whatever the campaign finance issue is."

The idea that labor's get-out-the-vote drives and internal communications give the Democrats a great electoral advantage is lodged deep in the psyche of Republicans. But it's estimated that, in all, business outspent labor by anywhere from six-to-one to eleven-to-one in 1996. The Center for Responsive Politics estimates that the business-to-labor spending ratio was twelve-to-one in the 1998 elections. The Center does say that the number for business might be slightly inflated, but the fact is that business substantially outspent labor. The issue is one of the several instances in which politicians say something enough times they begin to believe it.

"To politicians the First Amendment means ensuring that they have the financial resources to do what they need to do," the business lobbyist said. "The First Amendment is a great issue: People may think politics is corrupt, but do you want your rights taken away? There's something unique about using the word 'rights' to Americans that rallies them. I think the opponents [to reform] believe it now—that First Amendment rights are threatened. They've said it so many times that it's in their belief system, but what it's really about is power."

ON THURSDAY, October 23, 1997, at the Phoenix Park Hotel, just off Capitol Hill, at its annual dinner the National Association of Business PACs gave McConnell its first Guardians of Free Speech Award. McConnell had recently beaten back the first attempt to bring up reform in the Senate, and he was greeted as a hero. The award was created to recognize McConnell's commitment to making sure that no pesky campaign finance bill passed, and that the ability of business PACs to play to the maximum in the political process wasn't disturbed. If this was done in the name of the First Amendment, the business PACs were happy to go along with the charade.

More than a hundred people—most of them business lobbyists—attended the seated dinner of cucumber and blue cheese salad, grilled salmon with champagne sauce, and a mousse dessert. The assembled group gave McConnell a tremendous ovation when he was introduced. For his part, McConnell profusely thanked his top aide, Tamara Somerville, who worked closely with him on the campaign finance issue; she had helped organize the group of outside interests who met in his office to plot how to kill the bill. McConnell called on Somerville to join him in receiving the award, which, teary-eyed, she did. Then McConnell launched into a fifteen-minute off-the-cuff speech about the importance of protecting the First Amendment from the predators of campaign finance reform.

This wasn't McConnell's first such award of the year. In February, at an NRA board meeting, he was given the Harlan B. Carter Award, named after the person who had coinvented the NRA's Institute for Legislative Action, its political arm. He gave an impromptu talk which displayed his relish for the fight to protect the First Amendment, to a group that made a similar use of the Second Amendment.

THE STRAINS within the ACLU over the *Buckley* decision and the issue of reform burst into the open in June of 1998 when nine former high officials of the ACLU—in fact, all the living persons who have served in these roles in the past thirty years (save one who was in the government, but was sympathetic with the others)—issued a statement breaking with the current ACLU leadership. That leadership, the statement said, "has misread the First Amendment as it applies to campaign finance laws." It went on to say that "significant campaign finance reform—including a soft-money ban—is constitutional." The former ACLU officials called for the overturning of *Buckley*, but stated that "even within the limitations of the *Buckley* decision, we believe that a significant campaign finance reform is both possible and constitutional."

The former ACLU officials also supported regulation of "issue advocacy." Their statement said, "We have come to believe...that the opposition to campaign finance reform expressed by the ACLU misreads the First Amendment." It went on to say, "We believe that the First Amendment is designed to safeguard a functioning and fair democracy. The current system of campaign financing makes a mockery of that ideal by enabling the rich to set the national agenda, and to exercise disproportionate influence over the behavior of public officials."

It said that the *Buckley* decision "inappropriately treats the spending of money as though it were pure speech," and "such an approach ignores the long-established Supreme Court rule that when speech is inextricably intertwined with conduct, the conduct may be regulated if it threatens to cause serious harm." (For example, the Court ruled in 1972 that the First Amendment doesn't protect burning draft cards even though it was a form of protest.) The former ACLU officials called the *Buckley* distinction between contributions and expenditures "untenable," and "neither analytically nor pragmatically defensible."

ACLU officials, including executive director Ira Glasser and Laura Murphy, the Washington director of the ACLU, fired back with an op-ed article in the *Washington Post*, in which they took on the former officials' substance—arguing that pending legislative proposals would curb speech—and also pointed out that the current board didn't agree with their view.

THE PRESIDENTIAL election system set up by the 1974 act actually worked well for the next couple of elections. But in the late eighties the parties started raising soft money big-time, and in the 1996 election they threw off all constraints. Both parties used soft money to make "issue ads" on behalf of their candidates—as if there could be such a thing—and raised large sums of it. And both parties made "issue ads" for their presidential candidates—which is legally questionable. (The presidential campaigns themselves actually made the ads and used the parties as funnels for the money.) A Democratic National Committee "issue ad" that ran in twenty-four states in 1995 and 1996 said, "Protect families. For millions of working families, President Clinton cut taxes. The Dole/ Gingrich budget tried to raise taxes on eight million. The Dole/Gingrich budget would've slashed Medicare $270 billion, cut college scholarships. The President defended our values, protected Medicare. And now a tax cut of $1,500 a year for the first two years of college, most community colleges free. Help adults go back to school. The President's plan protects our values."

Also in 1996, for the first time the congressional party committees used soft money to make ads for their candidates, thus using soft money for individual federal campaigns—which is also legally questionable.

In fact, virtually all of the Clinton financial scandals in his 1996 election—the large contributions from unsavory or possibly illegal sources, the heavy-handed fund-raising by the President and the Vice President—involved soft money. The amount of soft money raised by both parties in 1996—262 million—was three times the amount raised in the previous presidential election.

As OF THE 1996 election, the post-Watergate reforms—enacted to end the ability of the very rich to buy access, ambassadorships, and policy—had been rendered null and void. The overall limit of $25,000 on individual contributions in one year, or $50,000 per election cycle, became meaningless. The idea that there were any limits on raising and spending private money for presidential candidates who accepted public financing was rendered obsolete.

Various attempts were made to reform the law in the years between 1974 and 1996. There was a kind of ritual to those legislative struggles: reformers would offer reforms, opponents would oppose, and nothing would happen. The legislative fights were marked by a high degree of hypocrisy, because it was generally understood that nothing would happen. Members would offer amendments knowing they were being proposed to amend a doomed bill, or would offer amendments that sounded as if they would bring about reform but were intended to make the bill unacceptable to a majority. These maneuvers gave people a free vote—a chance to appear to be for reform, in the knowledge there was no danger that reforms would pass.

After 1996, things changed.

4

————■————

The Money Culture

Indisputably, the greatest change in Washington over the past twenty-five years—in its culture, in the way it does business, and the ever-burgeoning amount of business transactions that go on here—has been in the preoccupation with money.

Striving for and obtaining money has become the predominant activity—and not just in electoral politics—and its effects are pernicious. The culture of money dominates Washington as never before; money now rivals or even exceeds power as the preeminent goal. It affects the issues raised and their outcome; it has changed employment patterns in Washington; it has transformed politics; and it has subverted values. It has led good people to do things that are morally questionable, if not reprehensible. It has cut a deep gash, if not inflicted a mortal wound, in the concept of public service.

Private interests have tried to influence legislative and administrative outcomes through the use of money for a long time. The great Daniel Webster was on retainer from the Bank of the United States and at the same time was one of its greatest defenders in the Congress. But never before in the modern age has political money played the pervasive role that it does now. By comparison, the Watergate period seems almost quaint.

61

THERE WAS A time when people came to Washington out of a spirit of public service and idealism. Engendering this spirit was one of John F. Kennedy's most important contributions. Then Richard Nixon, picking up from George Wallace, and then Ronald Reagan, in particular, derided "federal bureaucrats." The spirit of public service was stepped on, but not entirely extinguished.

But more than ever, Washington has become a place where people come or remain in order to benefit financially from their government service. (A similar thing could be said of journalists— and nonjournalists fresh out of government service—who package themselves as writers, television performers, and highly paid speakers at conventions.)

Probably not accidentally, the phenomenon of people cleaning up after, and from, government service also took on new proportions in the 1980s. (Several of Richard Nixon's alumni went to jail first.) The late Clark Clifford, the former Truman aide turned lawyer–wise man, minted money in his law office overlooking the White House. But Clifford was unusual for his time. Many of John F. Kennedy's alumni went on to—or back to—practicing law elsewhere, teaching, or doing philanthropic work. Jimmy Carter's alumni weren't in great demand. (Carter himself became an exemplary ex-President; unlike Gerald Ford and Ronald Reagan until he became too ill, Carter didn't use his former office to clean up, but continued his service in other ways.)

THERE USED to be a time when people joined presidential campaigns because they believed in the candidate. Now, an increasing number join campaigns with visions of the fame and fortune that might come their way afterward. The Reagan and Bush administrations produced several people who profited from their experience and contacts—but some of them, such as former Secretary of State James Baker, were wealthy before, and Baker probably would have flourished anyway.

Since his government service, Baker has done well as a partner in the Carlyle Group, a highly successful venture capital firm based in Washington (and which has attracted a number of former high administration officials), as a member of corporate boards, and as an attorney at his family's prosperous Houston firm. An institute at Rice University has been named after him. Like Henry Kissinger, Baker can open the door of international potentates for his clients and partners, and he also conducts business with these noteworthies. He specializes in Middle Eastern and Central Asian countries—for example, Kuwait and Azerbaijan—with which he built strong relationships as a result of the Gulf War.

Having worked for the Clinton White House, however, hasn't necessarily turned out to be particularly lucrative. An exception, of course, is the case of George Stephanopoulos, who became a famous public figure and a national heartthrob while he was still serving Clinton. When he left, he got a nearly $3 million book deal, plus a prominent television perch at ABC, plus a lot of well-paid public speaking engagements. But, in general, Clinton White House aides were not in great demand, and several spent a lot of time trying to arrange their postservice "packages." (People in this category do not take jobs so much as they put together packages.)

IN 1998, according to the requirements of the Lobbying Disclosure Act of 1995, there were close to 11,500 lobbyists wandering the halls of Congress. (Until the act went into effect, there were no real figures on how many lobbyists populated Washington.) However, this number isn't inclusive. A lot of people say they don't lobby—but they do something that seems a lot like it. Megafixer Clark Clifford solemnly maintained that he didn't lobby. Superlawyer Robert Strauss made the same claim. Perhaps these eminences were above betaking themselves to Capitol Hill to navigate the marble floors or to wait outside the Senate or House chamber, or a committee room, with the riffraff, hoping to nab a target, but they knew the power of their names and their phone calls and their social connections. And they could always send minions to do their bidding with the lawmakers or important staff members, who knew who sent them.

In the past, law firms didn't engage in lobbying to the extent they do now, and sometimes the firms hired nonlawyers to do their influencing. And now there are small firms established for the purpose of lobbying just one member, or one Congressional committee; they're usually staffed by people who had been close to the member, in one case by a powerful congressman's reputed mistress.

MORE THAN EVER, corporations or other interests that want to influence the Congress hire former Members of Congress or their aides as lobbyists, in order to ingratiate themselves with the current members. The former members have distinct advantages: they can go on the floor of the House or Senate and use their chambers' official dining rooms; even better, former House members can use the House gym, where a lot of business gets done. (A study by the *New York Times* found that in the 1970s only three percent of members who left Congress for one reason or another went to K Street—the downtown corridor that has come to symbolize the lawyer-lobbyist complex—and in the nineties twenty-three percent did so.)

The Buying of the Congress, a book by Charles Lewis of the Center for Public Integrity, published in 1998, said that from 1991 to 1996 at least fifteen percent of former Senate aides and at least fourteen percent of former senior House aides became registered lobbyists. The main sources of this pool of access-sharks were the "money committees," such as the House and Senate Commerce Committees, which handle such issues as banking and telecommunications. Sometimes the former aides so draw on their expertise and are so drawn into the legislative considerations that they in effect still act as staff members, writing legislation, except for a lot more money.

Sometimes a geographic region is spotted as an opportunity. In recent years, Latin America—with a growing economy, increased privatization, need for expensive "infrastructure" projects, and increased demand for U.S. goods (the second-largest market after Canada)—has become more and more attractive to Washington's lawyers and lobbyists. According to the *National Journal,* in the spring of 1998 former Clinton National Security Advisor Anthony Lake, who had supposedly returned to an academic life, and a former Commerce Department official, David Rothkopf, who had specialized in "emerging markets," formed their own consulting firm, which charged clients at least $250,000 a year for "strategic and political advice about investments in Latin America."

According to the same article, a Washington law firm, Verner, Liipfert, Bernhard, McPherson, and Hand, has fielded three of its former political stars—Bob Dole, Lloyd Bentsen, and Ann Richards—to drum up business in Latin America. So a former presidential candidate, a former vice-presidential candidate, and a former governor became, without apparent embarrassment, hustlers exploiting a new target of opportunity.

ANN WEXLER, one of Washington's premier lobbyists, knows a lot about how Washington has changed in the past twenty-five years. One day in the fall of 1997 she talked to me over lunch about how the new role of money has transformed Washington. Wexler, six-tyish, has short-cropped dark hair, brown eyes, and more energy than most people, in part because she enjoys life as well as the game. She has prospered as the head of her own firm, which she started the day after she left the Carter White House in January 1981. In 1983 she was astute enough to acquire as her partner Nancy Reynolds, who had worked for Ronald Reagan for ten years.

When she left the White House, Wexler, who had been in charge of "outreach"—working with outside groups in support of Carter's objectives—took with her what was believed to be the biggest Rolodex in town. She now has twenty-five lobbyists working with her, and in 1997 recruited as president former Representative Bob Walker, who had just retired from Congress and was one of Newt Gingrich's closest associates.

"This whole thing blew apart in the eighties, when congressmen could raise all this money," Wexler told me. "Before, they'd attend twenty-five-dollar barbecues.

"It was the development of PACs in the eighties—when people figured out that if they gave money through the PACs they could get access, they could get their phone calls returned. Just as the unions used dues for political activity, businesses began to use salary deductions for PACs. [Wexler's firm, like similar lobbying and law firms around town, has its own PAC.] The Hill figured it out. If you're a committee chairman, you could raise fifty thousand, even one hundred thousand dollars. Then they started leadership PACs—that's another extortion. Then the leader uses the money to try to gain higher office."

Under this last innovation, congressional leaders and would-be leaders and powerful committee chairmen created their own PACs, which they used to dole out money to win gratitude and advancement within their chamber—and to maintain power. Recent examples are former Senate Majority Leader George Mitchell and House Majority Whip Tom DeLay. DeLay's bestowing of campaign funds—especially on the class of 1994—helped him win his leadership post in 1995, and to maintain it.

One of the first things then–House Appropriations Committee

chairman Bob Livingston, of Louisiana, did when he decided in the spring of 1998 that he would like to succeed Gingrich as Speaker was to establish his own PAC (B.O.B.S.PAC, for "building our bases"). As Appropriations chairman, Livingston was in a position to raise a great deal of money, and he did. Livingston contributed to over ninety Republican House candidates: $5,000 from his PAC, $1,000 from his own campaign funds (he usually ran for Congress virtually unopposed), and served as a conduit for earmarked checks from business PACs to Republican candidates.[*]

Rivals within the same party for a higher leadership post compete to be the more beneficent. In 1998, Republican leaders raised a great deal more money than their Democratic counterparts did; they were the ones in power. Over the two-year election cycle, Republican leaders raised more than nineteen million dollars for fifty leadership PACs, while Democratic leaders raised a mere $328,000.

Wexler said, "We're dealing with a system where the members don't feel they can raise the money where they live. There's a panic among members. I get calls for money from people I've never heard of. The system's out of control."

THE ISSUE before the Senate in the spring of 1998 was a freighted one, a matter of historical importance. The question was whether to expand NATO, the North Atlantic Treaty Organization, founded after the Second World War to provide stability in Europe, which it had done successfully. The proposition was to include Poland, Hungary, and the Czech Republic, with other countries in Central Europe and the Baltics to follow in 2010.

There were strong reasons not to do so. Russia, whose cooperation the United States needed in all sorts of spheres (Bosnia, Kosovo, Iraq, and arms control, among others), and whose own stability was very much in the interest of the U.S., was vehemently against it. Russia saw a threat on its borders, and an insult. Moreover, by expanding NATO the original members became committed to the defense of countries or areas whose defense might lack public support. A successful alliance was in danger of being destabilized.

"We'll be back on a hair-trigger," said Senator Daniel Patrick Moynihan, who usually saw further than most of his colleagues.

[*]Livingston never became Speaker (see chapter 13).

New York Times foreign affairs columnist Thomas L. Friedman in 1997 called the expansion "the Whitewater of the Clinton foreign policy."

By the time the matter reached the Senate floor in late April 1998, the Clinton Administration had so committed the United States to the new policy that to turn back would have been an embarrassing retreat—in the eyes of the country and our allies. The three countries had already been formally invited to join NATO. The administration had rushed into the policy without thinking it through—in large part to head off certain ethnic-American voting blocs from going to the Republicans, in particular to Bob Dole, who was espousing the expansion.

In turn, the administration used these groups to drum up support in the Senate for the expansion.

But there was another force behind the approval of NATO expansion: defense contractors. The enlarging of NATO promised a lucrative new market, a welcome boon after business had fallen off with the end of the cold war. Even the Contract with America, the Republican agenda presented by Newt Gingrich and others after they took over the House in the 1994 election, called for NATO expansion and encouraged greater "inter-operability of military equipment." Translated, that meant that the new NATO members would have to buy sophisticated weapons from American defense companies. But since these countries couldn't afford them, according to Lars-Erik Nelson in the New York *Daily News*, the Pentagon had established a $15 billion fund to guarantee loans to these countries to buy the weapons.

According to a March 30, 1998, article in the *New York Times*, by Katharine Q. Seelye, a study done for the *Times* found that the six largest military contractors had spent $51 million on lobbying fees—which included not only the salaries of in-house lobbyists but also fees for others from outside the firms—from 1996 to the end of 1997. In that period, the six companies also expanded their contributions to congressional campaign committees. The defense industry was in fact the most generous contributor to the congressional campaigns, the *Times* said, having lavished $32.3 million on them since the collapse of communism in 1991.

Not all of the lobbying was for NATO expansion, of course, but that was the industry's main concern in those years, because of the lucrative new markets. If donations by computer and technology firms that do military work were added, the *Times* said, the total would "dwarf the lobbyist effort of any other industry."

The chief lobbying group on behalf of NATO expansion was the U.S. Committee to Expand NATO, whose president, Bruce L. Jackson, was also director of strategic planning for Lockheed Martin. The *Times* also said that arms manufacturers gave support to the ethnic groups who backed NATO membership for their native countries.

The Senate approved the expansion on April 30 overwhelmingly—by a vote of 80–19—after a few hours of debate spread over four days.

A GREAT DEAL more attention has been paid to the effects of the system on the politicians who raise money than on those who are asked for it. But some will talk about what befalls a contributor, or a potential one.

Nick Calio, the Republican lobbyist, who has some very large corporate clients, says that the rate of being hit up for money by Members of Congress has "increased significantly every year."

"Every request breeds another request," he adds. "If you show that you can produce, then you become a reservoir, and people come to dip in. And if you show any capacity to raise soft money and a crunch comes they come right back to you, because you've shown you can do it. And it gets difficult because you go back to the same people over and over again—your clients. And some people don't want to hear about it. They dive for cover when you call."

"LOOK AT THE list of Texas politicians," a former Republican Member of Congress said. "Texas has a long tradition of gaining power through using financial resources." He added that Dick Armey, the House Majority Leader, from Irving, Texas, as well as Tom DeLay, from Sugarland, Texas, just outside of Houston, "have used money to gain power." At the same time, another Texan, Bill Archer, of Houston, Texas, was chairman of the Ways and Means Committee, one of the most powerful committees in the House. The tradition of Texas leaders dispensing funds goes back to at least the late fifties, when Lyndon Johnson, of Texas, and Sam Rayburn, of Texas, ruled the Senate and the House respectively.

After the Republicans retook the House in 1994, DeLay became famous for keeping a list of contributors to the Republicans and refusing to grant audiences to anyone who hadn't forked over. He also tried to change what he saw—not inaccurately, given the forty-year Democratic domination of the House—as the Democratic-leaning culture of the lawyer-lobbyist community by refusing to see lobbyists who hadn't added Republicans to their firms after the Republican takeover. DeLay called this his "K Street Strategy."

In the fall of 1998, House Republican leaders, DeLay especially, brazenly objected to the naming, by the Electronic Industries Alliance, a major trade association, of a former Democratic congressman, David McCurdy, a moderate, as its president. A prominent soon-to-be-former Republican congressman, Bill Paxon, wanted the job. The association's board went ahead and named McCurdy to the post anyway. Gingrich, Armey, and DeLay ordered their staffs not to communicate with the association. Paxon was hired by the powerful law firm Akin, Gump, Strauss, Hauer & Feld, where he would join such eminent Democrats as Robert Strauss and Vernon Jordan.

In October of 1998, Representative John Linder, then chairman of the National Republican Congressional Committee, the political arm of the House Republicans, confirmed to *Roll Call,* a Capitol Hill newspaper, that the Republican leadership was blocking legislation of interest to the electronics association. The leaders were also spreading the word on K Street, he said, so that others would get the picture. Linder also said that he had told the National Association of Home Builders, one of the biggest and most powerful lobbying groups, that the Republican leaders would be less interested in working with them because they had hired a Democrat to run their organization.

MEMBERS OF CONGRESS—and the lobbyists who aim to please them—have come up with the relatively recent innovation of persuading people to donate money for university professorial chairs in their name when they retire.

I first heard of this a couple of years ago from the "Washington representative"—that is, lobbyist—for a major defense contractor, who was complaining about it to some of his counterparts. I later called him to ask how this gambit worked.

"Oh, man," he replied, "the bane of our existence." But first he started talking about another annoyance—the leadership PACs. He said, "One of the banes right now is the explosion of leadership PACs, in which leaders feel they have to curry favor with other members by giving them money. Now, even younger members feel that to get ahead they have to create a fund to butter up their own colleagues—especially if they don't have a tough reelection race—so that if there's a race for a leadership position or a committee chairmanship then you have chits you can call in. I can tell you that most industry PACs, like the one we have here, don't mind giving to members. It's money we've solicited from our employees and it's managed by the company's PAC board. We look at their records and see if we want to give to an incumbent. If it's someone we don't favor because of his voting record, we will go out and invite someone else to run." He said that the representatives of several military contractors, and some other corporate representatives as well ("we're all pretty close"), will get together to recruit a candidate.

"So there is this regular drumbeat for PAC money for people who are running, the drumbeat for leadership PACs, and then there's the drumbeat of the parties for soft money. Soft money is a bottomless pit. Each party has an entry fee [for attending their special events], usually fifteen thousand dollars. So we tend to throw fifteen thousand in the DNC pot, and the same for the RNC, and for the four party congressional committees—the Republican and Democratic House and Senate campaign committees. Usually, the money's for a dinner, so we probably contribute for six dinners. We tend to give a hundred thousand in soft money, and we get beat up as a poor contributor."

Then he turned to the subject of the chairs. "Now we're finding that not only do we support some members throughout their entire public life as long as they're helpful to us, but the year they retire there's a flurry of activity. It's now typical that when a member retires, the member thinks it's wonderful to have a chair endowed in his name at a university in his state. It's a big money deal, and we're usually very easy. Senior members who retire almost always get a university chair. It amounts to buying a table for a dinner for ten, fifteen, twenty thousand dollars—or they may ask for a hundred thousand or even a million. There's no limit. This is a charitable contribution to a university to endow a chair." (Therefore, it's tax deductible.)

He told me that a chair had been endowed for Sam Nunn, the

former chairman of the Senate Armed Services Committee, at Emory University after he retired from the Senate in 1996. And he was expecting to be asked to contribute in the fall of 1998 when Strom Thurmond, age ninety-five, was to retire as chairman of the Senate Armed Services Committee.* "Every company will be expected to throw in fifty to a hundred thousand dollars." Some chairs are dedicated by the lobbyists to a Member of Congress while he is still serving.

I asked the defense lobbyist what the point was of trying to please a member who was retiring. There were two reasons for doing so, he said. The first was—and this would be particularly applicable to defense contractors—it spreads goodwill in the state. "The bigger the company's presence in the state, the higher the contribution," he explained. "Second, it's another excuse to have a dinner where you can go elbow-to-elbow with a Member of Congress. We all do it."

Even if the member is going to retire?

"They have tons of their colleagues there, and it's a warm and fuzzy dinner."

The gift bans, or limits, enacted in recent years, including a limit on the price of meals that can be accepted, have driven lobbyists and members to find other avenues for purposeful socializing. So, besides the retirement dinners, special projects provide a means to please members of Congress and to spend a lobbyist's idea of "quality time" with them.

In 1995, Senator Daniel Inouye, the ranking Democrat on the Defense Appropriations Subcommittee, got the idea that the battleship U.S.S. *Missouri* should be towed from its mooring in Bremerton, Washington, to Pearl Harbor, in his home state of Hawaii, to be used as a memorial of the Japanese attack in 1941.

The defense-contractor lobbyist said, "There's a push within the industry to contribute funds to establish the *Missouri* as a memorial for visitors to the Pearl Harbor area. He [Inouye] gets folks to call the companies and ask for contributions to the memorial, and he gets great credit in the state. We also contribute to military museums in the states, and monuments and commemoratives."

---

*Thurmond retired as chairman of the Senate Armed Services Committee on January 5, 1999, and handed the gavel over to Senator John Warner, of Virginia.

And then there are the charitable dinners. "If you look at the dance cards around town," he told me, "there's the leukemia fund or the heart fund that members or members' wives have become associated with. You give for the dinner. It's a 501(c)(3) [tax deductible]. The charitable dinners become a way to spend time with a member.

"We spend several millions of dollars a year on contributions that aren't political."

Not precisely.

BUT OF LATE the interests and their favorite lawmakers—at least the most powerful ones—haven't waited for retirement to set up and contribute to a chair or, better yet, an "institute" in the politician's name. Thus, corporations can also curry favor with the politician by donating to a chair or institute while the politician is still in his prime.

Early in 1999 such an institute was being established in the name of Trent Lott at the University of Mississippi, his alma mater. Currying favor with the Senate majority leader through (tax-deductible) donations is obviously a good investment. The majority leader schedules legislation, appoints people to sensitive commissions, leans on committee chairmen to push certain bills—and this is just some of his power.

Among those who pledged large donations to the Trent Lott Leadership Institute were MCI WorldCom, a large telecommunications empire, which, under the law, could make direct donations to any federal politician of only $10,000 in PAC money. And MCI had a lot of concerns about congressional policymaking on telecommunications issues. Lott, for his part, appointed an MCI representative to a commission studying whether the Internet should be taxed. The plan was that major donors would have rooms named after them in the new building.

According to *Congressional Quarterly*, a similar institute had been established in the name of Jesse Helms, the North Carolina Republican and vengeful chairman of the Senate Foreign Relations Committee. Happily for Helms and Wingate College, his alma mater, foreign funds—supposedly illegal in American elections—could be donated to this enterprise. According to *Congressional Quarterly*, among those foreign governments that had contributed were Taiwan ($225,000), and Kuwait ($100,000).

And the University of Louisville has established the McConnell Center for the Study of Leadership, and a chair named the "McConnell Chair in Leadership," for the Kentucky Senator and ardent foe of reforming the campaign finance system. The university declines to reveal the donors.

Via such worthy-sounding and ego-enhancing projects, the possibilities for the politicians shaking down access- and favor-seekers, as well as corporations and foreign governments seeking access or favors, are substantial.

ANOTHER HIGHLY successful Washington lobbyist said, "One of the things that is amazing to me is the charities." Senators' wives, he said, "have wonderful charities. I mean, great, heart-tugging charities."

"When Senator So-and-so's wife calls your office and puts her arm around your neck about this wonderful charity and a black-tie event in the Mayflower Hotel ballroom, you get the drift. It's tables, not tickets, ten thousand to fifteen thousand a table. If you want to be a platinum donor, or an underwriter of the dinner, you give twenty-five thousand. You give a hundred thousand and you might get to sit next to the senator."

I asked about the benefits to the lobbyists of all this.

The lobbyist replied, "The senator probably feels he's done good works, and you give the money because, one, you want to be looked on favorably by the senator's wife and, two, it's part of the game around town called 'buying access.'"

VICE PRESIDENT Al Gore established a fund for a chair at the University of Tennessee in the name of his late sister, Nancy. In its early years, the fund-raising for the chair was run by Peter Knight, Gore's chief fund-raiser in 1992, campaign manager in 1996, and in between and since a prosperous lawyer-lobbyist, and a major fund-raiser for Gore's campaign for the presidential election in 2000. After controversy inevitably arose over Knight's role in raising money for the chair, the fund-raising was taken over by the University of Tennessee.

A FORMER Democratic congressman, a man still in his forties, had joined one of Washington's largest law firms. Over lunch in March 1997, he said, "Two things have changed so dramatically in the last dozen years: the severity of this town and the money chase. It goes together. All the races are about ethics—the other guy's ethics. They weren't like that before—going through people's financial records. Campaigns changed from the mid-eighties on—the harsher the better."

In his current position at a well-heeled law firm, the former congressman said, "I get an average of two calls a day" from candidates seeking money. "Our own PAC is one of the largest in the country—it's just huge. We're in play. We're popular. The CEO of our biggest client called the managing partner of the firm the other day, and we sent over fifteen thousand for a table at a Republican dinner. The money flow in the last half-dozen years is so much greater than it had been."

THE FORM of lobbying has shifted in the last few years. The definitions have become more vague. People who call themselves consultants say they do not lobby. But they can make a ton of money planning strategies for influencing Congress, which usually involves P.R. of some sort: ad campaigns, press conferences. Consultants are hired by companies and trade associations to offer what is generally called "strategic advice." A person who would seem to be a lobbyist told me that he very rarely goes to Capitol Hill. "It depends on how you position yourself," he said. "Now it's more a matter of assessing the situation; we can't operate without a strategy." There are now so many consultants in Washington that a couple of years ago a friend of mine, himself a consultant, was hired by a large corporation to sort out its numerous consultants.

A man who was flourishing in the consulting business in Washington told me in 1998, "You see more and more people getting into the business and you think it's very competitive. But it's not. There's so much business. There are a lot of companies who have representation in Washington today who didn't have it before. Microsoft had no one until 1995; now it has about sixty [representatives]. Even if other companies' increases in consultants aren't as dramatic as Microsoft's, there's a long list of them."

THE FUND-RAISERS that take place on Capitol Hill virtually every night that Congress is in session—usually a half dozen a night—are commonplace, but there are of late new, more ingenious mechanisms for raising and donating money.

The Capitol Hill fund-raisers have the benefit of convenience, of course. They're held close enough to the Capitol itself that members can rush across the street and down two or three blocks to the Capitol Hill Club (for the Republicans) and the National Democratic Club (for the Democrats) between votes. Many of the fund-raisers for individual members of Congress are sponsored by interest groups.

On September 9, 1998, there was an Insurance Industry Meet and Greet for candidate Greg Walden, a challenger for a congressional seat in Oregon; it was held at La Colline, an elegant French restaurant near Capitol Hill. On September 16, there was Congressman Dan Miller's Florida Citrus Breakfast (cost, $500) at Miller's home on Capitol Hill. On September 17, there was a Cigar and Wine Tasting Reception for candidate Mark Nielson, a Republican challenger from Connecticut, hosted by the Associated Builders and Contractors (cost, $1,000 for a PAC and $500 for an individual). On September 22, the American Trucking Association held a reception for Representative John Peterson, a Pennsylvania Republican. Actually, in September, the Trucking Association sponsored three fund-raisers for Republicans and one for a Democrat.

On the whole, few fund-raisers for Democrats were sponsored by interest groups. The Republicans controlled the Congress, after all. Yet Democrats nearly kept up with the Republicans in the number of fund-raising events that September: thirty-seven for the Republicans and thirty for the Democrats.

Thomas Boggs's law firm, Patton Boggs, occupies an entire nine-story building on M Street, N.W.—prime real estate. Boggs's office, on the top floor, opens onto a large balcony and has a splendid view of Washington west to Georgetown. Two things about Boggs's office caught my attention: the expensive paintings and the large stack of pink phone slips on his desk. Boggs, indisputably one of Washington's top superlawyer-lobbyists, is large, heavyset, with a round, pinkish face, blue eyes, dark wavy hair, and a look of prosperity, down to his Gucci loafers. When we spoke in the summer of 1998 about fund-raisers, Boggs said, "I go to a bunch of them."

Why?

"Just to show up and say, 'I like you. You're a good guy.' And to network. That's far more important. If a tax bill is being written up, people there will know what's in the tax bill. It doesn't matter so much who is the member the fund-raiser is for, but he's the cat-alyst for getting us there."

Boggs laughingly explained, "The best time for a member to hold a fund-raiser is right after a recess, because nobody has seen anybody. September is a big month, it's like going back to school."

Boggs's firm itself holds a host of fund-raisers. Another lobby-ist says, "They must have events every single day. I get a half-dozen invitations a month from them." Boggs laughed and said, "He's probably right."

But methods of fund-raising have taken new forms in recent years. People in lobbying firms also raise money for Members of Congress by conveniently bringing together in intimate groups the member who is being helped (with money) and the client who wants help from him. Some Members of Congress hire their own professional fund-raisers, who work from computerized lists. Some lobbying firms even put themselves on contract to raise money for a Member of Congress.

"It's a little bit shady," one lobbyist said. "They're in effect working for that member and for their client."

Patrick Griffin, who headed the Clinton White House congres-sional liaison office from January 1994 until February 1996, and then returned to the lobbying firm he had started in 1987, told me that he doesn't go to the fund-raisers on the Hill, because he doesn't have to.

"I just send the money," he said, and he laid out his own approach to fund-raising. "I have fund-raisers all the time—some-times jointly with somebody. I'll have a lunch for a member where I can raise ten thousand dollars. I'll have ten, fifteen people at most. You bring in your client. That's more effective than the big gang-bang." It's a more convenient way to discuss business.

Griffin continued, "Some interests don't have enough money to contribute to everyone they're interested in, so they might contribute to the party committees, who then invite them on a golfing or skiing weekend, where a number of members might be present. People see you around, and you get quality time with the members."

THE POPULAR conception is that money is exchanged for a vote, but while that no doubt happens sometimes, there are subtler ways by which a Member of Congress can attract—and help—donors. "All we really expect is access," one lobbyist said to me. He was playing it down a bit, but access is the gate to influence. And there is much to try to affect besides actual votes in the Congress. Regulations by government agencies, over which Members of Congress can have powerful influence, can be just as important. An affected industry may be struggling to head off the promulgation of a new rule, and it might seek legislation, or other forms of pressure, that would prevent it. A lobbyist gave me a not-so-hypothetical example: a senator who has historically been for side A might agree to be helpful to side B—"because he doesn't want to completely alienate them and he might even get their support"—by asking the agency for a study before the rule is issued. This gives side B time to carry on its campaign.

"Does the money then come in from side B?" I asked.

"That's why he does it," the lobbyist replied.

This lobbyist said, "A lot of it isn't visible. Members can be responsive to lobbyists' needs without having to support their legislation in the end. A member can make a client or company happy by looking like he's trying—making a phone call to an agency, asking a question at a hearing, writing a letter. You might try to find a way to neutralize someone.

"The point is," the lobbyist continued, "money isn't all about votes. There are a lot of ways to make people happy. The sophisticated lobbyist and the sophisticated member understand that."

LATELY, indirect ways of using money to influence a Member of Congress have come into vogue. A lobbyist for very big interests told me, "What does a savvy lobbyist do? He remembers that the most important thing for a Member of Congress is to get reelected." So the lobbyist would point out the "back-home reason" for a member to vote a certain way. To reinforce the "back-home" argument, lobbyists have created grass-roots support, or the appearance of it, for the corporation's or industry's position.

This approach, pioneered by the lobbyist Ann Wexler, has spawned another new industry in Washington: whole companies whose sole reason for being is to stir up grass-roots support for their client's position. Professional political operatives are hired to mobilize the local citizenry around an issue—economic, environmental—that affects, directly or indirectly, the client's business. Such groups are often organized to counter environmentalists who are objecting to a new plant or supporting a certain regulation.

The people, organized from outside, are encouraged to call on their representative in Washington or in his home district; to write letters, send faxes, make phone calls, organize town meetings, get someone in the area to write a letter to the editor, or even an op-ed piece—all to create the illusion of "grass-roots support." Even the National Association of Broadcasters, which ostensibly represents local stations but is dominated by the networks and their owned-and-operated stations, has retained a Washington company specializing in "grass roots."

But despite the importance of this relatively new form of influence/pressure, another lobbyist told me, it has to be paired with money. Pat Griffin said, "You can do money alone, but it helps to have grass-roots support. You can have money without grass roots, but not the other way around."

Of course, organizing and executing a campaign is expensive in itself. So these "grass roots" efforts, sown and nurtured from Washington, are another, indirect, and sometimes deceptive, way for interests to spend money to further their agenda.

As the "grass roots" method became widely used, a still newer approach was added, as was a new term in the lobbyists' liturgy, "grass tops."

"Grass tops" are the opinion-makers in a town or an area who are called on to help the cause of a lobbyist or local company. A lobbyist said, "Sometimes they have to be induced, and sometimes they're paid—that's not uncommon." These "grass roots" and "grass tops" efforts, in which Washington pros stir up, and even pay, people who might not be motivated to take action on their own are sometimes referred to by the more honest—or cynical—lobbyists as "Astroturf."

A lobbyist explained, "New techniques get invented as old ones get discounted."

GIVEN ITS combined money and power and ability to create ostensible grass-roots activity, the broadcast industry has become, in the words of Senator John McCain, "the most powerful industry in Washington." The broadcasters have been able to resist McCain's efforts to get them to provide free airtime for political campaigns or to pay anything at all for their ultravaluable use of the traditional broadcast spectrum, making the United States one of the few countries that gives away the broadcast spectrum—a public asset—for nothing. (Parts of the spectrum for more specialized uses, such as cell phones and paging systems, are now auctioned off in order to bring in government revenue.) The broadcasters have also been able to fend off any serious impositions on the money they make off political advertising—even though they are required to offer such advertising at a reduced fee.

SOMETIMES the issue giving rise to a "grass roots" effort is largely manufactured. In one instance in the mid-nineties, involving state regulation of securities, a lobbyist who was involved said, "A campaign was manufactured on an issue that wasn't fully drawn, but the lobbying campaign forced it to be drawn. It had all the elements of the most sophisticated campaigns. The industry was willing to put aside fifteen to twenty million for it. This was an example of a completely manufactured crisis and solution."

He continued, "Sometimes you're trying to convince the Congress that there's a groundswell, but there's nobody behind it. If you have to make it up, you hope you don't get found out. It's like the Wizard of Oz—there's nobody there but you and the smoke and the whistle."

FROM TIME TO TIME, to the delight of "downtown" Washington, there's a big legislative fight that engages armies of lobbyists and consultants on both sides. For them, such titanic clashes are heaven-sent.

The Telecommunications Competition and Deregulation Act of 1995 was a classic. The purpose of the legislation, which was backed by Speaker Gingrich and by Vice President Gore, was to open up the telecommunications industry to competition. It would affect the general public a great deal because it dealt with how we are entertained, how we get news, how we're educated, how we communicate with each other. But those, of course, were not the questions that the Congress was addressing.

Al Sykes, who was chairman of the Federal Communications Commission during the Bush Administration and is now president of Hearst News Media and Technology, said, "The issues became company versus company or industry versus industry, where in the final analysis there should be only one constituency—the public."

The fight unleashed vast amounts of money in contributions to the Members of Congress. It was also a vehicle for raising a great deal of soft money for both national parties, for all four congressional campaign committees (Republican and Democratic House and Senate), and for the state parties at the direction of the national parties. In the 1995–96 election cycle, during which numerous telecommunications issues were still being considered, the telecommunications industry gave three times as much soft money as it had in the previous election cycle. "Darling," said one lobbyist who was involved, "no other issue created more soft money."

The telecommunications fight pitted competing economic interests—long-distance telephone (MCI, AT&T, Sprint, GTE) against regional Bells, cable, Hollywood, broadcasters (large vs. small)—as they fought over the spoils. The interest that was hardly heard in the struggle was the public's.

A former telecommunications official said, "When the Congress gets into specific industry legislation, most members don't know much about it, and neither does the public, so members are much more pushed and pulled by the lobbying campaign. Look at members of the Communications subcommittees; they get large amounts of money from their local carrier, and a long-distance carrier, and a competitive carrier, and the cellular business. That works in favor of nobody doing anything because members don't want to 'work against our friends,' or you get a hodgepodge, butchered legislation. The 1995 act was butchered legislation."

Members of Congress have for the past couple of decades openly referred to the committees that handle telecommunications issues—the House and Senate Commerce Committees—as "lucrative" committees on which to serve, right up there with the tax-writing House Ways and Means and Senate Finance committees.

The selling point of the telecommunications bill was that it would "benefit the consumer" by creating more competition, and thus the market would lower prices. But so far the result has been mergers more than additional competition, and there's been no significant reduction of prices.

Senator McCain told me that he had opposed the telecommunications bill. "I thought it wasn't deregulatory, it was regulatory. Everyone from the Vice President to the congressional leaders said it was the greatest thing to happen to consumers. The result?

Phone rates have gone up. Cable rates have gone up. The bill took care of every special interest in the communications industry, except for the average person who owns a telephone or watches cable or makes a long-distance call."

PERHAPS THE longest-running jamboree has been the struggle between commercial banks and investment banks over something called the Glass-Steagall Act, which was passed in 1933, in the wake of the 1929 crash. The idea was to keep banks out of the stock market. Their participation in the market was one of the reasons cited for the 1929 crash—whether rightly or wrongly has never been resolved. The law also prevented commercial banks from getting into venture banking, and ever since the law was enacted the commercial banks have fought to enter the investment, bond, and insurance businesses. The fight over changing the law has gone on for at least two decades and has involved masses of lobbyists on both sides.

The money that poured in became a strong incentive for Members of Congress *not* to resolve the impasse. The financial, insurance, and securities industries combined are among the largest contributors to their campaigns: the Center for Responsive Politics, a monitoring group, said that during the 1997–98 election cycle the financial businesses, through their PACs or through individual donations, on both sides of the issue contributed over $70 million in hard and soft money to Members of Congress, the political parties, leadership PACs, and anywhere else they could put it (more to Republicans than Democrats). And individual donors associated with the financial service industry contributed almost $62 million to federal candidates, PACs, and federal parties for the 1998 election. Of course, "grass-roots" operations were created to carry on the war between the wealthy institutions.

A lobbyist for very large interests told me, "Senator Y is either for or against repealing Glass-Steagall. If you are for keeping Glass-Steagall the way it is, then you are friends with investment bankers; if you are for changing Glass-Steagall, your friends are the commercial banks.

"In the midst of trying to convince the senator which side of Glass-Steagall to be on, the senator calls you to buy a ticket or take a table for a dinner. If you're the corporate head of General Motors, what's ten thousand dollars? Most of them have dinners where the senator pats you on the fanny and says, 'Thanks, pal.'"

The lobbyist continued, "All this money. A man or woman in Congress has tens of thousands of issues to address. They are banged on by people on both sides of that issue. By meeting with all the groups involved they've created a constituency for money. They keep lists of those who have lobbied them, and go back to them to solicit their help in their campaign.

"I would have to conclude that in a lot of the fights there are no real people involved. Sometimes the outcome little affects the average citizen. It's a battle of corporations. You can get into an abstract discussion about the effects on the economy. Bunk. It's a decision between the very wealthy and the very rich. That's true of Glass-Steagall. It was true of the struggle between the Hollywood studios and the television networks over syndication rights and production. That Ping-Pong match lasted over twenty years."

A merger between Citicorp, a major bank, and Travelers Group, which dealt with securities and insurance, announced in early April 1998, required a change in Glass-Steagall. Egged on by lobbyists in support of the merger, the Congress decided to take another look at the law. In May, the House, by a one-vote margin that reflected the balance of power of the interests, passed a revision of the act. Senator Alfonse D'Amato had opposed changing Glass-Steagall in the past. But when the merger of two of his largest corporate constituents was announced, D'Amato, the chairman of the Senate Banking Committee and up for reelection in 1998, said he wasn't interested in having the Senate take up the matter until after the election. That way, the money would keep flowing.

The lobbyist said, "That's what everyone out here on K Street thinks." Thus, with the banking system in increasing turmoil as the industry was changing through mergers and the international financial system threw numerous shocks into it, Congress held off acting so as not to cut off lucrative sources of campaign funds. D'Amato received $2.9 million from both sides of the financial industry in the 1997–98 election cycle.

THERE IS, among lobbyists, a theological argument of sorts over whether it is better to give hard money (limited amounts) or soft (unlimited amounts). Because of the rise in the collection and use of soft money in recent years, the issue of PACs has almost been forgotten. But their continuing utility hasn't been lost on the lobbyists.

David Rehr is the vice president for public affairs for the National Beer Wholesalers Association, which is particularly powerful because there are beer wholesalers in virtually every congressional district.

Rehr told me, "We don't do soft money. It's a bottomless pit. It's never enough. Both sides play you against each other. Hard money is much more valuable, because it actually goes for electing someone. Giving a candidate ten thousand dollars [$5,000 in a primary and $5,000 in the general election] directly is much more useful. Soft money is more amorphous. If you go up to Congressman John Smith and say, 'John, we're going to give you ten thousand dollars,' it's much more valuable to him than if you give an amorphous fifty thousand in soft money to the national committee. The only way you get attention with soft money is it has to be really big: three hundred, four hundred, five hundred thousand, a million—that gets people's attention."

In a document—with holes punched for insertion in members' fund-raising notebooks—in the National Republican Congressional Committee's March–April 1998 newsletter for Republican members and their allies, Rehr sets forth "Six Steps to Maximize PAC Receipts Before November 1998." It provided an interesting window on the world of business contributions.

Rehr wrote, "At the NBWA, we generally receive ten to thirty invitations for events per week, dozens of telephone calls from professional PAC fund-raisers...and requests from other corporate and business association representatives serving on incumbents' PAC steering committees....The growth of so-called 'Leadership PACs' in both the House and Senate has further increased the competition for PAC dollars. You need to elevate yourself above your peers to maximize your PAC support....As an incumbent you have tremendous resources to maximize your PAC support from the business community."

In the past couple of years, some corporations have decided to stop giving soft money, for similar reasons. The money is unaccountable; there's now more scrutiny of big soft-money donors; there's no end to the requests; and a donation of hard money directly to a candidate is more welcome. But most of these corporations planned to put more soft money into "issue ads" for the 1998 race, another indirect way of influencing the Congress.

The Business Roundtable, an organization of the two hundred largest U.S. companies, increased, by about $300,000 per company, the amounts the members paid for dues, and ran ads against the "Patients' Bill of Rights," to reform managed-care programs, and against an international agreement reached in Kyoto, in 1998, to reduce the hazards of climate change. The Business Roundtable spent $5 million on issue ads alone in 1998.

But if one wants to please a presidential candidate, or party chairman, or chairman of one of the congressional campaign committees, soft money is in order because it's easier to get hold of and can be raised from individuals and labor unions and corporations in large amounts. And, at the least, big donors get access. Big-time donors or fund-raisers are also willing to steer money, as directed, to states where the President needs help. And, as was shown in 1996, they receive gratitude, access, and perhaps more.

A FORMER Democratic Member of Congress said, "What's so often misunderstood about the way we finance our campaigns is it doesn't affect big decisions, such as how to fix Social Security. It's the smaller things, which don't get reported—on spending bills, on tax bills, on authorization bills."

As an example, a proposal that the government charge meat packers fees for inspecting meat and poultry has never been enacted. The impasse has continued despite recent incidents of meat and poultry causing health crises—E. coli, salmonella. But the meat and poultry industry have strongly opposed paying a fee to upgrade the inspection system. And they have opposed giving the government authority to level criminal fines on meat packers and poultry producers, and the Congress has rejected giving that authority.

"The opposition is bipartisan," says someone familiar with the politics of these issues. "These things die in the Agriculture Committees, which are made up of people who represent agricultural interests. The committees generally reflect one perspective. So these proposals don't get the free flow of debate. That's where the power of money is.

"By and large, it's in the secondary issues—the ones that may affect the public the most. These are the issues where Members of Congress are less free because of the financing of campaigns."

ONE WEARY lobbyist says, "When I retire, I'll never write another check. I do it now because it's the cost of doing business."

5

———•———

A Painful Lesson

On one wall of Fred Thompson's office on the fifth floor of the Dirksen Building is a drawing of Sam Ervin, inscribed with the words, "To Fred D. Thompson—With deepest appreciation for the magnificent work you did for the Senate Select Committee on Presidential Campaign Activities." It was signed by Ervin on August 8, 1974—the day Richard Nixon announced his resignation as President.

This tribute from a Democratic committee chairman to the counsel for the opposite party was of another era, as Thompson was to learn painfully.

In the late afternoon of July 7, 1997, the day before the hearings were to begin, Thompson, sitting in his office, looked tired. His face was paler than usual, the sacks beneath his eyes puffier. He was wearing a white shirt with French cuffs, a dark tie, and trousers that were navy with a wide pinstripe. His thinning hair was longish and slightly curly at the nape of his neck.

Interviewing Thompson always had an aura of danger. The enormous man would tilt back his large wing chair, which was covered in blue cloth with a pattern of burgundy and cream fleur-de-lis, to a forty-five degree angle, giving the sense that at any moment it might fall over backward, taking him with it. But his height gave him balancing powers that less towering mortals dare not test. His office also contained a standard Senate-issue burgundy leather sofa, a large desk, and photographs of his three children.

I asked Thompson if he had a theory of the case.

After a long pause, he replied, "I bring it down to very simple terms. I think it's about power and it's about money and what people will do to meet the increasing demands for money."

And then Thompson told me, "Probably tomorrow, but, if not tomorrow, very soon, we're going to have a statement on behalf of the committee that is going to deal with China." He continued, "It's going to set out some things and it will paint a picture."

It was important to Thompson to hold hearings that would "paint a picture"—as a way of making sense of the morass of material about campaign finance abuses. That was a huge challenge. Unlike Watergate, or the Iran-Contra episode, the finance scandals had no story line. Thompson somehow had to depict a sprawling mess. He wanted to show that the Democratic National Committee "had no safeguards." He told me, "I think the picture will emerge that there was almost a deliberate attempt to not interfere with [John] Huang's fund-raising, no matter how he did it."

Thompson was referring, of course, to one of the main figures in the Democrats' fund-raising scheme, a former employee of the Riadys. He had been a Commerce Department official and then a fund-raiser for the DNC, and had been in and out of the White House often, and was a major target of the hearings. The early testimony was to focus on Huang's activities. Thompson and his staff had deliberately spread the idea that Harold Ickes, formerly Clinton's deputy chief of staff, would be an early witness, as a way of titillating the press and of trying to fake out the White House—in Thompson's words, "to keep the White House from working [other witnesses] over." Huang, who had taken the Fifth Amendment, was one of forty-five figures in this story who had either taken the Fifth Amendment or left the country. Never before had a congressional hearing been treated with such disregard.

In our conversation just before the hearings were to begin, I asked Thompson what he was worried about.

After another long pause, Thompson said, "I'm looking at a vast landscape out there. How long is a piece of string?"

Unhappy that no television outlet planned to cover the hearings in real time, Thompson said, "I think the Beltway crowd misconceives the effect of concentrated TV on the American people on things they'd only heard vaguely about." He knew he needed "a bombshell" to get people's attention, and felt he would have one in the opening statement he was preparing.

While we were talking, Bonnie Sansonetti, Thompson's executive assistant, slipped into the office and handed Thompson a note. John Glenn was on the phone. Thompson took the call in another room. Thompson had asked Glenn if he wanted to join him in the opening statement, but in this phone call Glenn said he hadn't seen it yet. Thompson told a staff member to let a Glenn staff member read the draft.

Thompson returned to our conversation. He looked a little worried. "I'm getting concerned that the Democrats are going to object to my doing this." Still hoping that the Democrats would sign on to his statement, Thompson said, "I may have gone beyond where they're willing to go. I hope it won't come to that."

Tilting back perilously, talking about his proposed statement, Thompson said, presciently, "It will raise more questions than it will answer."

BY THIS TIME, relations between Thompson and Glenn had been poisoned by partisanship beyond the control of either man. A number of people, including Thompson's close friend John McCain—who kept in touch with Thompson daily, offering him moral support—suggested that Thompson should have courted Glenn more. But given the pressures on both men, it's unlikely that idea would have worked. Besides, Thompson had grown resentful of the Democrats' tactics of complaining about his treatment of them, when he was going beyond what his party leaders thought he should do, and he wasn't much in the mood for courting.

Thompson had a gruff side, and his resentment fed the gruffness. Perhaps no matter how the Democrats were behaving, he shouldn't have let resentment in the door, but he did. And others' voices were whispering in Glenn's ear that Thompson wasn't treating him fairly. Susan Collins, the Republican committee member from Maine, remarked to me, of Glenn and Thompson, "They're both good men, but also very proud people, easily offended, and jealous of their prerogatives."

The committee Democrats had been pushing for authority to issue more subpoenas. The number of Republican subpoenas inevitably outnumbered the Democrats', and now the Democrats were demanding thirty more. The Democrats' demands were part of their strategy to paint the hearings as "partisan."

At the same time, in meetings of Senate Republicans, other Republicans took Thompson to task for allowing the Democrats any subpoenas at all. When Thompson tried to talk to Trent Lott about his difficulty in getting Republican support for subpoenas for the Democrats, Lott instructed him to "touch base with Don"— meaning Nickles. (Lott had made sure that Nickles filled one of the openings on the committee to protect his interests.) Thad Cochran said, "Fred was willing to put himself at great political risk in the Republican conference by trying to be bipartisan."

ON JULY 8, the opening day of the hearings, Room 216 of the Hart Senate Office Building was jammed with press and spectators. TV cameras lined the hallways outside the room.

Thompson opened with the dramatic subject to get people's attention. He said, "I speak of allegations of a plan hatched by the Chinese government to pour illegal money into American political campaigns." In what was to be the largest problem created by Thompson's statement, he said, "Our investigation suggests it affected the 1996 presidential race." The members of Thompson's staff, who drafted the statement, thought that they were being very careful in using the word "suggests."

It wasn't at all clear what "affected" meant. If it meant that Chinese money *had an effect* on the result of the presidential election, Thompson was staking out territory he wouldn't be able to defend. Later in the hearings, Thompson tried to shake the implication that the Chinese money had thrown the presidential election.

During the course of the hearings, in response to Dick Durbin's needling criticism of his statement, Thompson said, "Since the senator has again referred to me individually, I feel I need to take a few minutes to respond. Every time the senator mentions the beginning of these hearings and what I said, the characterization gets a little bit further from reality....There is disagreement, I think, as to whether or not or to what extent the presidential races were involved in that. However, I do not think that evidence of a Chinese determination to affect our congressional elections is anything to celebrate. Something like that used to be a serious matter in this country. It never occurred to me that this would become a partisan matter." But Glenn wasn't about to put his name on a statement that suggested that the presidential campaign had been "affected" by Chinese money. So when Thompson phoned him about an hour before the hearings were to begin, Glenn told him that he wouldn't join him in the statement.

THOMPSON had been encouraged in his pursuit of the China issue by Harry Damelin, one of the majority counsels, who made the China "plot" his territory. Damelin, an attorney who had served as the chief counsel of the Permanent Subcommittee on Investigations of the Committee on Governmental Affairs, is a slim, intense man, with a decidedly Boston accent. Another Republican on the committee said, "Damelin was totally convinced that there was solid evidence" for the opening statement. In a conversation we had later, Thad Cochran, the Mississippi Republican, defended Thompson's conclusion: "He's not overstating what the facts show to a reasonable person who draws inferences. It's circumstantial evidence on which people can draw inferences."

In early 1997, Damelin, who had a security clearance, began poking around for what information the super-secret National Security Agency, which eavesdrops all over the world, might have. The NSA had intercepted sensitive satellite messages between Beijing and its embassy in Washington and had been finding information about Chinese involvement in U.S. politics. The NSA showed committee investigators intercepted material that to Damelin—and Thompson—clearly indicated that there was a Chinese plan to get involved in the U.S. electoral process. After much pushing, and a number of unenlightening briefings by the CIA and the FBI, these agencies finally indicated that in May 1995, they had picked up information that this decision had been made at very high levels of the Chinese government.

In early 1996, these agencies picked up more specific intelligence about the plan, including that it would use conduits to funnel money into this country, and that money would be transferred to some Chinese outpost in the United States. Part of the intercepted "plan" focused on congressional races, and mounting a major lobbying effort on behalf of the Chinese government. But, according to a knowledgeable source, the intercept by the intelligence agencies didn't specifically mention the presidential election.

The FBI also picked up information electronically and through live informants that the Chinese were making inquiries about certain senators and representatives, and about funneling contributions to them. Thompson and Glenn were briefed on these revelations, as were the House and Senate intelligence committees. Seven Members of Congress were warned that they might receive illegal contributions, but the warnings were so vague that it wasn't clear what the members were supposed to do about it. The Members of Congress weren't given any names of potential donors to look out for.

In one of the curious episodes of this story, in June of 1996 two staff members of the National Security Council were briefed on the plan by FBI officials, before there had been any public scandal, but, it was said by the White House, they didn't pass the information up the line.

According to a knowledgeable source, the briefing "was so low-key and so uninformative—basically it said that China was thinking of ways to influence our political system—that it wouldn't attract attention." The national security staff people also claimed that the FBI briefers had told them not to pass the information on—which seems absurd, and which the FBI denied. This, of course, protected the President and other top White House officials from charges that they had known about the "plan" all the while.

In an even more bizarre episode, the White House, through White House counsel Charles Ruff, asked for a briefing by the FBI. Louis Freeh, the director of the FBI, objected, saying that he was conducting a criminal investigation and people in the White House were involved. The clear implication was that the director of the FBI distrusted the country's highest officials.

THOMPSON'S INVESTIGATORS—Damelin and two others who worked with him—had their eye on someone less publicly mentioned than John Huang. In March of 1997, *Newsweek* ran a story that mentioned Ted Sioeng, an Indonesian businessman who was now a citizen of Belize but had substantial business interests in Asia, and some in the United States, and was believed to have ties to the Chinese government.

A subsequent *Newsweek* piece said that Sioeng "may have been a conduit" for some of the "hundreds of thousands of dollars" that intelligence agencies traced from mainland China into California banks and that he used some of those funds to make political contributions. Until then, Thompson's investigators had some intelligence about the plan, but no name; now they had a name.

The investigators found that one of Sioeng's daughters, Jessica Elnitiarta, members of his extended family, and family controlled business had given the Democratic National Committee a total of $400,000 during the 1996 election cycle. (As a nonresident foreign national, Sioeng couldn't make contributions himself, but his daughter was a resident alien, and therefore eligible to contribute.) Investigators later found that Sioeng and his family bought a pro-Taiwan, Chinese-language newspaper in California and turned it into a pro-Beijing paper. And Sioeng had won from the Chinese goverenment the exclusive right to distribute its Red Pagoda Mountain cigarettes in the United States.

Damelin and the other investigators started subpoenaing bank records and talking to lawyers for Sioeng and his daughters. The hope was that Sioeng, who had left the country, would talk to them somewhere outside the United States. In the course of these conversations, the investigators learned that Sioeng had given a large contribution to a Republican California politician, Matt Fong, who was running for state treasurer in California in 1995.* (That money was returned when Fong learned through press accounts that the money had a questionable origin. The Sioeng family's contributions to the DNC weren't returned.) The plan envisioned that the Chinese would seed people at various political levels, currying their favor through contributions via conduits. From various pieces of information, the investigators concluded that Sioeng was one of the conduit contributors and was the connective with the presidential campaign.

It was this information, and the investigators' assessment, that led to Thompson's statement that "our investigation suggests" that the plan involved the 1996 presidential race, as well as congressional campaigns. When I asked later why they didn't just say so in July, or sometime after that—when the statement was being challenged by Democrats and by a substantial part of the press—the reply was that there was still important information that the intelligence agencies hadn't given the investigators. Another possible

---

*Fong lost a race for the U.S. Senate in 1998.

reason was that their case wasn't all that strong. Anyway, Sioeng never did talk to the investigators.

The Clinton-Gore campaign had treated Sioeng as a valued friend. Though he could speak little English, he was placed next to Gore at the famous Hsi Lai temple event in Los Angeles in April of 1996, and he was also seated next to Clinton at one fund-raising dinner—forty-eight of Sioeng's friends and business associates also attended—and was at the head table of another. Such prime seats aren't given away—especially to someone with whom the President and Vice President can barely converse. After one of the dinners, Clinton wrote to Sioeng, thanking him "for being there when you are asked to help."

The temple event was organized by Maria Hsia, who had escorted Gore on a trip to Taiwan in 1989. John Huang, whose purported connections to the mainland Chinese government were under scrutiny, also helped arrange the event at the Taiwan-based temple. Though the hearings were looking for mainland Chinese influence on our politics, they kept bumping into Taiwan. This distinction was never underlined. And it may not have been much of a distinction; there was considerable traffic—business people, agents—back and forth between Taiwan and the mainland. A committee investigator said, "If you're using conduits, that doesn't mean the person isn't aligned with China."

Thus, though the China issue *was* a distraction from the underlying corruption and destruction of the campaign finance system that had occurred in 1996, it was symbolic of the Clinton campaign's desperate, anything-goes hunt for cash, and it was fraught with great danger for Clinton.

INTELLIGENCE INFORMATION is like clay that can be molded into different shapes. The menace can be enlarged or reduced, one part can be made larger than another, and then reshaped again. The evidence is sometimes hearsay—as was some of the evidence that came to the committee—and the information given out by the agencies is often accompanied by protestations that if they went further, intelligence sources would be compromised. "Compromised" sometimes means that "sources and methods" would be revealed—and intelligence officials encourage the listener to believe that that means an agent would be killed. This puts the intelligence briefer at a tremendous advantage.

BEFORE THOMPSON and his staff drafted his opening statement, Thompson had asked FBI Director Freeh and CIA Director George Tenet if they would testify before the committee on how China was trying to involve itself in our political system. The officials, unsurprisingly, said no—the last thing they would want to do was to get in the middle of a fight between the Republican Congress and the Clinton administration. But they did agree to work with Thompson and his aides on a statement to be issued by the committee—as long as their "fingerprints" didn't show.

The CIA, keeping its political skirts clean, told Glenn's people that they had cleared such a statement for Thompson. When they received what they thought was clearance of the statement from the CIA and the FBI, with some sections redacted, Thompson and Damelin assumed that the agencies would back them up. It didn't work out that way.

"We were screwed," Damelin said to me later.

THOUGH THOMPSON HIMSELF was never able to prove in the course of the hearings that any Chinese money had actually gone into the 1996 presidential election—that was to come out later, through prosecutions—there was abundant circumstantial evidence that such contributions had been made. Much of the foreign money that came to the Democratic National Committee could be traced to wire transfers from Hong Kong, the parking place for much of the money that goes in and out of China.

The Democrats, of course, couldn't let stand the implication that Chinese money may have helped the President. Following Thompson's opening statement, Glenn, talking to reporters in the hallway outside of the committee hearing room, said, "I thought it went a little farther than where I would go based on what I know." The urgent task for the Democrats now was to discredit Thompson as well as his hearings.

NOT LONG AFTER he made his opening statement, Thompson sensed that in drawing so much attention to the China issue he may have made a mistake. It was attracting so much press interest and Democratic fire that he was having difficulty getting people to focus on other aspects of the hearings. His friend Thad Cochran said, "It wasn't that Fred had big, explosive information. It was his interpretation of material. He chose to start with China because it was a blockbuster, it would get attention, and show these were serious hearings, not just about violations of FEC [Federal Election Commission] rules."

Thompson hadn't considered that he would have to prove his opening statement conclusively. He told me, with evident frustration, and even a tinge if bitterness, months after the hearings were over, "It became in the press an *accusation*, a *charge* I had made." He believed that evidence was evidence, and that there was enough evidence—bits and pieces of it in intelligence reports—to make his claim. He realized, he said later, that "This was a political exercise, not a legal exercise. The only evidence worth considering in this town is *conclusive* evidence. People go to jail all the time on the basis of strong circumstantial evidence." But since he couldn't reveal the classified information that he felt supported his statement—whether or not it would have been accepted as supporting his statement was another matter—he was on the defensive. He told me, "I didn't realize that times had changed and people would do what they did."

If Thompson actually thought that his statement would go unchallenged, he would be more naive than he seems. More likely, he took a chance. He thought he had enough information to go on. He *had* told me before the hearings began that his statement would raise more questions than it would answer. What with potential witnesses fleeing the country or taking the Fifth Amendment and the intelligence agencies protecting certain information, he didn't know whether he would be able to prove his statement publicly. Moreover, he didn't anticipate the dimensions of the effort that the White House and the Democrats would mount against him. He was thinking back to the Watergate hearings, until this time the talisman of his political experience, and to the relatively nonpartisan Iran-Contra hearings. But in its new approach to hearings, the Clinton administration was changing the whole relationship of the executive branch to investigations by Congress.

Thompson was right. Times had changed.

THE SQUALOR THAT the Thompson hearings had to deal with was extensive. The hearings also had their comic aspects. By the time they opened in July, there had been stories in the papers about mysterious movements by Huang, a former employee of the Indonesian-based Lippo group, headed by the ethnic Chinese

Riady family, which had business dealings with China. The Chinese government owned half of a Lippo group bank and had given the company significant financial help. Lippo had placed part of its business in, of all places, Little Rock, Arkansas, with the eventual result that Huang had an unusual amount of access to the Clinton White House.

Yah Lin "Charlie" Trie, the former proprietor of one of Clinton's favorite Little Rock eateries, the Fu Lin Restaurant, was now a swaggering deal-maker and fund-raiser. Trie had brought a Chinese arms dealer to one of Clinton's coffees for donors. On the same day, Trie also escorted the arms dealer to a meeting with the late Ron Brown, then the Secretary of Commerce, to discuss expanding trade with China. Trie also raised nearly a half million dollars for the fund to help pay the Clintons' legal bills. But, it turned out, his contributions had to be returned because they had been coerced from a religious order with headquarters in Taiwan, or had other foreign origins, so they violated the Trust's own guidelines.

On June 18, 1996, Pauline Kanchanalak, a Thailand-born businesswoman, had coffee with Clinton, bringing along three associates, foreign nationals, for what was described as a meeting about "U.S. policy toward China." Also attending were John Huang and other DNC officials. Kanchanalak and her sister-in-law donated $135,000 to the DNC that day. (Six days later, Kanchanalak donated another $50,000.) This seemed a clear instance of selling one of the most rare and sought-after assets of this country—the President's time.*

The access-selling that went on in connection with the 1996 election, therefore, was well beyond just being tacky. People were expected to pay $50,000 on either the day before or the day after attending a White House coffee with the President—in the Map Room, or the Roosevelt Room, near the Oval Office, of the White House. The coffees became such an intrusion on the President's

---

*As a result of the Justice Department investigation of some figures in the tableau, on July 13, 1998, Kanchanalak was indicted by a federal grand jury sitting in Washington for making campaign contributions despite the fact that she was neither a U.S. citizen nor a permanent resident. (Also, despite the fact that she was neither a citizen nor a permanent resident, she had been made a member of the DNC's finance board of directors, which afforded her privileges to attend special events, such as the President's fiftieth-birthday gala, in 1996.)

time that then–deputy chief of staff Evelyn Lieberman wrote a memo to the staff saying that in order to make time for them, staff briefings of the President "may be considerably truncated or eliminated." (In his deposition, Richard Sullivan, the former Democratic National Committee finance director, said, "The coffees were such sort of nice events that you were hoping that—and generally people came out of there motivated to help to a greater degree than they were before they went in there.")

A businessman named Johnny Chung, an American citizen born in Taiwan, deemed "a hustler" by a staff member of the National Security Council, was later found to have visited the White House forty-nine times between February 1994 and February 1995. According to press reports, he liked to "hang around" Mrs. Clinton's office, something no ordinary citizen could do.

It was Chung who characterized the whole business with his immortal imagery: "The White House is like a subway. You have to put in coins to open the gates." And it was Chung who handed Mrs. Clinton's chief of staff, Margaret Williams, a check for $50,000 that Williams forwarded to the Democratic National Committee. Two days later, Chung attended one of Clinton's radio addresses.

The one occasion on which Clinton showed any outward unease about all this unusual traffic occurred when Chung brought six prospective business clients into the Oval Office following a radio address. We later saw, on a White House tape, Clinton hugging Chung on this occasion. But Clinton decided he didn't want any distribution of a photo of him with Chung and his friends. Other Chung cronies were more fortunate: He managed to get two Chinese nationals who were beer company officials into a White House Christmas party (the check he handed to Ms. Williams was to help Mrs. Clinton liquidate her Christmas entertaining debt to the DNC). A photo of these smiling men with a smiling President and Mrs. Clinton was displayed as the beer company's advertisement in Beijing.

THAT THE CHINESE had a plan to become more involved in American politics was undisputed by members of both parties. Less agreed upon was whether the plan had been implemented or, more controversial, that it involved, much less "affected," the 1996 presidential election. This became the heart of the issue.

If China did have some sort of plan to get more involved in American politics, how serious—or unusual—was it? There were a few—very few—precedents. There had been the famous XYZ Affair, which involved efforts by the French foreign minister during the presidency of John Adams to exact bribes from three distinguished American representatives in exchange for audiences. The affair led to an undeclared naval war between France and the United States. But most countries with a passionate interest in political outcomes in the United States—such as the Central and Eastern European countries—worked through émigré communities here. Or, in the case of Israel, its very strong supporters here. The U.S. Communist Party and communist parties in other countries were partly funded from Moscow, and we had our own history of financing foreign parties—including some pretty unsavory ones, usually as an alternative, or a perceived one, to the communists.

The Taiwan lobby has a long history of trying to influence political decisions in the United States, and the intercepts of the Chinese "plan" indicated that it was the issuance of a visa to the Taiwanese President in 1995, largely at the insistence of Congress, that set the Beijing government off in search of more political influence. But if China did in fact interfere in our elections through illegal contributions, and if the President of the United States encouraged that interference, even indirectly, or deliberately turned a blind eye, that's a highly serious matter.

PART OF THE PROBLEM in sorting out the meaning of the intelligence data was the strange behavior of Louis Freeh, the FBI director. On the Friday of the first week of hearings, Thompson phoned Freeh with an appeal that he state publicly that the FBI had cleared his statement. Freeh told Thompson he would get back to him.

Late that afternoon, as Thompson's staff was gathered in his office, a letter to Thompson, with a copy to Glenn arrived by fax, signed by a middle-level official at the Justic Department. It said, "As you know, that review...was only for the purpose of protecting classified information....You neither requested nor received assessments of the accuracy of any conclusions you drew from information available to the committee. Those conclusions, of course, are your own."

Thompson exploded.

Andrew Fois, the Assistant Attorney General for Legislative Affairs, whose name was on the letter, wasn't in a position to send on his own such an insulting message to a committee chairman.

Even Glenn Ivey, Minority Leader Daschle's tough-minded representative to the hearings, thought that the letter had gone too far, that it was too blatantly political. In fact, according to a Justice Department official, Fois's correspondence was routinely cleared by the Attorney General, who in this instance would have asked, "Has Louis seen this?"

Upon receipt of the letter, a furious Thompson called Freeh to complain. Freeh informed Thompson that he had stopped an even worse letter and indicated that he didn't entirely agree with the one that was sent. "You should have seen the one they wanted to send," Freeh informed Thompson. "The one they wanted to send," drafted with the participation of the FBI, was even more condescending, instructing Thompson on what he could say.

But I was told reliably that Freeh had been read every word in the letter and had approved it, and so had CIA Director Trent, but both men declined to sign it. (Thompson's request had even been to Freeh, and under such circumstances Freeh might well sign the response.) I was also told reliably that Freeh told Reno that he hadn't cleared the substance of Thompson's statement, but had simply looked out for revelation of any classified information. But apparently he didn't tell Thompson that.

That Sunday, on ABC's *This Week*, Glenn revealed the Justice Department letter to Thompson. Referring to Thompson's statement, Glenn said, "I've been on the Intelligence Committee now for almost nine years, and I don't like to comment on these things. I think that it's a dangerous practice." Glenn also said, "Well, he swung a broader loop on some of the conclusions than I would swing. I would just leave it at that."

On Monday morning, Thompson made an angry call to Glenn. "What you're doing is unforgivable, John," Thompson said. "There's no excuse for your behavior. You're not helping the situation." After that, there was no possibility that the two men would trust each other.

THE REAL PROBLEM seemed to lie in a misunderstanding about what exactly the agencies had approved.

In an interview I had with him after the first two weeks of the hearings, Thompson insisted that his statement had been cleared by the intelligence agencies. He believed that Freeh had cleared his statement, period. "This is all Louis's fault," a dispassionate witness to these goings-on said. "Louis should have conveyed to Thompson that he was doing him the favor of reviewing it for intelligence, but not clearing it substantively." This person continued, "Louis should have seen this coming. He played both sides. He didn't want to antagonize Thompson. Louis believes he has two bosses—Reno and the Republican leadership."

Freeh was caught in a hard place. He was dealing with an explosive issue, one with enormous stakes for the Clinton administration and even the Democratic Party. When the Democrats, in league with the White House, threw down the gauntlet on Thompson's statement, Freeh wavered.

A senior Clinton Administration official told me that there was real tension between the FBI and the Justice Department about the nature of China's involvement in our elections. Despite Freeh's skittishness about the Thompson statement, the FBI was known to think that there was serious evidence of Chinese involvement in our politics, and perhaps spying on Huang's part. "Justice's take on what was in the information was that Louis was pushing it too hard," the official said. (This division was to show up in the open split revealed later between Freeh and Reno on whether an Independent Counsel should be appointed to look at the whole Clinton-Gore and DNC campaign finance operation in 1996.)

Thompson learned that Leonard Weiss, Glenn's chief aide, was spreading the word to reporters that Thompson had refused to make one change in his statement requested by the agencies: In the sentence, "However, other parts of the plan direct actions that are illegal under U.S. law," the agencies wanted "are" changed to "may be."

AFTER THE FIRST two weeks of the hearings, Thompson wasn't a happy man. In the interview we had then, he told me, "People now look at everything in terms of whether it confirms the Chinese plan. But the Chinese plan is not in dispute. The next election, it could be another country. The real question is, Did we have a 'For Sale' sign up? The Democrats have set up a situation where if we don't show that John Huang reported to [Chinese President] Jiang Zemin, it isn't true. I hope the agencies will be able to say more at some point. They now claim they're investigating and ring down the curtain. We've kind of put things in play and I'm hanging out there. But I'm not a reckless man."

6

———■———

"Now Let Me Get This Straight"

On July 28, the Thompson committee members met with intelligence officials in the "secure room," Room 410, on the fourth floor of the Capitol. Sitting at a horseshoe-shaped witness table before the senators were CIA Director George Tenet, olive-skinned, with dark hair, graying in front; Freeh, with crew-cut, dark hair, bushy eyebrows, and a very serious mien; and Lt. Gen. Kenneth A. Minihan, the director of the National Security Agency, who had graying hair and wore steel-rimmed glasses, and whose blue uniform held rows of ribbons, three medals, and three stars. Their aides sat behind the officials. Thompson had called the meeting in order to sort out the dispute over the Chinese plan. It went on from 4:30 in the afternoon until 8 P.M., amid much tension.

A great deal was at stake: Thompson was hugely concerned that intelligence back up his statement; Glenn was hugely concerned to establish that even if there was a Chinese plan, it didn't involve the presidential election; Freeh was hugely concerned not to offend either man. The three officials were questioned as a panel. They conferred frequently with their aides. Like Freeh, Tenet was in a difficult spot; he had served on the Democratic staff of the Senate

Intelligence Committee and on the Clinton White House National Security Council staff, and he was now serving a Democratic President, and answering to a Republican-dominated committee. So he said little, but what he did say seemed to support the Democratic position. Minihan said less, pointing out that his agency simply collected information and relayed intercepted messages.

Freeh gave each side something to claim afterward.

Picking up from Thompson's opening statement, Glenn asked, "Is there any evidence that Chinese money affected the presidential election?" Levin and Durbin dwelled on the same point, about "evidence"—absolute evidence that Chinese money had affected, or even gone into, the 1996 Democratic presidential campaign. But no one, not even Thompson, was claiming that. He had said "our evidence suggests." The intelligence representatives said there wasn't much such evidence.

In the meeting, it was pointed out that the FBI's evidence of an involvement in the presidential race was fragmentary: that "a person of known reliability"—i.e., an informant—had heard from another person "of unknown reliability" that someone (Sioeng) had put money into the presidential campaign. But this didn't confirm the point that the Chinese government had actually put money into the presidential campaign.

Thompson said to Freeh, "Now let me get this straight; I don't want to mislead some folks"—and the Democrats spun afterward that he had said, "I may have misled some folks," and made much of it. But, according to enough reliable witnesses, that wasn't what he had said.

The intelligence officers confirmed that Damelin had gone to them to clear the statement, and that at their request some points had been deleted. But as the intelligence officers, in particular Tenet, in response to the Democrats, kept their distance from confirming absolutely that Chinese money had gone into the presidential campaign, Thompson became angry.

Slowly, Thompson said, "Louis, you reviewed the statement personally."

"Right," replied Freeh.

"Would you have let me go out there and read a statement that contained inaccuracies?" asked Thompson.

"No, sir, I wouldn't," Freeh replied.

Thompson's question was artful, leaving Freeh with only one

possible response. The trial lawyer in him was showing. But the response was good enough for Thompson's purposes.

Freeh said that the FBI hadn't questioned Thompson's statement about the possibility that the plan "affected" the presidential contest because it was preceded by the words, "Our investigation suggests"—which Freeh said he took to mean Thompson's and his staff's investigation, not that of the intelligence agencies.

Thompson called on Damelin to explain how they had arrived at their conclusion about what the evidence "suggests," but Damelin didn't convince anyone who didn't want to be convinced.

The real issue was the quality of the source for the "suggestion" that the Chinese tried to affect the presidential campaign.

"Fred got very agitated," said one senator who was in the meeting. "They danced around a lot."

But, in the end, Freeh seemed to be confirming Thompson's statement.

In answer to a Democrat's question as to whether there was any evidence of Chinese involvement at the presidential level, CIA Director Tenet said, "No." Freeh, on the other hand, said "there are reports" to that effect. Another senator said afterward, "From that meeting you could take whatever you wanted. It was very strange."

Afterward, the Democrats painted the meeting as a debacle for Thompson. The Republicans argued otherwise. Senator Collins told me later, "Fred got a bum rap. The agencies did clear it."

Durbin said to me the next day, "What happened was stunning." Referring to Thompson, he said, "The floor fell out from under him." Glenn's aide, Leonard Weiss, who attended the meeting, was known to be telling people that the meeting had been a disaster for Thompson.

To rub it in, the next day, Jim Jordan, the committee Democrats' press secretary, handed a note to Paul Clark, Thompson's press secretary, asking if Thompson would like to join in a statement with Glenn in which Thompson recanted his charge. Clark declined on the spot on Thompson's behalf, saying that Thompson was standing by his original position, and then Clark wrote a note to Thompson, who was conducting that day's hearing, about what had transpired. Thompson read the note twice and quietly handed it to Glenn. Glenn read the note and immediately left the room with Weiss and Jordan in tow, and in the anteroom behind the dais, he told off his aides. This was too much even for him. He returned to the hearing room and told Thompson to forget about it.

"We didn't need any gigs like that around here," Glenn said to me shortly after. "We're trying to get things on a better footing."

MONTHS LATER, suddenly, the FBI found new information about Sioeng that had been in its files for two years. At another intelligence briefing, on September 11, the committee was informed about the "new" FBI material on Sioeng. Thompson was enraged at this belated discovery. The new information suggested that Sioeng had a closer relationship with the Chinese government than had been previously confirmed—that, as a "cultural agent" of the Chinese government he had ties to a Chinese Communist Party committee that did "outreach" to overseas Chinese. Later, according to the committee majority's report, committee investigators also found that a substantial portion of Sioeng's and his daughter's funds were wired from Hong Kong.

Opening the September 11 intelligence meeting, Thompson expressed his displeasure not only that this latest piece of evidence had just turned up, but that the Democrats were continuing to bait him about his opening statement. So he challenged Freeh once again: The FBI *had* vetted his opening statement, and was there anything wrong in it?

Freeh replied that Thompson's was a conclusion that he was free to make based on the facts.

Carl Levin slyly suggested that maybe the FBI should have told Thompson that "'that's not the conclusion our investigation comes to.'"

Thompson accused Glenn of leaking classified information, as revealed in news reports about the previous intelligence briefing.

Glenn said that he hadn't authorized release of any classified information. (Actually, Thompson had Weiss in mind.)

And then an angered Glenn said, "I wasn't the one who raised China as the premier campaign finance issue."

RENO AND FREEH were so embarrassed by their belated disclosure about Sioeng that Reno shook up her task force for the campaign finance investigation, bringing in Charles La Bella, an assistant U.S. attorney in San Diego, to head it. The FBI sent out a teletype to its offices across the country asking for any information they might have on the China matter. That they had just got around to doing this seems absurd, as is the fact that in the computer age one field office didn't know what the other one was doing, and headquarters didn't know what the field had turned up.

And then, on the afternoon of Friday, November 7, after the hearings were over, still more new information was relayed to Thompson, Glenn, and a few key staff members by Freeh and Reno's deputy Eric Holder. Some of the information remained classified and was locked away as a separate committee document, along with other material the Republicans couldn't get cleared by the intelligence agencies. According to well-placed sources, the new information alleged that Maria Hsia (who had escorted Gore to Taiwan and arranged the event at the Hsi Lai temple) had recruited someone in the California state government to be an "agent" for China. This information also held that when another Chinese agent, normally based in the United States, was fleeing authorities in France and was about to be apprehended, Hsia had obtained phony papers to get him out of that country. The new material suggested that the Riadys, according to the committee's final report, had a "long-term relationship with a Chinese intelligence agency." All of this information, sources say, was in the FBI files before the committee began its hearings.

The committee report cited "unverified information" indicating that John Huang "may possibly have had a direct financial relationship with the PRC government." Until then, the only name that the intelligence agencies had confirmed as connected with China was Sioeng's. The Republicans put in their final report only those parts of the new material that the intelligence agencies cleared. In several instances, the report used their exact wording. The agencies had warned that if the report went beyond what they would approve, if asked, they would say that the information was uncorroborated or too weak, and Thompson and his staff had no interest in going through another version of the Battle of the Opening Statement.

MY OWN SENSE is that there was enough evidence to buttress Thompson's point that the Chinese made an effort to insert illegal foreign funds into the 1996 presidential campaign, even if they didn't actually "affect" the election. Large amounts of foreign funds, thought to be illegal, apparently came into the campaign through an interlocking set of conduits, several of whom had ample and unusual access to the White House. Thompson may not have proved in the course of his hearings that any of the money came from the government of China, for which he was much chided—but what he did show was disturbing enough.

IN EARLY 1998, with hardly anyone noticing, Washington's narrow band of attention had now turned to the President's sex scandals— Charlie Trie, who had left the country and then returned, Maria Hsia, and Johnny Chung were indicted, as a result of the Justice Department investigation. Hsia was indicted for the money-laundering at the Hsi Lai temple (the temple was named an unindicted co-conspirator). Chung was indicted for illegally funneling money into the DNC. (In all, Chung had given $366,000 to the DNC, all of which was eventually returned.)

In May 1998, in the course of plea bargaining with the Justice Department, Chung revealed that $100,000 of his contributions to the DNC had come from a Chinese aerospace executive—a lieutenant colonel in the Chinese military—who had given him $300,000.* Chung's revelation set off an explosion, particularly because his testimony was juxtaposed against a developing story about whether Clinton had been too lax in giving waivers to U.S. satellite companies to use Chinese rockets. The most controversial waiver had gone to Clinton's largest contributor, Bernard Schwartz, of Loral Space and Communications, Ltd. Since 1995, Schwartz had donated more than one million dollars to the DNC.

Clinton had courted too much danger. Whether or not it turned out to be the case that Schwartz's contributions led to the waiver, which had been opposed by the Justice Department, here was a possible real, and significant connection between money and policy. (In 1996, Clinton had switched the authority over such technology transfers from the State Department to the more business oriented and politically attuned Commerce Department.) The fact that national security may have been involved gave the combined stories traction and provided the Republicans with a big political

---

*Later Chung told prosecutors that the $300,000 had been ordered into his bank account by the head of Chinese military intelligence, whom he said he met through the lieutenant colonel.

issue. Thompson received congratulations for having been right about the Chinese contributions, but he didn't gloat. And whether or not it was the case that there had been a trade-off, Clinton had brought the worst suspicions on himself.

THOMPSON'S OPENING STATEMENT wasn't the only thing that hadn't gone well for him in the first two weeks of the hearings. "Sullivan was a disappointment," Thompson told me in the interview after the hearings had begun, referring to the first witness, Richard Sullivan, the former finance director of the Democratic National Committee. "He essentially changed his story."

We were talking on a Friday afternoon, and Thompson was planning to fly later in the day to Nashville, as he often did on weekends. He had a condo there, and his three children and five grandchildren lived there; and his mother lived nearby.

On the basis of the deposition Sullivan had given to members of the committee staff, Michael Madigan, the chief Republican counsel, had recommended Sullivan as the lead-off witness. Madigan told Thompson and colleagues that Sullivan would express his outrage over the strange business of the hiring of John Huang as the vice finance chairman at the Democratic National Committee, despite his dearth of training and experience. The appointment followed a meeting between James Riady and the President; another between and Riady and Don Fowler, the chairman of the DNC; and calls from Harold Ickes, then the deputy White House chief of staff, who was essentially running the Clinton-Gore campaign. There was also a follow-up inquiry by Clinton to DNC officials. Madigan told reporters the day before Sullivan was to appear that he would be "the John Dean of this investigation."

But when Sullivan testified, nothing occurred on the order of former White House counsel John Dean's telling the Ervin committee of his concerns about the Nixon White House, and of his own report to the President that said, "There is a cancer growing on the presidency." Nor, in fact, was there to be a Clinton insider such as Dean, who would offer the Thompson committee anything like the evidence Dean had given the Ervin committee.

That Sullivan toned down his testimony from the way he had spoken during his deposition may have come as an unwelcome surprise to Thompson, but it wasn't a surprise to the White House.

Talking to me after Sullivan's appearance before the committee, a White House aide said, "People go into a deposition with the committee's lawyers and point fingers, and then, all of a sudden, in the hearing room, the lights and cameras are on, and your lawyer has worked you over, told you to cool off."

Such "working over" was a hidden but critical dynamic in the Thompson hearings, and it wasn't limited to Sullivan and his lawyer—or, in fact, to the Thompson hearings. The White House aide said lawyers for other DNC officials knew what Sullivan was going to say and had informed the White House. The lawyers serve more than one master. "The lawyers all talk to each other. They all talk and they say [to their client], 'That's not what really happened, is it?' They don't say, 'Change the story,' they say, 'Change the tone.'" He added, "There's pressure among lawyers to tone it down."

Asked about the White House role in all this, the aide said, "I know there were White House lawyers talking to lawyers for Sullivan. We knew that his deposition hadn't gone well for us. And we knew that he was going to tone it down—that he would be much more reserved than in the deposition."

By this indirect method, if Sullivan was asked in the hearing whether he had spoken to anyone in the White House about his testimony, he could say no. This daisy chain of lawyers informing each other, and the White House, had been used during congressional hearings on the firing of the White House travel office, the FBI files, and Whitewater.

In his appearance before the committee, Sullivan, a pale, nervous thirty-two-year-old with wavy sandy hair and long eyelashes, did more than "tone down" his deposition. He walked back from a key part of it. In the deposition, Sullivan had said that one of the reasons he and Marvin Rosen, the finance chairman of the Democratic National Committee, were concerned enough about John Huang to take him off the fund-raising job in July was that Huang was inserting foreign nationals into presidential events. They were worried—with good reason, as it turned out—about the perception. "We are not all that pleased with the fact that he put a couple of foreign nationals into a small dinner with the President," Sullivan said in his deposition, "because of the possible perception." Sullivan added that he and Rosen "both had a sense that the press could make a story...about the President having a small dinner at which foreign nationals attended."

Yet when Sullivan appeared before the committee, he said, "The reason I took him [Huang] off the events was because we were in great need of federal dollars, and John was not raising as many federal dollars as we needed." That is, Huang wasn't raising enough hard money—the federally regulated money that can be given only in limited amounts and is necessary for certain expenditures.

This seemed improbable on its face. Thompson was very perturbed. In frustration, he boomed questions to Sullivan, reading portions of his deposition back to him, but Sullivan's wall of noncommunication held. From Thompson's view—and the press's—Sullivan had been a flop.

Expectations of drama, always dangerous, led the Thompson hearings to a letdown and a widely held consensus that with its first witness the committee had blown it.

PUTTING ON a compelling congressional hearing requires certain skills, which lawyers don't necessarily have. During the course of most congressional hearings, there is a natural antagonism between the lawyers and the political advisors. Trial lawyers— which the lead lawyers were—tend to approach hearings as if they are court cases. They attempt to build a case, no matter how tediously. They are more apt to score legal points than paint a picture for the public. Hearings need a producer, someone with a larger sense of what will have an impact on a wider audience—a sense of political theater.

On those occasions when the Thompson hearings did become theater—sometimes accidentally—they came alive, and the press and the public paid more attention. But Thompson, as he himself commented from time to time, was also up against the public's substantially diminished attention span since the Watergate days. Television as it has evolved has led people to expect fast-paced stories and resolution of a conflict in twenty-two minutes; *Seinfeld*, the most popular program of the era, consisted of short sequences that made a quick joke.

And the hearings were conducted under conditions of total war. Despite a slipup from time to time, the White House had now perfected the technique of getting out material adverse to itself before the committee did. To drive the point home, Lanny Davis, the White House "spin" man, stood in the corridor outside the hearing room pronouncing that whatever the committee had produced that day was "old news." The preemptive leaking by the Clinton White House became so prodigious that, on occasion, Thompson and his staff took to trying to preempt the preemption by leaking their discoveries first. Sometimes the press's dismissal of a story as "not news" disregarded the fact that, but for the hearings, the information wouldn't have come out at all.

And even if some of the specific facts had been known before—assuming that the public followed all of the stories as closely as even the press did—the hearings fleshed them out, or put them into patterns that were instructive. But the public got to see little of this. The networks ran stories only sporadically. Public broadcasting declined to run the hearings. The new Fox cable channel, in a P.R. ploy, announced it would cover the hearings, and it did give more continuous coverage than any other commercial outlet, but it broke away whenever something more audience-grabbing occurred—such as the murder of fashion designer Gianni Versace.

C-SPAN aired the hearings gavel-to-gavel, but according to its agreement with Congress, had to check out when the Senate or the House went into session. The Senate, at this point, often convened at 10 A.M. Fanatics could catch the whole business starting at ten or eleven at night on C-SPAN, and a remarkably large number did.

Thompson told me in July 1997, "It's the fate of public hearings that you have to have continuing blockbusters to keep interest alive."*

The public was led to look for specific crimes rather than patterns. This was in keeping with the press's tendency, and also that of investigators, to search for the "smoking gun" in a room full of smoke.

The real story of the 1996 campaign was the agglomeration of stories of questionable money coming into the Clinton-Gore campaign; of White House tours, coffees, and dinners given for some people who shouldn't have been allowed near the place. White House aides explained that the clearance system had broken down, which, even if true, was an alarming thing to confess. But there

---

*The impeachment of a President might be considered a "blockbuster," but according to a survey by pollster Andrew Kohut, only 15 percent of the American people said that they had watched all or a lot of the impeachment trial of President Clinton.

were also instances where national security aides warned against giving access to the likes of the shady Roger Tamraz, the "hustler" Chung, and Grigori Loutchansky, "a Russian mobster,"only to be overridden.

Thompson resented, with reason, that after twenty-four hours his hearings were largely written off in the press. He minded that, when he was trying to present a broader picture, the press had made "the story of the week" the testimony of an employee of Hip Hing Holding, Inc., an unprofitable California company connected to Lippo. Julia Utomo, a slip of a woman, produced proof of a check to the Democratic National Committee for $50,000 in laundered money, through John Huang in 1992. It had done so mainly because this was fresh news.

Thompson was also irritated with some Republican committee members for trying to wring an avowal that Huang was a spy from two hapless CIA briefers who had given Huang intelligence briefings while he was at Commerce. (The CIA briefers testified while hidden behind a ramshackle screen that was once used to hide mobsters). Following the briefings, Huang would walk across Pennsylvania Avenue to the offices of a company owned by Lippo to use the telephone and fax machines and to send packages.

Thompson said to me, "It's like asking the guy who removed the tape at the Watergate whether he had seen Richard Nixon."

SOME WHITE HOUSE aides were nervous about White House spokesman Lanny Davis's whirling outside the committee room. Some Democrats on the committee called the White House to complain. But the real problem, a White House aide told me in the early days of the hearings, was that almost no one was willing to defend the White House publicly. "We don't have surrogates out there," the aide said. "Do we have friends who would go out on a limb for us now? We don't have people knocking on our door."

That's what it had come to in the matter of the President, even by 1997, before the biggest scandal yet broke, and before his most prodigious lying. Too many people who had attempted to speak for him had been burned, their reputations damaged by their unknowingly putting out incomplete or inaccurate information.

WHEN I asked Thompson, in our interview after the first two weeks of the hearings, what he thought he was up against, he replied, "I think I'm up against, at different times, in different ways, by different people, efforts to change the story, confuse things." He alluded to the fact that he had pushed other Republicans to go along with him on the widening scope of the hearings and on giving the Democrats some subpoenas ("we didn't have to") and said, "If the Democrats are insistent on pulling this thing down in the mud as far as they can and Torricelli-ize the whole hearing, I'll be damned if I'll let them keep doing that." He added, "They haven't one time tried to help explain the necessity of these hearings."

THE COMMITTEE that Thompson had to try to manage was a mélange of the able and the incompetent, the honest seekers of truth (few of these on either side) and the partisan scrappers, the naive and the nearly paranoid. On the dais in the large, austere, marble-and-wood hearing room in the Hart Building, which was maintained at a freezing temperature so that the senators wouldn't be uncomfortable under the television lights, the Democrats sat to Thompson's right, the Republicans to his left. His only real allies on the committee were Senators Susan Collins and Thad Cochran.

Collins, who had raven hair, blue eyes, and a porcelain complexion, was a lot lovelier and livelier than she came across on the television screen. During the hearings she, more than anyone else, caught Thompson's little jokes, usually said in passing. The white-thatched Cochran looked like a stereotypical senator—in an era when almost no one else did. He attended as often as he could, to give Thompson moral support and someone to talk to.

Sam Brownback, of Kansas, was a freshman who had been one of the Republican radicals elected to the House in 1994; he was still in the process of coming to terms with reality, and he wasn't much of a force on the committee.

And Brownback had his own problems with the hearings. He had been a beneficiary of Triad Management Services, which fed conservative donors' contributions into donations of its own, or into ads. It provided conservative donors a means of exceeding the legal limits on contributions, and was thus, in effect, a device for laundering money. Brownback's family reportedly had exceeded the donation limits for his Senate campaign through contributions to Triad. Another committee member, Don Nickles, had appeared in a Triad promotional video.

Pete Domenici, of New Mexico, was often otherwise occupied in his role as chairman of the Senate Budget Committee. A smart man and a highly respected senator, Domenici would join the hearings, ask a line of questioning—often combined with an odd display of temper—and then depart.

Don Nickles, age forty-nine, energetic, and none too bright, would come in, in shirtsleeves—despite the frigid temperature in the committee room—ask questions, usually highly partisan, in a yapping manner, and then he, too, would depart.

Arlen Specter, of Pennsylvania, was a loner. A moderate, he antagonized others with his heavy-handed style. Robert Smith, a big lump of a man from New Hampshire, was probably the dimmest light on the Republican side. Next came Robert Bennett, of Utah, whose own claim to history was that he had been Howard Hughes's representative in Washington and arranged the famous donation of $150,000 from Hughes to Richard Nixon. Bennett was the most convinced that John Huang was part of a spying plot.

Thompson longed for a Howard Baker on the Democratic side, someone of the opposite party who was serious about the inquiry and had an open mind. Joseph Lieberman, of Connecticut, who from time to time expressed concern about misdeeds of the Clinton campaign, came closest, but, unlike Baker, he didn't have the standing of ranking Democrat, and he was usually out there all alone. Glenn and Levin had seniority over him, and as the hearings went on they took a purely partisan role—playing out the White House strategy.

The thin, white-bearded Weiss, who looked like a figure in an El Greco painting, was never far from Glenn's ear. Whatever the merits of Glenn's complaints over the number of subpoenas the Democrats would be allowed to issue, and about the few days given the Democrats to call witnesses (there were no Republican days in the Ervin hearings), Glenn didn't distinguish himself as he raised repetitive and streamlike complaints. Glenn rarely used periods when he spoke. Sadly, after a while he became a whiny bore.

Carl Levin was one of the fiercest partisans on the committee. Though Levin had his own contacts with the White House, he pursued a tit-for-tat, the-Republicans-did-it-too strategy that even the White House didn't favor—because, a White House aide said, "We couldn't sell it." He added, "Our primary concern was to shut down the Republican hearings." It was odd that a man as smart as Levin would, through repetitive citations of a past Republican misdeed or two, allow himself to look so foolish.

Thus, Lieberman was in a lonely position. A serious and deeply religious man, his face often wore a worried look, his voice conveyed concern. Lieberman was disappointed and frustrated by his fellow Democrats' combative approach to the hearings. He felt that they were defending the indefensible. And he was more sympathetic toward Thompson than the other Democrats. "I trust Fred," Lieberman said. "He engages in partisanship a little bit, and engages in showmanship a little bit—as we all do—but his instincts are good."

After Lieberman came Daniel Akaka, of Hawaii, often a room-emptier because of the thinness of his thought; but Akaka did serve to warn his colleagues, and the press, against talking in generalities about "Asians." Durbin, who had a youthful face and a soft voice, and a midwestern plain-spokenness, came across as a nicer guy and less partisan than Torricelli, but he was just as fierce in protecting the Democrats' interests. He became the designated tweaker of Thompson about his opening statement, going so far as to say, "The element here that I find difficult to follow is one that the chairman opened this hearing with, relative to the so-called Chinese plot." Torricelli, with a beaked nose and dark, alert eyes, usually made sharp partisan points. Max Cleland, of Georgia, was a paraplegic as a result of Vietnam and one of the nicest people on the committee. But he was out of his depth.

The two lead counsels, Madigan for the Republicans and Alan Baron for the Democrats, did most of the questioning by the legal teams. Madigan was curly-haired and taut. Baron, blond and handsome, a former prosecutor, often outlawyered Madigan. In fact, Thompson came to admire Baron's work. Baron cultivated Madigan; they attended basketball games together.

THE ROTUND, blustery Haley Barbour, former chairman of the Republican National Committee, appeared on July 25 to discuss his role in obtaining a $2.1 million loan for the National Policy Forum, a think tank closely allied with the RNC, from Ambrous Young, a Taiwan-born businessman based in Hong Kong, with a token business in the United States. A larger contingent of reporters than normal turned up to hear him testify. Here was the potential for a good show. Barbour did not disappoint. Barbour had to explain how, having sat on Young's yacht, *Ambrousia*, anchored in Hong Kong harbor, discussing the loan for the NPF from Young, it didn't occur to him that he was receiving foreign funds.

Despite Barbour's protestations that the money hadn't been used for federal races, which would have made it illegal, the funds had in fact gone through the NPF into the Republican Party's account for nonfederal races, which indirectly went to helping candidates for the House of Representatives. Barbour's folksy belligerence, delivered in his honeyed Mississippi accent, which seemed broader than usual that day, was touted by his boosters as brilliant and received much television play.

"Senator, I don't mind being asked the factual questions. The hardest thing is when people say you have betrayed your country, you have betrayed your party. A senator has said that about me, and I resent it."

But the bluster seemed so calculated that in some minds it simply underlined suspicions.

DESPITE THE fashionable criticism of the Thompson hearings, the first month's worth established, with more detail and color than before, the Clinton campaign's desperate chase for money. Still, during the August congressional recess, Thompson and his staff reviewed the situation, and there was much that wasn't to Thompson's liking. "We had what I thought were rotten days, especially at first," Thompson told me later. Tom Daffron, Thompson's chief of staff and close advisor said, "We kept telling our lawyers, 'If we close in New Haven, we may never get to New York.'" So decisions were made in the course of the August review: The committee would place more emphasis on box office appeal and less on lawyers' cases.

STILL, SHORTLY after Congress reconvened in September, Thompson quietly took some steps designed to put an end to his own hearings. And he did it in an extraordinary way.

7

---◼---

Shutdown

Shortly after the Congress returned in September 1997, Fred Thompson approached Bob Torricelli on the Senate floor to open quiet talks about an "endgame" for the hearings. Thompson was running out of witnesses for the first phase of the hearings, about activities in the 1996 presidential campaign, and the next phase was nearing collapse. The second phase, which Thompson had considered highly important, was to examine the role in the 1996 elections of outside and supposedly independent groups and congressional campaign committees and evidence of possibly illegal coordination among them in the 1996 elections. But the groups to be examined were resisting being called before the committee.

Thompson's opening of talks with Torricelli in September stemmed from a brand-new situation in American political life. A combination of forces was leading to something without precedent: the shutdown of hearings by people and groups whose political power the hearings threatened. It was all done very secretly, and it was obscured by a cover story. The real story has never been told.

By the close of the first round of the hearings in July, Thompson had concluded that he had wasted too much time trying to work with Glenn. In dealing with Glenn, Thompson actually had no one to deal with; Glenn had disappeared as an individual entity. So Thompson made the on-the-face-of-it surprising decision that he could do business with Torricelli, one of the most partisan Democrats on the committee.

Thompson was searching for a way out of the hearings soon, and his retreat would appear less like one if it was cloaked in bipartisanship. In Thompson's view, Torricelli represented the interests of the liberal groups, in particular the AFL-CIO, that were resisting the committee's subpoenas.

Torricelli and Thompson had already had an unusual, private human exchange amid all the partisan crossfire. In July there arrived on the desk of Tom Daffron, Thompson's chief of staff, an envelope of clippings, scraps, some of the material quite personal, some of it politically sensitive, that appeared to have been taken from Torricelli's trash. Accompanying the material was a note saying, "If you want to see more, put an ad in [a New Jersey paper] saying, 'Wet birds never fly at night.'"

When Daffron asked Thompson what to do with the material, Thompson told him to send it to Torricelli right away. So Daffron called Torricelli's chief of staff, Jamie Fox, and told him to come get the material. "Senator Thompson doesn't want to play this way," Daffron said as he handed Fox the material.

Later that day, at an otherwise roiling intelligence briefing of the full committee, Torricelli told their colleagues the story and said, "It was the most honorable thing I've seen in public life." Torricelli told me later, "It did change the tone. I was the most contentious person on the Democratic side. He's an honorable man."

SPEAKING OF THEIR endgame discussions in the fall, Torricelli said to me, "Thompson withstood the pressure for a while, but he was losing his Republican constituency for the hearings." According to a well-placed Republican strategist, Mitch McConnell was still pressing his view in meetings of Senate Republicans that any discussion of the campaign finance scandals only increased pressure for campaign finance reform, so the hearings were neither good policy nor good politics for the Republicans.

And by the fall Thompson and Lott were barely speaking. Earlier in the year, aware that Lott's staff was leaking derogatory things about him (Lott had his own representative sitting in the hearing room and in the meetings of the committee Republicans) and because he was receiving no support from the Republican leaders, Thompson went for help to Connie Mack, of Florida, the chairman of the Senate Republican Conference. Mack, a descendant of the famous manager of the Philadelphia Athletics, and a Gingrich ally, was soft-spoken and gentle, and Thompson thought that Mack would be able to bridge the canyon between him and the other Republican leaders.

"We're not going to be able to get the job done if I have to fight Democrats and Republicans the whole year," Thompson told Mack. Daschle, the Senate minority leader, was working with the committee Democrats, Thompson pointed out, but he himself was receiving no support from his own leadership. He knew that the leadership was saying that if the investigation was opened up to look at the coordinated expenditures of congressional committees with supposedly independent groups, the Democrats would go after Al D'Amato, who, it was believed, as head of the National Republican Senatorial Committee in 1996, had led the way in questionable coordination.

After hearing Thompson out, Mack suggested that the leaders and Thompson get together. Thompson told me, "Connie was the one person in the leadership who was trying to hold things together." But such a meeting never happened.

Mack told me later, "I really think Fred tried to play this thing straight." Mack added, "In his mind, in order to have a credible hearing, he had to have the perception that this was a fair and equal pursuit of the issues." As for Thompson's decision to seek an end to the hearings, Mack said, "I think Fred just came to the conclusion that wherever he looked there was no support for continuing them."

By early September, Thompson also had little support among the committee Republicans. Nickles was the most persistent opponent of investigating the Republicans' allies. He would rather close down the hearings. Other Republicans were complaining about the committee's "hassling" of two conservative groups—Americans for Tax Reform, headed by Grover Norquist, and Triad. (Toward the end of the 1996 election, Norquist received $4.6 million in soft money from the Republican National Committee, most of which he put toward a supposedly nonpartisan "issue ad" on Medicare that was actually designed to help the Republicans.)

THOMPSON WAS becoming increasingly frustrated with the lack of cooperation by the Justice Department on the China issue. Few witnesses were being given immunity so that they could testify before his committee. Moreover, with the hapless Indiana Congressman Dan Burton warming up for his own hearings, Thompson and some other Republicans were uncomfortable about sharing the stage with him. They feared what Torricelli called "a loss of prestige by association."

The White House, of course, had a strong interest in curtailing the hearings, and Torricelli was in close touch with the White House. The White House's reasons for desiring an early end to the hearings went beyond whatever embarrassment they were causing: At the very time that the endgame strategy was being discussed, Attorney General Janet Reno was considering the appointment of an Independent Counsel to examine whether Vice President Al Gore had violated the law by soliciting contributions from the White House, with some of the funds, the committee had discovered, going into a hard money account. The law prohibits the solicitation of funds on federal property. So the hard money was significant because Reno had adopted the seemingly odd theory that since soft money wasn't covered by the election laws (it was a loophole), apparent violations involving soft money weren't violations of the law. But it was clear that the Campaign Finance Reform Act of 1974 didn't intend that unlimited money from corporations and unions as well as individuals be used, as it was in 1996, to destroy the limits on the books. (An inquiry into whether Clinton also improperly made calls soliciting money from his office was begun in mid-October.)

If the Reno theory were taken to its logical conclusion, even foreign money in the form of soft money, which virtually all of it was, wouldn't be illegal. But the Justice Department also took the position that the statute that banned foreign contributions covered soft money and thus it prosecuted some such contributors, including Charles Trie, Pauline Kanchanalak, and Maria Hsia.* The distinctions between hard and soft money as far as the phone calls

---

*In September, 1998 a U.S. district judge held, contrary to the Justice Department, that prohibition against foreign contributions did not apply to soft money donations. This threw into question prosecutions of contributors of soft money of foreign origin.

were concerned, or about which rooms in the White House were federal property (from which fund-raising calls were considered okay), as opposed to private residence (from which the fund-raising calls weren't okay), were silly and based on an antiquated law. The real point was that Gore—and Clinton, who also apparently did so—shouldn't have been making the calls at all. Calls from the holders of the highest elected offices in the land added to the aura of shakedown that permeated the entire campaign finance system.

Another reason the White House and the committee Democrats were eager to shut down the hearings, Torricelli explained to me, was that the hearings might be putting pressure on Janet Reno to appoint an Independent Counsel in the Gore case. Reno went back and forth on whether to appoint an Independent Counsel on Gore's phone calls. "The hearings haven't affected 2000," Torricelli said. "An Independent Counsel is another matter."*

Also at that time in September, the Democrats were trying to give the appearance that they were about to hold hearings on Triad, the conservative fund-transfer organization, but that was, Torricelli said, "a bit of a bluff," to worry the Republicans. Some Democrats were worried that if they explored Triad, which involved two Republican committee members (Nickles and Brownback), the Republicans might open fire on possible irregularities in some Democratic members' campaigns. "It was a situation of mutual assured destruction," a Democratic strategist said.

Another incentive for the Democrats to pull the plug on the hearings was that the last part of the first phase of the hearings was supposed to be about possible quid pro quos. This would have involved people around Gore and a major Democratic contributor. So Clinton and Gore, for various reasons, were all for shutting down the hearings.

MEANWHILE, the interest groups who were to be called in what Thompson called Phase 2 had banded together in a most unusual coalition to put an end to the hearings by defying the committee's subpoenas. The groups' defiance had its origins in a subpoena the committee had issued to the AFL-CIO on May 23. The labor fed-

---

*On December 2, 1997, Reno said she would not appoint an Independent Counsel to investigate Clinton's or Gore's calls, then reopened the question on Gore because a new bit of evidence surfaced, and then, on November 24, 1998, again said she would not name an Independent Counsel for Gore.

eration had been resisting, arguing that it was too broad. (Issuing broad subpoenas, followed by lawyers arguing over the breadth, is common in civil litigation.)

After considerable wrangling over which other groups should be called, the committee had decided on July 30, just before the August break, to subpoena twenty-five groups, at both ends of the political spectrum, including the National Right to Life Committee, the National Council of Senior Citizens, the National Education Association, and EMILY's List, which supports Democratic women candidates who support abortion rights. The committee's action doomed the hearings on the role of the groups.

The AFL-CIO was also declining to accept the committee lawyers' offer to negotiate over the breadth of the committee's subpoena. The Democrats, thinking this was a clever move, insisted that the subpoenas to the groups on the right be just as broad as the AFL's.

In fact, the AFL-CIO had no incentive to negotiate. As Torricelli explained it to me, "The AFL knew that the broad subpoena would never be enforced by the court, so it didn't make any sense to them to narrow the subpoena. There was no incentive to compromise."

In early September, Thompson issued an order to the AFL-CIO to produce documents. The next step would have been for the committee and then the Senate to vote to hold the AFL-CIO in contempt—but this wasn't going to happen. Not only would no committee Democrat vote for a contempt citation, but even two committee Republicans—Don Nickles and Bob Smith—had quietly voiced their objections to such a move. Neither was exactly a friend of labor, but they didn't want to establish a precedent for moving against groups that were their friends. The Democrats had an equivalent reaction: some, especially from rural states, were loath to take on the National Rifle Association. Not that the Democrats would get any more support from the NRA than Don Nickles would from the AFL-CIO, but these Democrats—in particular Carl Levin, who is from Michigan, where gun militants are particularly strong—didn't want to take on such a politically powerful group. (The NRA was not subpoenaed.)

The result of the new batch of subpoenas was the formation of a new coalition, united in its refusal to comply with them. The organizing of the coalition, and its strategy, were coordinated by

James Bopp, the Terre Haute–based general counsel of the National Right to Life Committee (NRLC), and Arthur Spitzer, the legal director of the ACLU.

Bopp was staying in the Marriott at Metro Center, in Washington, on July 31, when he got news of the subpoena for the Right to Life Committee. He told me, "I had monitored the Thompson committee's debate over whether or not they were going to investigate lawful activities by citizens groups." The NRLC clung to the literal interpretation of the famous footnote in the *Buckley* decision: No matter how much an ad appeared to be, or clearly was, aimed at affecting the election or defeat of a candidate, if it didn't use those few words in the footnote, it wasn't an "express advocacy" ad.

The National Right to Life Committee opposed pending reform proposals to expand the category of ads that should be paid for with hard money to include ads that, even if they didn't use the specifically forbidden words, were unmistakably ads for or against a candidate. Other officials of the NRLC, Bopp told me, had been "talking to members of the Thompson committee, expressing their concern about investigating people who hadn't done anything illegal." The group had a sympathetic audience among some committee members, in particular Nickles.

When Bopp received the subpoena, he said, "I said to myself 'They will rue the day that they served Right to Life with a subpoena.'"

The first thing Bopp did was to contact the ACLU, "because," he said, "I felt that they would agree that the investigation constituted a violation of First Amendment rights." Bopp and the ACLU had worked together on various issues over the years, including against campaign finance reforms. So Bopp and Arthur, the ACLU legal director, set out to coordinate their and other groups' responses to the subpoenas.

Aware that the AFL-CIO was stalling its subpoena, Bopp and the ACLU made common cause with the labor federation, and then made contact with other subpoenaed groups, "to determine," Bopp said, "whether they shared our concern on the issue." There followed a series of meetings of attorneys for more than twenty groups that had been subpoenaed, chaired by Spitzer and held in law firm conference rooms around Washington.

On September 3, shortly before Congress reconvened, a press conference was held by the representatives of various groups, left to right, under the auspices of the ACLU and including the Association of Trial Lawyers of America, the NRLC, Citizen Action, the Teamsters, and Citizens Against Government Waste, represented by the muckraker columnist Jack Anderson. They announced that they wouldn't comply with the committee's subpoenas.

Torricelli told me, "Once the AFL lawyers figured it out, the rest followed. The AFL has very deep resources. It could fight the subpoena legally until the hearings were a distant memory. The groups didn't want to settle, and they saw that they could hide in the shadow of the AFL." So the groups played for time. The hearings, after all, were bound by the Democratic-imposed cutoff date of the end of the year.

But once the groups formed their coalition, it was doubtful that even if Thompson's committee investigation continued into the next session—or for five more years—the Senate would have voted to hold them in contempt. Each side was protecting its allies. Torricelli said, "All the groups on the right were complaining. The political pressure became too intense." Thompson, facing reality, capitulated. Baron and Madigan met with representatives of the groups on September 18 and told them they wouldn't be investigated after all.

The result of all this evasion and protection was a new kind of lawlessness. It made even some of the partisans uneasy. Dick Durbin said to me in an interview, "One of the things that has happened here that is of historic moment is the collapse of the subpoena process."

Torricelli said, "The United States Senate is going to have to live with this precedent. Subpoenas are going to be ignored."

In an interview, Thompson called it "a new level of audacity."

Meanwhile, Torricelli and Thompson talked to their fellow committee members and got the agreement of most of them to close out the hearings soon.

IN THE HEARING ROOM on Friday morning, September 19, committee aides passed out a statement issued in the names of Thompson and Glenn, announcing that the committee would now turn to the subject of campaign finance reform. That was the cover story for the shutdown. The stated rationale was that reform legislation would soon be coming before the Senate and the committee should make its own contribution to the debate. This was hogwash, of course. The statement deliberately left vague what would follow a four-day seminar on campaign finance reform. The actual intention was to conclude the hearings after that.

Glenn Ivey, Daschle's aide, was standing outside the hearing room that morning, attempting not to look too pleased. Earlier in the year the Democrats had expected Thompson to hold hearings until the end of the year and then ask for more time, and they had been prepared to give him three additional months. Now they had an opportunity to shut the hearings down soon, and any extension was out of the question. An end to the hearings before Congress was to adjourn in early November (the committee Democrats made it clear that they wouldn't stay around after that), was a windfall.

Leaning up against a wall outside the hearing room and speaking softly, Ivey said to me, "This has got to be historic in the annals of investigations. You can shut down a whole avenue of investigation. Some people are already saying it's the triumph of defensive politics, and spin control, by the Democrats."

But Ivey was concerned that if the press or the Republicans beat up on Thompson too badly for curtailing the hearings, he might feel constrained to resume them.

On the Senate floor, Thompson had told a small group of Democrats, "In order to keep peace on my side I can't close the door on more hearings." He might have to call Ickes if he got too much criticism for not having done so, he said, or something new might turn up."We could shut off the lights the day before something big comes up."

Torricelli told me, "Thompson reserved the right to return to Phase One, but it was implicit that that wouldn't happen. He couldn't say publicly that Phase One was over, and he couldn't tell other Republicans he wouldn't call Ickes."

Don Goldberg, the White House aide, also standing outside the committee room, was also trying not to gloat. If he did, he told me, "That would make it hard for Thompson to complete this deal. But obviously we'd like to end things as quickly as possible. Especially given the last couple of weeks. Jesus!"

IN THOSE past two weeks, the committee had produced several embarrassments for the White House.

It had brought out that Gore had raised "hard" money from the White House, and the hearings on Gore's appearance at a fund-raiser at the Hsi Lai Temple in Los Angeles weren't helpful to Gore. The hearings showed more fully than before the contortions that Gore's staff had gone through to not call the event arranged by Maria Hsia and John Huang, who were there, as was DNC Chairman Don Fowler a "fund-raiser." The money wasn't raised while Gore was there; the event was community outreach. While the testimony went on, the Republican side displayed large color photographs of Gore at the event, which were bound to turn up in a campaign against Gore's attempt for the presidency.

David Strauss, Gore's former deputy chief of staff, told the committee, "We were involved in many sorts of fund-raising activities to lay the groundwork for fund-raising events, that were not fund-raisers per se." The committee Democrats tried to establish that Gore wouldn't necessarily have known that the event was a fund-raiser, but Gore is smarter and more alert than that. Another person who attended the event with Gore had no doubt that it was a fund-raiser. One document described the event as a "fund-raising lunch for VP."

Fund-raisers, of course, aren't supposed to be held at tax-exempt places of worship. But the real problem with the event at the temple was that donations, ostensibly from the monastics, were reimbursed—laundered—by the temple's tax-exempt funds. (A donation of $5,000 that had originated from the Hsi Lai event, was returned by the DNC. The reason stated on the return form, "It's a temple, you idiot!")

The temple charged $5,000 per couple to attend the lunch with Gore and to have their picture taken with him. About $45,000 was raised *before* the lunch. On September 4, when Man Ho, the temple's chief administrative officer, a tough, small woman with short-cropped hair, wire-rim glasses, and dressed, as were the other two witnesses alongside her, in a cinnamon-colored robe, appeared before the committee, another big audience turned up. Man Ho testified to the committee that "John Huang thought that the temple could contribute more," that he needed to take $100,000 back to Washington that day. So temple funds were given to the nuns to contribute. Man Ho also testified that Maria Hsia "said the event was approved at the White House."

This wasn't the only event that raised questions about Gore's instincts. The matter of his phone calls from the White House had led to his famous press conference in March, in which he uttered "no controlling legal authority" seven times, a legalism that made sense only to him and his new counsel, and also to a changing story about how many calls he made. The number went from "a few occasions" at his press conference to forty-six by the end of August. In politics, the only thing worse than a bad answer is a changing answer.

At the end of the hearings on the temple event, Thompson commented, "As long as you didn't have a table set up in the pulpit collecting checks, you don't call it a fund-raiser," and he returned to the main point. "If that's the situation, if that's the law, which I don't think it is, that's clearly something we need to address. So, I think a lot of productive things can come out of this."

Actually, Thompson was depressed. He thought that he had the word of CNN that it would provide live coverage of the testimony of the three temple nuns, in part to balance the live coverage it had given to Haley Barbour. His despair sometimes showed through during the hearings. At other times his huge body would shake with barely suppressed laughter—as at a characteristically long-winded question by Specter that one of the nuns asked him to repeat. Though Thompson believed that the hearings were having an impact on public opinion—and there was evidence that he was right—he assumed that televising of them would have had more. "The only way to have an impact is to have enough out there to shame people," he told me.

OTHER EVENTS in the hearing room had also given the hearings more traction in the fall, and embarrassed the Clinton Administration. Roger Tamraz, the shady financier, entertained with his testimony on September 18, and provided good one-liners for television stories. (Tamraz was wanted in France in connection with the collapse of a bank, and in Lebanon for embezzlement, and Interpol had an arrest warrant out for him.) He had contributed $300,000 to the Democrats in July of 1995, and, over the strenuous objections of Sheila Heslin, a staff member of the National Security Council, he had managed to get into six events with the President, even if he hadn't succeeded in getting the help he sought for building an oil pipeline from the Caspian Sea.

When he was asked by Lieberman, "So, do you think you got your money's worth? Do you feel badly about having given the three hundred thousand dollars?"

The Lebanese-born Tamraz replied, with complete aplomb, in what improbably sounded like a Yiddish comedian's accent and timing, "I think next time, I'll give six hundred thousand."

Or, when asked by Levin whether he was unhappy that he didn't get his desired one-on-one meeting with the Vice President, Tamraz replied, "Not really. Because if they kicked me from the door, I will come in the window."

Tamraz did obtain a hearing, at the President's request, relayed through former chief of staff and then senior advisor Thomas "Mack" McLarty, with Energy Department officials about his plan to build his pipeline.

The real point about Tamraz was that what he did wasn't very different from what a lot of donors do: buy access. Because he was colorful as well as shameless, Tamraz had a real impact, as did the intense testimony by Heslin about her futile efforts to keep Tamraz from getting the access.

The strong effect of Heslin and Tamraz came as a surprise to Thompson and his staff, who had put them on only because they were scratching around for witnesses.

ON THE SAME MORNING that the announcement of the switch in committee plans was made, the White House suffered another embarrassment. The committee heard from Warren Meddoff, a pudgy man wearing a diamond pinky ring who had a story to tell that was bizarre, but not, in essence, unlike other stories involving Clinton fund-raising. The pattern was becoming clear. At a $1,500-a-seat fund-raiser in Miami, Meddoff had handed the President a business card on which he had written, "I have an associate that is interested in donating $5 million to your campaign." Even as things went, this was a huge amount.

According to Meddoff, the President of the United States "took two steps, looked at it, came back, and asked if he could have another one of those cards." A few days later, Harold Ickes called Meddoff from *Air Force One*. Meddoff made clear to Ickes that his associate wanted to make the donation "in a tax-favorable way," which led to a fax from Ickes to Meddoff citing various tax-exempt groups sympathetic to Clinton's cause to which his associate could donate the money and take a tax deduction.

Ickes's fax raised questions, among other things, about the groups' tax-exempt status. Increasingly, another way that corporations and big donors get around the legal limits and get a tax deduction in exchange is by making large contributions to tax-exempt groups whose ostensible purpose is to "educate" the voters, or to "get out the vote," but actually have close ties to one party or the other.

Ickes's memo also raised questions about his issuing such directions from the White House. Meddoff claimed that Ickes later called and said that he had sent the fax in error and asked Meddoff to shred it. Ickes, in his deposition and in his testimony said that he didn't recall asking Meddoff to destroy the fax.

And Meddoff got a talk with a staff member of the National Security Council about some concerns of the company he worked for, a subsidiary of a Danish company that supplied vehicles and spare parts to governments. After that, Meddoff said, a Democratic fund-raiser for Florida asked him to donate another $25,000 to the Inaugural Committee, with the promise that if he made the donation he could attend a private dinner with the President and the Vice President. Donations to presidential inaugural committees were another way around the legal limits on contributions.

The frenzied access-peddling by the Clinton campaign led to other disturbing stories. There was Yogesh Gandhi, who claimed to be a descendant of the sainted Mahatma, who wished to give Clinton a bust of the great man and a $325,000 donation. He had hoped to make the presentation at the White House, but the NSC was warned by the FBI that the man was a fraud and that the foundation he purported to head consisted of himself. After the NSC received and passed along the FBI warning and after Gandhi arranged to donate, through John Huang, the $325,000, the President of the United States slipped out of a fund-raising dinner at the Sheraton Carlton Hotel in Washington to accept the bust from a Gandhi designee in an adjoining room. (The money was later returned.)

The picture of the President slipping into side rooms to reward shady donors with a chance to be in his presence is not a pretty one.

Eric Hotung, a Hong Kong businessman, donated $100,000 to the DNC and got invited to a White House dinner and was given a private briefing by a National Security Council official and a photograph of himself with National Security Advisor Samuel Berger.

On a Friday afternoon in early September, Michael Mitoma, the former mayor of Carson, California, told a nearly empty committee room about a Korean businessman, John Lee, who was eager to meet with Clinton and offered to buy all the seats at a $50,000-a-plate dinner at the Sheraton Carlton that was being arranged by John Huang. (Mr. Mitoma was involved because he wanted Mr. Lee's company, the Cheong-Am Corporation, an electronics firm, to build a new plant in his city.)

Lee was permitted to buy only five seats, but he flew from Korea for the event anyway. At the Sheraton Carlton, Huang opened the envelope to check on Lee's contribution but told Mitoma that there was no room at the dinner. The embarrassed mayor said he told Lee "it was not such a great idea to eat American food with a bunch of stuffy people" and suggested they go out for Chinese food.

As it happened, there were two fund-raising dinners starring the President at the Sheraton Carlton that night.

And Lee's long trip to Washington wasn't totally futile: between the dinners, Clinton slipped into a holding room to have his picture taken with Lee. It could be argued that this wasn't much for $250,000, but why was the President posing with the man at all? Was this a way of taking his money, knowing it was at best legally ambiguous? Didn't the President wonder about the source of the funds? Or did he not care?

AFTER A LONG struggle between the Thompson committee and the White House, videotapes were released to the committee on October 4. They showed Clinton greeting various questionable contributors in the Oval Office or at a coffee, or addressing himself to foreigners at a fund-raising dinner. Their release followed a suspicious failure by the White House counsel's office to alert Janet Reno to them while she was still deciding whether to appoint an Independent Counsel on Clinton's and Gore's phone calls.

The committee's inquiry into the White House's tardy presentation of the tapes proved fruitless, except for showing how wan the excuses were. The White House Communications Agency, able to patch the President through to anyone, anywhere in the world, apparently couldn't handle a four-page fax from the counsel's office. (It said it had lost the page asking for tapes.) White House aides had to be aware that taping Clinton greeting visitors was routine. (It was even done to me when I had an interview with him.) The tapes left little room for doubt that the President was aware that questionable money was coming into his campaign.

But Clinton is one of our history's great deniers. He floated like a butterfly above his own embarrassments (at least until his denials caught up with him in the Monica Lewinsky case). During his first press conference after the 1996 election, he had refused to address the growing finance scandal and tried to portray the Democratic National Committee as an utterly separate entity.

He said, "I'm not trying to disclaim responsibility, but I am trying to point out there's a difference between what the party does and what the campaign does"—even though the two were tightly entwined. Referring to the DNC, he added, "That was the other campaign that had problems, not mine."

Is it possible that President Clinton, one of the smartest men ever to inhabit the White House, was unaware of the stream of foreign visitors and large amounts of money produced by Huang and Trie and Chung? Did no staff member warn him? One Clinton staff person told me that he and another staff member did notice the chain of Asian visitors, but didn't say anything about it to Clinton. (One of Clinton's great failings was a reluctance to appoint grown-ups who would speak frankly to him.)

This staff person said, "You have to understand, we were hearing the death rattle"—the much overstated parlousness of Clinton's political situation in 1995 and 1996. Even if he needed the money that didn't sanctify all means of obtaining it.

Clinton's panic after the Republicans swept the 1994 congressional elections, and the Republicans' historical advantage in fundraising, set off an obsessed quest for money. This money-hunger has often been attributed to Clinton's then-Svengali, Dick Morris, and his expensive advertising campaign in 1995. But even one of Clinton's closest advisors confirmed to me that the frantic fundraising effort would have occurred even if Dick Morris hadn't returned to the President's side to help him get re-elected.

A Democratic operative close to the White House agreed: "The President is a winner. He'll do anything to win."

If Clinton cautioned Huang or Trie or Chung—or the Riadys—about being meticulous in observing the fund-raising laws, there's no evidence of it. Speaking to a dinner arranged by Huang and attended by a large number of Asians, many of whom didn't speak English, Clinton thanked "those who come from other countries to be with us tonight." A high administration official who didn't serve in the White House and who attended a dinner of the Democratic Business Council in 1995 found it odd that at his table he was surrounded by Asians who spoke little English. (In exchange for a contribution of $10,000 by individuals and $15,000 by corporations, business leaders were invited to several dinners a year with the President.)

In one of the tapes we saw Arief Wiridinata, the landscape architect/gardener who was to become famous for donating $450,000 to the DNC, greet Clinton at a coffee with "James Riady sent me." Clinton acted as if Wiridinata's appearance and message were nothing out of the ordinary.

Clinton knew that Charlie Trie had turned in a substantial amount of suspect money to his and his wife's legal defense fund. This information wasn't made public, deliberately, until after the 1996 election. (The money was returned.) Trie continued to raise money for the DNC. In fact, only a few days after the alert to the White House about Trie's fund-raising for the legal defense fund, he sat at the head table with Clinton at a fund-raising dinner. (The DNC later returned $645,000 that had been raised by Trie.)

The intelligence agencies allowed Thompson to say in the committee's final report that Maria Hsia "was an agent" of the Chinese government and that Ted Sioeng "worked and perhaps still works" on behalf of the Chinese government, and that the Riadys had a long-term relationship with a Chinese intelligence agency. There were plenty of warning signs to the President and the Vice President and the President's staff, but apparently they weren't heeded. It's hard to accept that such heedlessness was accidental.

It seems inconceivable that the President wasn't briefed about people whom he was about to meet with in a small group. In fact, the President *was* briefed before at least some of the coffees. In going through papers that Ickes released in the summer of 1997, I came across two sets of memos, three pages each, to the President giving fairly detailed biographies of people who were coming for coffee.

Is it possible that such hustlers as Huang and Trie and Chung never bragged to the President about the money they were bringing in or mentioned its sources? At one dinner, Clinton praised

Huang and said, "He has never told me anything that didn't come to pass." Is it possible that no one asked these men where they were getting the money? Or did they not want to know?

Clinton's attitude toward the risk he was running in his fund-raising was of a piece with that aspect of his character that was reckless, took chances, that lived on the edge. Often cautious about policy, he took risks on other things (including, it later emerged, his sex life). He was accustomed to getting away with taking risks.

A former administration official described to me Clinton's mind-set as follows: "If no one is going to catch you, you take the chance. It is very risky, but you have to figure out the risk calculation. If someone might write about it, then you live closer to the edge in terms of sex and money. To him, something's not a problem if he doesn't get bad press about it."

So Clinton took a chance on letting people in his orbit raise highly questionable funds from highly questionable people. This is an alarming trait in a president, and, as future events were to show, can wreak havoc on his presidency.

GLENN IVEY, Daschle's aide, turned out to have been prescient.

Trent Lott was furious at Thompson for veering off into hearings on campaign finance reform. "Trent went crazy," another Republican senator said. "He never forgave him for going off on his own." It may seem odd that Trent Lott was unhappy with the hearings and then was unhappy when Thompson and the others moved to close them down. But the last thing Mitch McConnell wanted was hearings on campaign finance reform.

The Republican strategist added, "No matter what Thompson did, people didn't like it because they didn't like him from the start, and if there's any ambiguity to the call, he's going to be questioned."

He added, "There's a lot of cognitive dissonance in internal Senate politics. The same people who were saying, 'How dare he continue?' were saying, 'How dare he stop?' Within the Republican leadership the preponderant view is that Thompson has not managed this properly."

"Lott doesn't say much in public sessions," the Republican strategist said, "but when he sends a signal, it's unmistakable."

One unmistakable signal from Lott was an article in the conservative *Weekly Standard* in early October, titled "Has Fred Thompson Blown It?" Capitol Hill savants could tell that the article relied heavily on unattributed statements by Lott or Lott's staff. It quoted an anonymous Senate Republican aide as saying, "This is easily the worst congressional investigation in public memory." It described Thompson's "about-face"—deciding to hold hearings on campaign finance reform—as only the latest of his actions that "mystify and enrage congressional Republicans and conservative partisans." The article continued, "Senate Majority Leader Trent Lott is the foremost among them." It went on to say that "Lott has concluded that selecting Thompson to lead the investigation...has been the biggest mistake of his tenure....Now the majority leader's frustration with Thompson is so great that he'd like to shut down the hearings before any more damage is done."

No one I asked could recall such an open attack by a Senate leader on one of his committee chairmen. (When Thompson defeated Lott earlier in the year over whether the hearings should be broadened to include "improper" activities, an obviously thin-skinned Lott criticized Thompson in the Nashville *Tennesseean*, Thompson's hometown paper.)

The Republican strategist said, "Thompson wanted credibility and reached out to Democrats and got the worst of both worlds. The Democrats didn't appreciate it, and the Republicans thought he was going too far." Pointing to the larger historical context in which all this was happening, he added, "Part of this has to do with the changing nature of the Senate in the last ten years."

He summed up Thompson's situation: "The ultimate truth is that Thompson is in an untenable position, period."

All of this raises the question of whether there can ever be a dispassionate, nonpartisan, and close-in examination of the campaign finance system by the Congress.

THE REACTION of several Republicans against Thompson's "throwing in the towel"—even though some had wanted the hearings shut down—convinced Thompson that he had to renew the investigation. Ickes had to be called. Yet when Thompson reopened the hearings, some of the Democrats felt betrayed—even though Thompson had left himself an opening for calling Ickes. Ever the realist, Torricelli said, "It was more difficult to get out of this than he calculated. But given the forces at work, this had to happen." (When the committee's tentative decision to shut down the hearings was made, Torricelli had called Ickes and told him that he was off the hook.)

Thompson had been reluctant to call Ickes, because he knew that a clever, combative witness who didn't want to get pinned down wouldn't get pinned down. Nonetheless, there was box-office—and press—demand for Ickes, who would probably put on a good show, and his appearance was eagerly awaited. The heated exchanges between Ickes and some committee members received more attention than other, more revealing, testimony.

The thin, pale Ickes, wearing metal-rimmed glasses, with a bank of lawyers seated behind him, spoke rapidly in his fairly high-pitched voice, displaying his whiplike mind. By growling back at committee members who growled at him, he discouraged tough questioning. When the gentlemanly Thad Cochran asked him about his role in White House planning for the presidential campaign, the following, typical exchange occurred:

COCHRAN: Well, I am suggesting that it was a group, in that there were several individuals involved, and you began having regular meetings in the White House at the insistence of the President. He asked you to attend the meeting, and he asked the others to attend the meeting. Isn't that correct?
ICKES: I attended a lot of meetings with the President which could, under your definition—
COCHRAN: OK. Well, let me cut to the chase.
ICKES (continuing): Which under your—
COCHRAN: This meeting—
ICKES: Could I finish my answer?
COCHRAN: Let me clarify the question, if you are going—
ICKES: Senator, you—
COCHRAN (continuing): To just start a filibuster against my questions.
ICKES: Senator, with all due respect, you have asked me—you have asked me a question. I assume I get the courtesy of answering.
COCHRAN: Yes, you certainly do.
ICKES: Good.
COCHRAN: We are going to be very, very courteous to you.
ICKES: Good. I appreciate that.

ICKES'S MEMORY lapses were frequent, but more elaborate than most of the other witnesses'. When asked if he had been in a meeting with the President and Teamsters' president Ron Carey, Ickes replied, "I don't recall. I have been in a lot of meetings with the President with a lot of different people. I may well have been. I don't have a specific recollection as I sit here today."

Ickes was virtually the only witness to continually appear to concede the positive, only to turn around and envelop it in a cloud of ambiguity.

Only Nickles took Ickes on, on some sensitive questions about labor unions, but Nickles was no match for him. It had already been established that, to an extent previously unknown, Ickes was running the Democratic National Committee from the White House. Don Fowler, the DNC chairman, a longtime party reformer, was reduced to a sad helpmate. Fowler was only one of many honorable people who got muddied, or worse, because of their proximity to Clinton.

Another was Bruce Babbitt, an estimable man now Clinton's Secretary of the Interior. A former governor of Arizona who had run for the Democratic nomination in 1988, Babbitt had twice come close to being named to the Supreme Court by Clinton. Clinton's deliberations on this matter entailed long, soulful talks between the two men at the White House, only to have Clinton back off at the last minute. ("We're getting used to it," sighed Babbitt's wife, Hattie, also a considerable figure and an administration official.)

Now Babbitt was in trouble because it appeared that he was loyally covering for the White House's meddling in an Interior Department decision, and in the course of that had given two different committees two different explanations. A regional office of the Interior Department had recommended that a group of Chippewa tribes in Wisconsin be given permission for a new gambling casino (it already owned a failing dog track). A group of rival, wealthier tribes objected and hired a big-time Washington lawyer and former DNC treasurer, Patrick O'Connor, who took his case directly to the President. According to the pattern, the President directed Ickes to look into it. The Interior Department in Washington turned down the new casino, and the following day O'Connor, according to his diary, raised more than $300,000 for the Democratic National Committee. Babbitt gave conflicting responses to congressional committees over whether he had told an erstwhile close friend, whom the poorer Chippewas had hired, that Ickes was pressing for a decision and that the wealthier tribes had contributed a half million dollars to the DNC.

It was not unusual, another Cabinet officer told me, for Ickes to get involved in matters pending before Cabinet departments. And another told me that the Interior Department is the most politically sensitive of all, dealing as it does with such issues as land use, water rights, and commercial usage of natural resources. Governors and senators and representatives—and therefore the White House—take a great interest in its decisions. A Cabinet officer of a different department told me, "This is not Cabinet government. We have White House staff government."

Babbitt insisted that no one from the White House had lobbied him, but it didn't have to work that way, and there was a paper trail of calls from Harold Ickes's staff to Babbitt's subordinates. Watching Babbitt stumble around in his testimony before Thompson's committee was painful, and in the end, the whole thing won him an Independent Counsel and big expenses.

Ickes's powers of recollection were so poor, actually, that Thompson seriously considered referring him to the Justice Department on perjury charges. At one point, Thompson was considering sending nine names to the Justice Department on such charges, but in the end, he decided not to make any such referrals, but instead to point out in its final report the "inconsistencies" in the testimony of certain key witnesses, among them Ickes, Fowler, Sullivan, and Babbitt.[*]

TOWARD THE END of October, Thompson wrote Lott asking for an extension of the hearing, with no cutoff date. He did so knowing that he wouldn't get either one. Thompson also decided that despite their nonspeaking relationship, it was time that the two men swallow their pride and sit down in the same room. In Lott's Capitol office, Thompson said, "Trent, I wrote you this letter. You know as chairman of the committee I've got to take that position. But unless I get no cutoff date at all, I don't want an extension, and I ain't going to get no cutoff date."

Lott told Thompson what Thompson already knew, "The

---

[*]In September 1998, the Justice Department opened an inquiry into whether an Independent Counsel should be appointed to investigate whether Ickes had committed perjury before the committee; on January 29, 1999, Attorney General Reno ruled against it.

Democrats would never let that happen." Neither, of course, would Lott.

Thompson told me later, "I knew it wasn't going to happen and I didn't really care. We could have taken some time to develop other instances and held hearings on them, but they would have been labeled 'defunct' hearings, 'languishing' hearings. The P.R. would win if we wanted to take some time to look at other things."

SO THOMPSON decided again that the hearings should be shut down. Several potential witnesses were still declining to appear. The leader of a group of Cheyenne and Arapaho tribes in Oklahoma had been referred to a Gore fund-raiser Peter Knight by Nathan Landow, a major Democratic contributor, after they had a donated $107,000 to the DNC to help them reclaim some valuable land in Oklahoma. (The exploitation of Indian tribes by Washington operators, a sub-theme of the hearings, was never fully developed.)

Thompson had planned an investigation of a scheme whereby the DNC would provide financial help for the incumbent Teamsters head, Ron Carey, in his narrowly successful race for re-election against James Hoffa, the legendary leader's son, in exchange for Teamster donations to the Democrats. But that investigation was now stymied because of court proceedings in New York.*

The possible quid pro quos that the committee had planned to examine were, predictably, turning out harder to prove than had been thought. Quid pro quos are usually hard to prove, even if the circumstantial evidence is screaming. Some of the Republican staff members wanted to have an "immunity day," in which all of the people taking the Fifth Amendment would be called in to do so in front of the cameras. It was too easy to take the Fifth, some complained: their lawyers simply faxed it in. But Thompson was concerned that such a proceeding would make him appear to be grandstanding, even have a whiff of McCarthyism, and the idea was dropped.

By late October, Thompson had little choice but to end the hearings shortly. Congress was planning to adjourn soon. His party was giving him no support. Hardly anyone on the committee, Democrat or Republican, wanted the hearings to go on. Since the

*A federal elections officer had ruled the election a fraud and handed the case over to the U.S. Attorney's office. A new election was held on November 2, 1998. Hoffa won.

investigation was an add-on to the Senators' already busy schedules, many of them were simply feeling worn out. Neither Lott nor his Democratic counterpart, Tom Daschle, wanted the hearings to continue. Thompson himself, unhappy with what had become of his hearings, had become so tired that he lost control in a set-to with Levin during the hearing on October 23, on the White House tapes. Levin was once again trying to establish that there were precedents in the Bush 1992 campaign for what the Clinton White House had done in 1996. The two men shouted over each other:

THOMPSON: It is one o'clock—

LEVIN: Yes.

THOMPSON (continuing): And I am not going to sit here and go through another ten minutes of a prior campaign. It is clearly outside the jurisdiction. I know you believe everybody does it, and that the most important function that we have here is to demonstrate that, and that is all fine and good. You have done it consistently, but it is one o'clock. These gentlemen have got other things to do. We have White House counsel coming in here. And I am not going to sit here and listen to another ten minutes, even, of everybody does it and Bush or Reagan or Calvin Coolidge or anybody else.

LEVIN: Well, Mr. Chairman, we have heard you make representations that what happened in 1996 at the White House was unprecedented. We sat here and listened to you say over and over again that what happened in 1996 was unprecedented.

THOMPSON: All right. You say, then—

LEVIN: We have—

THOMPSON: You say, then, that—

LEVIN: If I could—if I could just—

THOMPSON: Well, why don't you just say that it was not unprecedented, and we will be even.

LEVIN: Very good. It was not unprecedented—

THOMPSON: All right.

LEVIN (continuing): The only way we are going to find out whether it was unprecedented or not is we do not deny the opportunity for us to show, indeed, it was unprecedented. Now, the allegations were made over and over again by Republicans that these events were unprecedented, and when it comes our turn to try to show, "Hey, wait a minute"—

THOMPSON: Do you have—

LEVIN: Excuse me, Mr. Chairman. That Bush hosted a Team 100 dinner on the State Floor of the White House, 1993, page after page—

THOMPSON: Do you have any evidence that there were money-launderers, convicted felons, or otherwise—

LEVIN: Yeah.

THOMPSON (continuing): Coming in and out of—

LEVIN: Yeah.

THOMPSON (continuing): The White House?

LEVIN: If we—

THOMPSON: Do you have any evidence of that?

LEVIN: Mr. Chairman, we are trying to get evidence of what President Bush did at the White House.

THOMPSON: Well, it is not going to happen. I am going to give you another five minutes or whatever time you have left here—

LEVIN: I am not going to take another five minutes.

THOMPSON (continuing): Then we are going to recess.

THOMPSON had displayed his temper in the hearings on other occasions, but he insisted privately that his anger was calculated. The Levin contretemps was of another order. Thompson knew he had lost control then, and Levin, too, was shaken afterward.

So, on Friday, October 31, after agonizing over the decision for days, Thompson pulled down the curtain on the hearings for good. In a crowded press conference in the Senate Radio-Television Gallery, a small room on the third floor of the Senate side of the Capitol, Thompson, speaking briskly, told the assembled press, "I am disappointed that we will not be able to lift the cutoff date," adding, in a bow to reality, "however, I can count."

Asked to evaluate his committee's role, Thompson said, "We should not measure ourselves in terms of scalps on the wall." But he claimed that the committee had dug up some "troubling stories," and that it had played some role—"I'm not saying we caused it"—in forcing the Senate to debate campaign finance reform.

Thompson had some suggestions for future investigations by Congress, and, noting that the committee had been beset by partisan fighting from the very beginning, he said, "Things have changed now. Some people consider it their role—regardless of the evidence—to play a certain role. That takes away from what you're trying to do." He added, "If the ranking member doesn't agree on the purpose of the hearing with the majority, it doesn't work. It worked on Watergate, but, unfortunately, that time has passed."

REPRESENTATIVE Christopher Shays, of Connecticut, a reformer, who invited Thompson to come to his district in the spring of 1998 (a number of reform Republicans did this, and even Don Nickles did, as well), said to me shortly afterward, "Thompson is a hero who hasn't yet got his recognition."

Shays criticized his own party harshly. "We, the Republicans, have blown it," he said, "The fatal flaw of the Republicans has been to only want to expose and embarrass the Clinton administration, rather than expose the system and reform it. Where the law is found wanting, we should change the law. Thompson, with his ethics, knew exposure had to lead to reform. The Republicans didn't like that and they shut him down."

DESPITE THE limited exposure the public had to the hearings they clearly had an impact. Enough people paid close attention to move opinion. Enough information and examples turned up by the hearings came through the cracks in the windows and doorways for the public to get the idea, more strongly than ever, that something was terribly amiss. The hearings made the case that the current campaign finance system was a disaster, corrupt, that the problems went well beyond the Clinton follies.

As the time approached in the fall of 1997 for the Senate to debate a campaign finance reform bill—which Lott had tried to avoid—there had been a change in the atmosphere. The rising public mood on the issue, and the embarrassments that the hearings produced, built pressure on Lott to allow the Senate to take up a bill. As the hearings were drawing to a close, an utterly partisan Democratic operative said to me, "Everyone's a second guesser. That's easy. And they did make mistakes. But they built enough momentum that a reform bill's about to be on the Senate floor and House leaders are having to talk about bringing a bill to the floor."

Joseph Lieberman, the independent-minded Connecticut Democrat, felt that Thompson had come off well, that he had wanted to do the right thing. Lieberman didn't share his Democratic colleagues' view that Thompson was running distorted, partisan hearings. He thought that if the Democrats were in control, they would have run the hearings the same way. He felt that the Democrats had got too much into the role of defense lawyers, which cut the credibility of both sides.

The hearings may not have set the country on fire, but they caused more politicians to not want to appear to be opposed to reform. The stream of stories about soft money raised through questionable means, of money purchasing access, of access-peddling, got through. The hearings showed graphically, as never before, that the campaign finance system had been destroyed. They gave texture and definition to that point.

Thompson told me, "The question has always been, What would be the effect on the American people of the array—the *array*—of stories. That's much more important than the details about whom you put on and what did you prove and smoking guns and the rest of it."

Thompson may have been building his own defense case then, but he turned out to be right.

8

— ■ —

Hypocrisy

Perhaps nothing has contributed more to cynicism about government than the hypocrisy of the politicians about reforming the campaign finance system. Numerous polls have documented that though majorities want the system reformed, they don't trust the politicians who are in the system to change it. And they've been proven right in not expecting the beneficiaries of a corrupt system to fix it. Each struggle for campaign finance reform since 1974 has met with ultimate defeat. So what reason is there for thinking there might be real reform? What reason is there to think that the politicians might behave differently?

Since the passage of the comprehensive—and for a while effective—campaign finance law in 1974, no subject in American politics has been as bathed in hypocrisy. Everyone is "for" it. But the form that "it" might take, in certain politicians' calculations, often amounts to a cosmetic change in the guise of "doing something," or to something they know the Congress won't pass, or gutting whatever laws remain. All these people at play in the fields of hypocrisy may not realize what they're doing to the body politic—or they may not care.

Disingenuousness defines many proposals, such as one, offered

142

in recent years by Republicans, to simply require faster reporting by the candidates of contributions. The information was to be posted on the Internet. Faster and more accessible reporting would be useful, of course, but it's no substitute for real reforms. And it still would take heroic efforts by news outlets and monitoring groups to translate and give form to the reports—to find out which contributor has ties to what groups, what the company a contributor is associated with actually does and what its legislative interests were—before an election.

The reporting ruse has had as its most vociferous backer an appropriately named House Republican, Doolittle (John, of California). Among Republicans, Doolittle came to be known as "the Mitch McConnell of the House." Reformers feared Doolittle's proposal because it sounded so plausible.

The hypocrisy practiced by both political parties took other forms as well. A member would declare support for reform, but manage to not have to actually vote for it if there was any real danger that a substantial bill would be enacted into law. Thus, people could vote for a bill they knew a president would veto, or that they assumed that the other chamber wouldn't pass, and still claim credit as a backer of reform. Beryl Anthony, a former Democratic Member of Congress, and a former chairman of the Democratic Congressional Campaign Committee, told me, "We used to say, 'What the Democrats pass, the Republicans wouldn't sign into law,' and 'What the Republicans pass the Democrats wouldn't sign into law.'"

Anthony told me of an incident in 1992 when House Democrats, about to pass a campaign reform bill, assured him, "'Don't worry, Beryl, this thing won't become law.'"

Anthony replied, "What if it does? We're screwed." (It didn't, because Bush vetoed it.)

In the late eighties and early nineties, Mitch McConnell moved to eliminate PACs, on the well-founded suspicion that the Democrats wouldn't let that happen in the end, because they needed the PAC money. "He no more meant that than the man in the moon," a business lobbyist told me. "It's an example of how this whole debate has become posturing." In 1993, McConnell even offered a bill to ban soft money and to impose tight controls on "independent expenditures." But now he vigorously opposed both changes.

Representative Bob Matsui, Democrat of California, explained to me, "All of it is making sure that the dead cat is not at your doorstep when all is said and done."

One curious aspect of all this posing was that so many politicians wanted to be seen as being for reform at the same time that they were saying that "the public doesn't care."

Another form of the hypocrisy was to proclaim that one was for campaign finance reform and not lift a finger to help get it passed by the Congress. The champ at this—at creating the greatest chasm between promise and performance—was Bill Clinton.

AN INDELIBLE SCENE from the Clinton-Gingrich fandango following the Republican takeover of the House was of the two pudgy, gray-haired, garrulous wonks at a more-or-less improvised town meeting in New Hampshire on a sunny Sunday afternoon in June 1995, shaking hands on Gingrich's proposal that they name a "blue-ribbon commission" on campaign finance reform. Clinton accepted "in a heartbeat." A commission was never formed, though Clinton, knowing that Gingrich didn't really want reform, made some let's-pretend moves toward naming commission members—exploiting, as he so often did, well-meaning and even distinguished figures. Clinton, who could change his position in a flash, was at least consistent in his cynicism on this subject.

"He supports it but he doesn't do anything," former Clinton aide George Stephanopoulos told me. "He's conflicted. He's feeling, rightfully, that 'everybody does do it.' He got outspent by two hundred million dollars in ninety-six." Clinton brought to the subject of the Thompson committee hearings the same attitude that he had toward campaign finance reform in general—"everybody does it," "I'm being picked on," etc. After insisting to me over a period of five years that Clinton had done some things about campaign finance reform—a line in a speech, a letter to Congress—another White House aide finally conceded in March of 1998, "The real answer is, No, we didn't do anything."

Rahm Emanuel, a senior aide to the President, told me in the fall of 1997 that several people in the White House, including Clinton (and himself), shared this view. "Nobody here thinks they get any credit for doing anything. We got no benefit for the lobbying reforms or the gift ban. Everybody pocketed it and said, 'That's not good enough.' It was different with the Brady bill. We got plaudits from the press. But lobbying reform and the gift ban just blew up in the ether. There is a group of people here who believe if we pass campaign reform it won't be appreciated. Therefore, there is some level of 'We can do this and if we reform the system we're not sure it will accrue to our benefit and we know we'll lose money.'" So the President, feeling, as he often did, unappreciated, abandoned the field.

The strongest opponent of reform among the President's advisors—according to four sources—was his pollster, Mark Penn. According to these sources, Penn kept telling the President that "the public doesn't care." Yet, though the issue rarely shows up on the top ten that people say they care about, it's also true that when the direct question is put to them of whether they think the political system should be cleaned up, or there should be campaign finance reform, the answer is a strong yes.

It has established that in 1996 the campaign funding issue, breaking as it did less than a month before the election and building as the election approached, cost the Democrats their chance to retake the House of Representatives. Ten days to two weeks before the election the Democrats appeared to have the House in hand. But the cascade of press stories, mainly about John Huang's activities at the Democratic National Committee, caused enough movement among voters to re-elect a Republican House, if with only an eleven-seat majority. This development, and others in 1998, suggest strongly that when the public is given a specific way to focus on the subject, it registers its opinion for reform.

MARK PENN'S position, about which he was quite vociferous, actually reflected a view held by other Democratic political consultants. The consultants, after all, prosper from the current system. The ad-makers make a negotiated, fixed percentage of the cost of purchasing expensive television time for ads—in addition to their fees for giving general advice to a campaign. (For the same reason, most consultants oppose proposals that television stations give candidates free airtime.)

A former White House aide (not Stephanopoulos) said to me, "The political consultants are trained to ignore the campaign finance issue. They think it'll send them to Section 8 [subsidized] housing. They insist it's not an issue. They resisted suggestions Clinton go with it. If Clinton had talked about it during the campaign, it might have arrested the slide at the end."

A colleague of Penn's said, "Penn's whispering into his [Clinton's] ear that nobody cares, which is wrong."

CLINTON'S ABANDONMENT of campaign finance reform is often attributed to a meeting in Little Rock shortly after the 1992 election with Democratic House leaders who urged him not to push for reform. But there's scant evidence that it ever would have been a priority for him once he himself was amidst the *Realpolitik* of big-time fund-raising.

In his first four years in office, Clinton rarely spoke about campaign finance reform and made little effort to get it. In the succeeding years, he did in this area what he did in others: He substituted what a Cabinet officer calls "stunts" for policy-making. But the gap between real and phony action on the part of the President may have been the greatest in the case of campaign finance reform.

In 1997, for the obvious reason, Clinton displayed an ostensible new enthusiasm for the subject. In his State of the Union address, he called upon the Congress to pass a campaign finance reform bill "by the day we celebrate the birthday of our democracy—July the Fourth." (Applause)

That didn't happen, of course, and neither did a number of other campaign finance reforms that Clinton called for in the comforting knowledge that they wouldn't happen.

In each case, his aides insisted that this showed that the President was truly sincere in fighting for campaign finance reform— really, truly sincere—until some of them finally gave up the pretense.

AS THE SENATE Democrats gathered for a caucus meeting in the LBJ Room of the Capitol, after the new Congress convened in January 1997, they needed to separate themselves from the Clinton campaign's scabrous behavior in destroying the campaign finance system in the 1996 election—and by extension their own national committee's. Many of the senators understood that those activities had kept the Democrats from regaining the House in 1996. The response to certain poll questions notwithstanding, it was becoming clear that supporting campaign finance reform was good politics. Besides, many Democrats were sick of the ever-rising demands of fund-raising. Some even thought that reforming the campaign finance system was the right thing to do. They had seen or experienced directly the campaign finance system hurtling out of control in 1996. And some of the ways it did so were to their disadvantage.

But the Senate Democrats were divided on what to do about campaign finance reform legislation in the new Congress. So were their House counterparts, but everyone expected the Senate to act first. The most obvious reform was a ban on unlimited soft money, which was at the root of most of the 1996 scandals. It was the frenzy for soft money that led to the coffees, the foreign funds, the visits to the Hsi Lai Temple and Ambrous Young's yacht. Yet this was the subject on which the Democrats were most divided.

Despite their mixed feelings and views, after 1996 the Democrats had to not just appear to be for campaign finance reform, but to actually be for it. A lobbyist with strong ties to the Democrats said, "After 1996, they had to be for it—and will have to be. But I don't think their souls have changed."

SENATE DEMOCRATIC LEADER Tom Daschle had no difficulty assessing the new reality. His challenge was to unite the Senate Democratic caucus, to keep the Republicans from riding over a divided minority. A Democratic strategist said, "Daschle believes that one of the most important weapons he has is the unity of his caucus. He'll go to great lengths to get it and he'll go to great lengths to keep it." He added, "It was difficult to get it on this issue."

Daschle believed that a party united on campaign finance reform would gain more support from the public, and, of more immediate importance, establish its bona fides with the public interest groups, in particular Common Cause, the "citizens' lobby" which had long pushed for campaign finance reform. And reform won support from the editorial boards of major newspapers, especially the *New York Times* and the *Washington Post*. While dismissing these papers as organs of the "elite," Republican strategists understood that they had considerable influence on the Congress, in particular on moderate Republicans from eastern states, and also on wavering Democrats.

At the Democratic Caucus in January 1997, Bob Kerrey, of Nebraska, the past and current chairman of the Democratic Senatorial Campaign Committee, and Bob Torricelli, who had joined Kerrey as vice chairman, rose to oppose banning soft money. The job of the people in those roles was to raise money, pure and simple.

Technically, Bob Kerrey was Mitch McConnell's counterpart, but, aside from a shared passion for raising money, McConnell the solemn expositor and Kerrey the blithe spirit had almost nothing in common. Kerrey, whose large, penetrating blue eyes drew attention, was an unconventional political figure. Unlike most of his colleagues, Kerrey, though a former governor of Nebraska and now a second-term senator, and briefly a presidential candidate in 1992, didn't seem to take politics, or himself, with puffed-up seriousness. His thoughts were sometimes hard to follow, but some of them were refreshingly iconoclastic. A genuine war hero, he had volunteered for the highly dangerous mission of the Navy SEALs in Vietnam, and had a leg blown off. He was frank but uncomplaining about having an artificial leg, and unselfconsciously participated in running contests.

Both Kerrey and Torricelli told the Democratic caucus in early 1997 that since the Republicans had outraised them in hard money—that is, strictly limited contributions—the Democrats couldn't afford to give up soft money. Democrats were more dependent on soft money than the Republicans were, and, at that, the Republicans outraised them in soft funds, too. But soft money constituted a higher proportion of the funds raised by the Democrats. Others in the room were sympathetic. Daschle was torn. It was a matter of sheer pragmatism.

Another pragmatic consideration was explained to me by the blunt Torricelli as we walked across the Capitol grounds during a lunch break in the Thompson hearings.

"There is no financial base for the core issues of the Democratic Party," he said. "I've said so in the Democratic Caucus several times. Civil rights, the environment, pro-choice—they have a voting constituency but they have no financial strength. In current American politics you can't survive without a financial constituency. One item on our agenda, education reform, is popular with the voters. That's why we're still alive. The Democratic Party is disproportionately funded by organized labor and our Jewish constituency. The Republicans have a small-donor base. We don't."

"Look at the Democratic Party agenda," Torricelli said. "It's the progressive agenda. Twenty years ago the Democratic coalition was able to compete even though it didn't have a big-money constituency—because the amounts were so much lower. And now we see a possibility of being taken out of contention."

And then he said, "If there's not the right kind of campaign finance reform, our survival will be in question. We'll have deep, thoughtful discussions about issues that will raise us money."

Torricelli added that all this, their pro-reform rhetoric notwithstanding, was why I sensed that Democratic leaders—Senate and House—didn't want to give up soft money. They didn't, Torricelli explained—pointing out that he shared this view—at least unless there were also curbs on "issue ads." Otherwise, the Republicans would still have the advantage in those, too. But, as Ed Gillespie, who had previously served as House Majority Leader Dick Armey's press secretary—one of the best I'd seen on Capitol Hill—and is now a lobbyist, pointed out, "The Democrats are trying to remove the Republicans' two greatest areas of advantage: soft money and issue ads."

Daschle's dilemma had another origin: Like some other Democrats, he was from a small state, in his case an essentially Republican one, and was dependent upon the national network of Democratic donors. Similarly, in the House, many blacks and Hispanics were dependent on wealthy contributors from outside their districts, and were loath to give up soft money.

At one point in the strategizing in 1997 on campaign finance reform legislation, the reform groups—Common Cause in particular—were willing to settle for only a ban on soft money. The theory was that past multipart bills had been too hard to get through the Congress, and that a simple ban on the greatest source of scandal would be hard to oppose.

But a Senate Democratic strategist said to me at the time, "If there were a secret ballot on soft money, only thirty-five or forty [out of forty-five] of the Democrats would be for it."

HOUSE DEMOCRATIC LEADERS were even more reluctant to change the rules of war by getting rid of soft money than were their Senate counterparts.

A House Democratic aide said, in the fall of 1997, "Most people in the House and Senate feel they've won by the current system and they don't want to change the current system, period."

Mark Mellman, the Democratic pollster, said that the Senate Democrats were beset by three competing viewpoints on what to do. A lot of them, Mellman said, would like to have public financing of congressional campaigns, along the lines of the presidential system (before it was destroyed), but know that isn't politically feasible now. The politicians feel that they can't sell it to the public, so they don't try.

"Two," Mellman said, "survival." Some Democrats, like Torricelli, felt that the "issue ads" that came in at the last minute nearly overcame their financial advantage over their opponents. Mellman said that the Democrats realized that far more was spent on ads to help Republicans than would ever be spent for them.

"Three," Mellman said, "utter contempt and distaste for what they have to do day to day to raise money. They hate it. There's nobody who doesn't think it's just a little bit unclean. They have to be exceedingly solicitous of some of the most difficult people in the world—who aren't even their voters."

THUS, THE INTERESTS of the two political parties were in direct conflict—except for a few Republicans who, like Fred Thompson and John McCain, thought that supporting campaign finance reform was the right thing to do, and those who also thought it was good politics. The prevailing view of most of the Republicans was that they would do best with the fewest limits.

Trent Lott was on record, after all, that he wouldn't be in national politics if he hadn't been able to raise a great deal of money to overcome the longtime Democratic hold on his state. He had also said that limits on fund-raising would hurt Republicans, who needed to get around the "news media with their prejudices." That, plus their self-inculcated views on the power of labor, led the Republicans to resist limits.

But everyone was "for" reform.

9

————■————

The Presidency

The President had just made an upbeat statement in the Rose Garden on the state of the economy. As had become his wont of late, he declined to take questions. As he strode purposefully back to his office, chin high—a manner he had developed well into his first term—a reporter called out, "Will you voluntarily give a DNA sample, sir?"

Clinton's failure to lead on campaign finance reform was of a piece with his general failure to lead. And his presidency contributed to the decline of the Office of President—even before the sex scandal. His wasn't the first presidency to do so, but Clinton's own contribution was substantial and of historical importance. His flawed presidency was another disappointment and added to the cumulative negative impact, coming as it did after the disillusionment caused by the presidencies of Lyndon Johnson and Richard Nixon over the Vietnam War and Watergate, the disappointment of the Ford and Carter presidencies, the societal divisions of the Reagan presidency (though Reagan himself remained popular). The limited vision of the Bush presidency was another disappointment. That Clinton remained popular during most of his presidency doesn't belie this point. Clinton laid waste to two of the office's most important elements: its mystique and its power to influence the public and the Congress.

Clinton's presidency has been a squandered opportunity. His formidable political skills and exceptional brain have gone more to self-preservation than to leadership—and this, too, was true well before he became enmeshed in the sex scandal that blew up in January 1998. If the definition of leadership is acting on things one feels strongly about and being willing to risk some political capital in order to achieve them, Clinton has come up short. In fact, with a few exceptions, it wasn't very clear what Clinton did feel strongly about.

No presidency has been as poll-driven as Bill Clinton's. When Richard Wirthlin polled for President Reagan, he did it two to three times a month—unless there was a crisis, during which he polled nightly. But there was another big difference. A Democratic political consultant says, "Reagan used polling to figure out how to sell his beliefs. Clinton uses polling to figure out what to believe."

At a time of unparalleled prosperity, and even into his second term, Clinton had given the country no sense of direction. The President enjoyed the political fruits of the prosperity, the longest peacetime economic expansion in history, accompanied by low inflation and low unemployment. His support of the 1993 economic plan, cutting spending and raising taxes, had something to do with that. His acceptance, in 1995, of the concept of the balanced budget—pushed on him by Gingrich and opposed by several of his aides, but urged on him by his then-guru, Dick Morris, to help his election prospects—helped push the budget from red to black (with the help of a surplus of over $125 billion in the Social Security trust fund). The surplus that showed up in 1998—and was announced a week before the election—gave Clinton the opportunity to provide the country with a grand vision, but he didn't do so. His State of the Union speech in 1999 continued his by-then habit of handing out goodies to all the Democratic constituencies, or hoped-for constituencies. His speech was a myriad of poll-tested proposals, most of them small in aim. He still had an opportunity to resolve two long-range and politically difficult problems: assuring the soundness of the Social Security and Medicare programs, about to be flooded by the "baby boomers." But in both cases Clinton chose the easy way out.

With his mini-proposals, his abandonment of any vision, Clinton had trivialized the presidency.

At the beginning of his second term, he formed a "legacy committee" of staff members to figure out what his legacy should be, which said it all. In the first few months, three "legacies" were trotted out: education, voluntarism, race (through a commission to conduct a national "discussion"). The first one he botched (and then gave away large parts of it in order to try to obtain a trade bill that Congress denied him anyway); the other two received at best fitful attention.

CLINTON DID LEAD in the first year of his first term on his economic program, spending a great deal of political capital on it. He also did so on the North American Free Trade Agreement (NAFTA), which was passed in late 1993. That was it. His capitulation on an energy tax as part of his 1993 economic program after House Democrats had walked the plank to support him—and he had promised them he wouldn't abandon them—left a legacy of mistrust among his own party. (Using a different metaphor, a Senate Democratic aide told me, "Clinton's left too many people out on thin ice and let them fall through.")

So deep was the lack of trust in Clinton after the sex scandal, even among former loyalists on Capitol Hill, that when Lawrence Summers, the Deputy Secretary of the Treasury, appeared before the House Ways and Means Committee in March of 1999 to discuss Clinton's still-vague Social Security plan, the normally polite, even elegant Representative Bob Matsui, Democrat of California, snapped at him, "I shouldn't be so supportive, lest you pull the rug out from under me."

Clinton's signing of a harsh welfare reform bill—Dick Morris told him that if he didn't he would lose ten points in the election—was an inglorious moment in his presidency.*

---

*The new law broke the sixty-year compact between the federal government and people in need of assistance, and turned the matter over to the states, with fairly loose guidelines. Welfare rolls dropped substantially in the first few years under the new law; no one could be sure to what extent this was due to the booming economy, or what portion of those who left the rolls had been thrown off and hadn't found jobs. Recognizing that the hardest cases remained on the rolls, in 1999 Clinton proposed some limited additional measures to give them training and help them find jobs.

For such a gregarious man, one so convinced of the effectiveness of his own charm, Clinton was strangely isolated. He made few friends in the Congress, at the same time that he took various steps that alienated the congressional Democrats, all of which left little sense of loyalty to him on Capitol Hill. Following the 1994 debacle, he accepted Morris's advice to "triangulate"—set himself apart from both the Democrats and the Republicans.

The "triangulation"insult to members of his own party was followed by the damage his campaign financing scandals caused the House Democrats, turning their near-victory in the 1996 House elections into defeat, thus imprisoning them in their hated minority status.

Clinton's ruthlessness and insouciance about the effects of what he did to others—he left a long line of casualties—did not bind any significant number of other politicians to him.

So when the sex scandal threatened to demolish his presidency, Clinton found at first few friends on Capitol Hill. And a Democratic senator told me in early September 1998, when Clinton appeared to be in serious trouble, "There's not that kind of bond in the Senate Caucus that people are rallying behind him."

In the House, only the Black Caucus stood firm at first. Clinton had a real rapport with blacks, based on his seemingly natural empathy and some of the things he did for the less advantaged, such as winning from Congress the earned income tax credit, which guaranteed everyone a minimum income—and despite the welfare bill. In September, John Lewis, one of Clinton's few friends on Capitol Hill (and Lewis wasn't a social friend), and other black Members of Congress told white Democrats in the House, especially Minority Leader Gephardt, who was keeping his distance from Clinton, that they expected more support of the President.

That the Democrats supported Clinton on impeachment—after a while—had to do with the fact that more than 60 percent of the American public approved of the job he was doing, even after Joseph Lieberman criticized him strongly in a Senate speech in September, and with their sense that the Republicans were, in the words of one House Democrat, "piling on." Besides, he said, "The people at home didn't care, they said 'leave him alone.'"

This Democrat said, "When they released the President's grand jury testimony is when I flipped." Clinton's taped grand jury appearance was released on September 21, 1998.

Bob Matsui told me, "My colleagues were outraged about their releasing grand jury information. Cynics think that Members of Congress don't get outraged, but there was outrage that these guys had overdone it."

THE SQUANDERED opportunity of the Clinton presidency was all the sadder, even tragic, not only because Clinton was unusually smart, but also because, unbeknownst to most Americans, early in his presidency he actually had a vision. I heard him talk about it frequently in small groups during his first year in office, and he did incorporate it in a few major speeches, but he never got it across to the nation. The vision was that every American would have a lifelong opportunity for learning and training. Clinton's capacious mind grasped very well the effects of the changing global economy and new technology on workers, rendering their current skills obsolete. He could be quite passionate on the subject.

But Clinton hadn't turned this vision into reality by the time of the 1994 elections. Then the Republican sweep of Congress traumatized him, and he abandoned his vision, leaving himself to the manipulation of the cynical strategist Dick Morris, who—with Mrs. Clinton's concurrence—was called to the rescue. This led in turn to the poll-inspired mini-proposals of the 1996 election: school uniforms, a second emergency number because 911 was becoming overloaded. A senior White House aide told me that Morris was adept at writing poll questions designed to get the answer he wanted—and then he turned them over to his pals, Mark Penn and Doug Schoen, the team he had brought in to conduct polls for Clinton after the 1994 debacle. (As far as can be determined, Penn was the first pollster to virtually camp out in the West Wing of the White House.)

In the end, a much slimmed-down version of his vision, what Clinton called "a G.I. Bill for America's workers," was approved by the Congress and signed by the President in a Rose Garden ceremony in August 1998. This partial success was barely noticed over the din of the sex scandal.

CLINTON BEHAVED oddly after his re-election in 1996. He didn't seem very interested in his job, or know what to do with a second term. (That led to the "legacy committee.") One White House aide told me that it was as if when he won re-election Clinton had passed the ultimate exam test, and then experienced letdown. This feeling of ennui, perhaps also affected by his tarred victory—the money scandal that had begun to break before the election was growing ominously—had an impact on those around him. When the President entered his first Cabinet meeting after the election, no one stood to applaud him.

By the time Clinton responded to criticism of his presidential lassitude with an activist State of the Union speech at the beginning of 1998, the second year of his second term, he had been smacked with the sex scandal. Though he maintained throughout that he wasn't distracted by it, he was, as he had to be, and, just as important, so was much of his staff. Whatever effectiveness with the Congress remained to him was diminished further in the course of 1998. The price for this was the loss of several proposals, including one for voluntary testing of school children, and "fast track" trade authority, which he had won in the past.

When the Senate in 1998 defeated most of the remainder of his education program, the voice from the White House was muffled.

By now Clinton knew perfectly well how to make effective use of the bully pulpit, but he didn't seem interested. He was distracted and disengaged. The President's influence on legislation to curb smoking was minimal at best, and the tobacco interests defeated the combined efforts of Clinton and Congress to raise taxes on cigarettes.

But being Clinton, and not having lost his political skills even as he lost his moorings, he managed to turn these issues into weapons to be used against the Republicans as the 1998 elections—which could be crucial to his fate—approached. As his confidence began to return from what was, as of then, the lowest point of his presidency—his having to admit publicly in August that he had lied to everyone and had dragged the country through seven months of needless turmoil and court challenges in order to cover up his sexual dalliances with a White House intern—he was obviously pleased to be able to return to utilizing those skills. The result was as it had been when the Republicans had mistakenly thought that they could beat him on the budget in late 1995 by shutting down the government: He flimflammed them again.

He won some substantive issues, including at least a part of his education proposal, but mainly he won the public-relations/political war. Though capable of copious self-pity—at an

October 1998 fund-raiser, mixing metaphors, he referred to the "hard, cold experience in the caldron that I have lived in for six years"—Clinton was the most resilient politician in memory. But tactical skills, however great, do not constitute leadership.

His self-pity—in evidence well before the sex scandal broke—was combined with an anger that had a strange hold on him, and went beyond his well-known temper tantrums. In September 1997, the *Washington Post* quoted someone who had attended a recent meeting of Clinton and his Cabinet as saying, "He said he'd been angry just about every day he'd been President." There was a petulance to Clinton that seemed adolescent. The boy who wanted to grow up to be President became President but never quite grew up.

Both the President and his wife, despite their triumph in 1992, came to Washington with grudges—against the press, against Washington itself—which, however justified, did them no good. Their lingering grievances only isolated them and caused them to make mistakes, such as appointing an inexperienced White House staff. And in the cases both of the press and Washington itself, there were numerous people who had helped Clinton win the presidency. Mrs. Clinton never got over her anger at the press's attention, during the New Hampshire primary, to Clinton's affair with Gennifer Flowers and his dodging the draft during the Vietnam War. The press can be an irritant, for sure, but it is an inescapable part of the presidency, and it can be charmed if not manipulated. Treating it as the enemy from the outset was simply not smart.

EVEN WITH HIS more activist program, Clinton wasn't providing the country with a sense of direction. David Cohen, the liberal activist, said, "Even in a time of tremendous prosperity, there is no sense of public purpose—in the Congress or the Executive. There are things Clinton has proposed but he's not taking us anywhere beyond those proposals."

He added, "In the global economy the movement of capital dislocates equity for a lot of people in this country and outside this country. There's no effort to address that in terms of what kinds of institutions and policies we need. There's only a sidelong glance. As for that bridge into the twenty-first century [Clinton's overused metaphor in his 1996 acceptance speech], we're not being led into it, we're drifting into it."

The Clinton presidency was characterized by "stunts." To show that he was "doing his job," or to distract the public from the less pleasant aspects of his presidency, Clinton's aides struggled mightily to produce a stunt a day: visiting a school; examining a housing project; talking to small businessmen; meeting with police. (Clinton was often shown meeting with police.) In and of themselves, these events were harmless and may have even done some good and been worthy uses of the symbolism of the office. But they weren't a substitute for an overarching purpose.

The stunts were a specialty of the Clinton White House staff, which knew more about putting them on than about governing. Leon Panetta, who had been the chairman of the House Budget Committee and then Clinton's first director of the Office of Management and Budget before he became chief of staff in late 1994, brought some order to the Clinton White House. But only so much order could be imposed. Panetta understood governing, and several Democrats mourned his departure after the 1996 election. But Panetta was worn out by the chaotic nature of the indecisive Clinton's decision-making and management, and the thinly experienced White House staff.

Richard Wirthlin, the Republican pollster, saw another consequence of Clinton's lack of leadership. Wirthlin argued to me that the fact that Clinton had changed course so many times meant that "the public doesn't react strongly with his changes. He's adroit enough. He's more able to smooth over gaps and contradictions than anyone before him. But there's a price: The whole concept of us as a nation has been eroded."

Wirthlin also argued that the lack of presidential leadership had intensified the "Balkanization" of Washington. "There always were interest groups, but the drive for self-interest—whether you're a senator, a House member, or an interest group—has been intensified. When there's no agenda, everything is up for grabs."

The total effect, Wirthlin said, was an "increase in people's cynicism about the system, and that weakens the system in terms of participation—not just in voting but also in expressing opinion and seeing how things work out."

WHATEVER ELSE can be said about the deserved downfall of Nixon, he did lead the country on some issues, such as the opening to China, and his family assistance plan, which would have provided a guaranteed income to everyone. But in the end, Nixon gave up on that proposal because of congressional resistance. He had liked the idea when then-White House domestic policy advisor Daniel Patrick Moynihan told him he was Disraeli—a conservative leader pressing reform—and Nixon did have a relatively progressive domestic policy, but Moynihan's intended makeover was never completed.

Jimmy Carter tried to lead on energy conservation and on arms control, but his astringent personality got in the way of being a highly effective President. Yet, after a very difficult struggle with Congress, he did win ratification of the Panama Canal treaty.

Neither Gerald Ford nor George Bush, Republican centrists, had any great government goals, though Bush tried to raise taxes, but was blocked by then–Minority Whip Newt Gingrich, and he did lead a resistant nation into the Persian Gulf War. Bush's own political demise occurred because he didn't know what to do with the huge support the quick victory in the Gulf had brought him— ninety-one percent approval. After his military triumph, to which there had been strong opposition, he went to the Capitol to make a special address to Congress—and had nothing to say.

Thus, the last great presidential leader was Lyndon Johnson, a man who enjoyed governing—who thrived on twisting congressional arms and cutting deals to advance his sweeping legislative agenda, to enact his vision, the "Great Society." He failed only when he finally pushed too far, something he had understood would happen. Though Nixon actually kept many of Johnson's Great Society programs going, it became fashionable to think that none of those programs had worked—some did—and that government couldn't really help people.

Ronald Reagan was a leader, but with his leadership came an antigovernment mood, a negativity about government itself, for which the country is still paying a price. His presidency tripled the national debt, to $3 trillion. And the cost of his policies was growing inequality among the classes, and an enduring skepticism about the role of government.

The boost that Clinton got from the 1998 midterm elections, in which the Democrats did better than anyone considered possible just two months after the height of the sex scandal, appeared to give him new opportunities to accomplish significant things, such as fixing Social Security, in his remaining two years in office. He seemed, momentarily, at least, to be freed from the sex scandal. But it was only momentary.

THE PRESIDENCY must have a certain aura of majesty and mystique, and that has been destroyed over the past twenty-five years. One could see the importance of these traits in the public's distinctly negative reaction to Jimmy Carter's carrying his own bags, and his delivering a presidential address in a sweater. Accessibility, and a sense that a president is in touch, are good things, but can be and have been carried too far. Excessive populism can undermine respect for a president and for his office.

Reagan understood the importance of making a presidential impression. His impresario, Michael Deaver, once told me that before Reagan made any entrance to a public event he quite deliberately threw his shoulders back. Reagan was a success at playing President. George Bush may have lacked Reagan's touch, but he had an obvious respect for the office.

Clinton's lack of dignity, not to mention his sexual recklessness, was an assault on the office itself. Dignity, and maintaining a certain mystique are important to a presidency because the public wants to respect its president, and because in order to get things done a president needs moral authority. Clinton threw away what moral authority he had remaining to him, which put his effectiveness in serious doubt. His extraordinary political deftness, and the blundering of his Republican opponents, kept him going, but he damaged the office as well as himself.

The mystique of the presidency, and Clinton's effectiveness, had actually begun to evaporate by the end of 1994, his first year in office. He had talked too much on television, had comported himself with less-than-presidential bearing. In the summer of 1994, White House aides told me worriedly that when Clinton was on television people in airports didn't stop to hear what he had to say. He had talked about his underwear on television and was seen wearing jeans as he emerged from *Air Force One*.

Clinton and his wife knew by the summer of 1994, in the course of the debate over their humongous and ill-considered health care plan, that he had a stature problem, that the difficulties they were having in getting the bill through Congress weren't the result of just the effective ads by the health insurance industry. They realized that Clinton couldn't get through to people with his arguments. (And

Mrs. Clinton made the colossal misjudgment of refusing to compromise with the Republicans in order to get a bill.)

Panetta and others argued that the President had to be more disciplined about his public appearances, should talk less. With his presidency dead in the water then, Clinton listened. When Panetta told him that he needed to look and be more presidential, pay more heed to the stature of the office, Clinton replied, "I've got to be more like John Wayne."

After a long struggle, Panetta finally got Clinton to wear a track suit when he jogged, rather than shorts that showed his fleshy thighs, and, after the reassessment, Clinton was rarely seen in jeans. Clinton did in fact work on his posture, carrying himself with more dignity, which sometimes came across as self-conscious. (On election night, 1996, on a grand stage in Little Rock, in a Mussolini-type setting, he came across as stiff as the statue in *Don Giovanni*.)

The odd thing about Clinton's carelessness with the office of the presidency from the beginning was that he revered it. He insisted on being called "Mr. President," and flinched when an old friend from Arkansas called him "Bill" in front of others. A serious student of the history of the presidency, he worried a great deal about what his standing would be in the future.

But changes in a president's bearing do not restore the authority and dignity of the Office. Some aides remarked that Clinton should be "like Harry Truman," but he couldn't be Truman if it wasn't authentic. The whole point of Truman's postpresidential popularity was that, in retrospect, he seemed authentic. How likely was it that Clinton would act as Truman did when he fired General Douglas MacArthur at a time when his standing in the polls was twenty-six percent?

CLINTON'S DEGRADATION of the office of the presidency also degraded our national discourse. Even in a time when people are said to be "turned off" Washington, what a president does affects the country's conversation. Certainly, public talk of the President's genitals, and of oral sex with an intern, and of whether the President of the United States considered receiving oral sex as constituting "sexual relations" had a devastating effect on the dignity of the office. Clinton's popularity and the blunders of his adversaries did not change that. After the sex scandal broke, Clinton's personal approval ratings were far below the oft-cited approval ratings of how he was doing his job.

PREVIOUS PRESIDENTS had lied to the public. Johnson did and Nixon did and Reagan did (about trading arms for hostages), and George Bush did (when he said that the fact that Clarence Thomas was black "has nothing to do with this in the sense that he is the best qualified [for the Supreme Court] at this time"), but Clinton's sustained lying almost ruined his presidency.

Actually, few Democrats on Capitol Hill believed Clinton when on January 26, 1998, five days after the Monica Lewinsky story broke, he denied having had "sexual relations with that woman." Among the disbelievers were some who expressed shock when Clinton later owned up to the affair.

That he told individual senators and congressmen as well as the public, his staff, and almost anyone who happened by, a bald-faced lie, assured that even if he survived politically his word meant even less than ever. This was a dangerous state of affairs for a presidency, which might at any moment have to call on the public to do something hard. (One person he lied to was Senate Minority Leader Tom Daschle, who, shortly after the Monica Lewinsky scandal broke, when Clinton's political survival seemed at risk, and several Democrats were on the verge of abandoning Clinton, called Clinton to ask if the story was true. Clinton assured Daschle that it wasn't, whereupon Daschle went on the line for Clinton.)

Clinton had succeeded for so long in talking his way out of corners, his confidence in his ability to outsmart others, was so strong, that he seemed to have come to believe that there was no corner he couldn't get out of. His series of evasive replies to questions about whether he had smoked marijuana, culminating, in the course of the 1992 campaign, in "I didn't inhale" was symbolic of his political career. His saying to the grand jury, in August 1998, in the course of the sex scandal, "It depends on what the meaning of the word 'is' is" entered the political lexicon right away.

And Clinton pushed his luck. Fending off charges that the White House had planted a story that some time ago Henry Hyde, chairman of the House Judiciary Committee, had had an extended extra-marital affair (a report that, while true, infuriated Hyde, who strongly suspected the White House). Clinton's press secretary,

Michael McCurry, said, "Everyone can blame the White House because [the perception is that] the White House lies about everything, that our credibility is zero."

In October 1998, when a Democratic representative briefing the House Democratic Caucus on dealings with the White House on the issue of how to conduct the census said that the President had promised to hold firm, her statement was greeted with laughter.

The egregiousness of Clinton's dishonesty about the sex scandal, as will be shown, made people suspicious of virtually everything he said or did—including his management of foreign policy.

MANY PEOPLE believe that the damage that Clinton did to the presidency can be erased if his successor is a figure who commands respect, has moral authority. But Clinton's time in office will leave scars, irrespective of his current popularity.

10

———•———

Tricks

John McCain's eyes had a certain look, which, along with his gentle voice, drew people to him. It was a slightly haunted, vulnerable look. McCain had endured, even prevailed over, five and a half years in a North Vietnamese prison. Most of those who knew him thought that he was remarkably normal for all that. Whatever the origin of the look in his eyes, it gave McCain, who is sixty-two, an aura of sensitivity that wasn't common among politicians. He seemed less glib than most.

Some critics, especially Democrats, thought that the press was too easy on him, since he had been one of the "Keating Five"—five senators who in 1987 had intervened in a federal investigation of a failed S&L owned by Charles Keating, a big contributor. Some people suggested that McCain's penchant for reform—he had pushed lobbying reform and the gift ban, as well as campaign finance reform—was born of an effort to compensate for his Keating problem. In any event, he worked hard at it, and McCain had long had a rebellious streak. Now McCain, a Republican senator from Arizona, was the sponsor, along with liberal Democrat Russell Feingold, of Wisconsin, of the lead campaign reform bill before the Senate. The McCain-Feingold bill had been introduced in 1995 and killed by a filibuster in 1996. It was a fairly comprehensive bill, but in 1997, in reaction to the new developments in the 1996 election, reformers wanted to add a provision to curb phony "issue ads" and to tighten the rules on coordination between campaigns and supposedly independent groups running ads.

"Over time, I became more and more alarmed at what I was seeing," McCain told me in a conversation in his office one afternoon in March of 1997. McCain's office is filled with Arizona-Native American tchochkes and pictures of his family. (He is in his second marriage.) "It's the influence-buying that leaves out the average citizen. *Buckley* is being misread," McCain said in his direct way. "If money equals free speech, there are a couple hundred million people in this country who don't have free speech."

"I admire Senator McConnell for standing up and saying he doesn't want reform," McCain said. "Others come up to me and say, 'I'm for reform, just not this one.'"

Being a reformer in an institution that doesn't want to be reformed can be a lonely position. "I'm very much isolated on this issue," McCain said. "A lot of people don't converse with me."

The two principles of his bill, he said, were to reduce the influence of money in politics, and to give challengers a more level playing field.

But most elected politicians, whatever their rhetoric, don't favor giving challengers a more level playing field. And one by one, the provisions that would have done that were eliminated from McCain's bill even before it went to the Senate floor. The most important provisions, to give free airtime and lower-cost airtime and free mailings, to candidates who *voluntarily* agreed to spending limits, were dropped in September of 1997. The National Association of Broadcasters got rid of the section on broadcasting without any real difficulty. At the behest of Democrats, mostly from small states, a requirement that Senate candidates raise 60 percent of their funds within their own states was also rejected. Tom Daschle, of South Dakota, was against it; he had raised 16 percent within South Dakota when he ran for the Senate in 1992 and a little under 14 percent in 1998.

A ban on PACs was first watered down, in May of 1997, at the suggestion of Susan Collins, a moderate Republican who supported reform but had had substantial PAC support in her race for the Senate. The revised proposal would have lowered the amount PACS could give from $5,000 to $2,000 per election. The goal of the bill's backers was to gain the support of enough moderate Republicans to prevail on the Senate floor. Finally, any new limits on PACs were eliminated altogether.

STEVE STOCKMEYER, sandy-haired, in his mid-fifties, and a jovial cynic—he sees the fraudulence in what many of the characters in the drama, himself included, were doing—was one of those powerful but unknown Washington figures who leave their imprint on national policy. He had been executive director of the National Republican Congressional Committee, then a lobbyist for the National Association of Broadcasters, and now was a consultant/lobbyist, with the National Association of Business PACs (NABPAC) one of his major clients. Stockmeyer played a large, if barely noticed, role in the campaign finance fights.

Operating out of his house in Virginia and equipped with ready access to a blast fax and political cunning, Stockmeyer helped kill the PAC ban in the McCain-Feingold bill. It wasn't very difficult. Democrats weren't keen on it, either. And he could call on vast troops and resources. In his capacity representing NABPAC, Stockmeyer represented one hundred and thirty PACs of corporations and trade associations that together had invested almost $60 million in the 1996 congressional elections.

Stockmeyer turned Democratic support of McCain-Feingold to his own purposes. On September 11, 1997, Daschle proudly announced that all forty-five Democratic senators now supported the bill. At that point, the bill still contained a curb on PAC contributions. So when Democratic senators called a corporation or a trade association to ask for a contribution, at Stockmeyer's urging, he told me, "They replied, 'You've put us in a very hard position because our board has said don't give to people who support the PAC ban or reduction, and you signed a statement that endorses a bill that limits PAC contributions.'"

Then, as Stockmeyer related the tale, the senator would say, "It does?"

Two weeks after Daschle announced Democratic support of McCain-Feingold, Stockmeyer told me with evident satisfaction, the limitation on PAC contributions was dropped from the bill.

When, in 1997, Representative J. D. Hayworth, Arizona Republican and former sports broadcaster, introduced a bill to reduce the amounts that could be contributed by PACs, the business PAC community was displeased. Hayworth had had a close race in 1996; labor had strongly supported his opponent, and business had helped him out with last-minute ads. Hayworth also had barely won in 1994, when he became a member of the famous Republican freshman class. So business PAC leaders went to remonstrate with him about his apparent ingratitude. Don't worry, Hayworth told them. He had been getting a lot of pressure for reform from home. Bear with me, he said. It's not going to happen. Having heard this kind of reply for years, other business PAC leaders called him, called his staff. The National Restaurant Association gave him a strong talking to. Hayworth decided not to push the bill.

Stockmeyer told me, "It made people think twice before they adopted this phony reform. When you come down on someone like Hayworth, it gets around the cloakroom."

Stockmeyer, with his long experience in politics, was also capable of disinterested reflection. And he had an arresting insight on the whole matter of money and politics. "There isn't anything in this whole business that couldn't be solved by individual politicians looking in the mirror," he told me one day. "They don't have to raise year-round. They don't have to raise more than their opponents. They don't have to raise more money than they need, or from people who have business before them. Nothing forces them to create the appearance problem."

But why would any politician take such measures unilaterally, I asked him.

"There are about a hundred and fifty competitive seats," he replied, referring to the Senate and House elections in each two-year cycle. "That leaves really four hundred not in contest. There are a whole bunch of people who don't need the money. After every election there's about a hundred million dollars left in campaign treasuries. If voluntary restraint doesn't work, they could put restrictions in the House and Senate ethics rules. They should also prohibit fund-raising from outside their district while Congress is in session. Their lives would be better; we could bill it as 'family-friendly.'" He chuckled.

BUT THE THORNIEST issue in reaching a consensus on the McCain-Feingold bill was how to get at the problem of "issue ads." The difficulty was how to draw up a provision that (1) might survive the Senate, the combined opposition of McConnell and the interest groups notwithstanding, and (2) might not be struck down by the Supreme Court.

The provision that eventually went before the Senate said that any broadcast ad that mentioned a candidate within sixty days of a primary or general election was a campaign ad, and had to be paid for with hard money, as was any newspaper or broadcast ad that expressed "unmistakable and unambiguous" support of or opposition to a candidate. This was known as the "duck test"—"if it walks like a duck, talks like a duck, then it must be a duck." Also, a state party that spent for voter registration activity within 120 days of a federal election had to use hard money. Get-out-the-vote drives for an election in which a federal candidate was on the ballot also had to be paid for with hard money. The breadth of this particular proposal worried even some Democrats. But the sponsors of the bill believed this was the only way to truly close the soft-money loophole. The McCain-Feingold bill also tried to deal with the problem of coordination between campaigns and supposedly independent groups taking ads.

FOLLOWING THE 1996 elections, opponents of campaign finance reform became concerned—with reason—that support for reform was building.

Steve Stockmeyer told leading congressional Republicans, "This is a time-bomb, guys. Why don't you pass a bill with a cap on soft money and a tightening of the restrictions on foreign contributions and some disclosure of who was sponsoring issue ads."

Stockmeyer told me, "My fear was that it was going to get out of control. For the last twenty years, there has been a postelection feeling of 'Oh, my God, we've got to do something.' This year more groups felt this really might be the time." Foes of reform worried that, as Stockmeyer put it, "When the establishment"—Common Cause and other reform groups, editorial writers—"gets going, it's like clockwork. The whole machine starts working. There was the sense this was happening."

SHORTLY AFTER the 1996 elections Mitch McConnel set out to make sure that a campaign finance bill wouldn't be approved by the new Congress. Using his leverage as chairman of the Republican Senate campaign committee, in January of 1997 he called in all nine newly-elected Republican senators for private chats on reform. He also made his views clear to senators up for re-election in 1998, who would certainly need his help.

As chairman of the Republican Senate campaign committee, McConnell was raising unprecedented amounts of soft money at the same time that he was objecting to its ban—also on First Amendment grounds. According to Common Cause, in the first six months of 1997 McConnell had raised $2.1 million in soft money, twice the amount that his predecessor, Alfonse D'Amato, had raised during the same period two years earlier. And D'Amato was notably adept at fund-raising.

But some other Republicans assessed the new, post-1996 situation in a different way. At noon on Thursday, September 25, 1997, Jim Nicholson, the chairman of the Republican National Committee, met with his "kitchen cabinet"—about a dozen Republican wise heads, including pollsters and consultants—for the sole purpose of talking about his concern that public support for campaign finance reform was growing, and that the Republican Party could be caught on the wrong side. "Republicans are very nervous," someone who attended the meeting told me.

"They don't know what to do about the campaign finance reform issue. They know they don't want it to become law. The Democrats seem to have made it an issue at the grass roots. But whatever the reality is, Republicans at every level are convinced that campaign finance reform is lethal for them. One person at the table said it would be the end of the two-party system. In the Republican structure, that's assumed. One state party chairman said he could never support Thompson or McCain in any presidential bid because of their efforts on campaign finance reform. The argument is that the Democrats have allies [labor] who do the basic functions for them—voter identification, get-out-the-vote, that only our party does, that our groups don't have their numbers. The fear is that people will start saying we're getting beat up on the issue at home, and in editorials, that the dam will crack. The concern is that if campaign finance reform doesn't come up this year, the Democrats will have the issue all next year."

The Democrats understood the situation the same way. Though there was still some unease within the Democratic Caucus about going along with a ban on soft money, one Democratic senator told me, "Daschle has done such a good job whipping this up that Democrats want to go with the tide."

TRENT LOTT had been holding off bringing up the campaign finance bill in the Senate, telling his colleagues, "Let's wait and see the effect of the hearings." At the same time, of course, Lott was doing his bit to make the hearings ineffective, or go away altogether.

But despite Lott's efforts, the Thompson hearings did contribute to the pressure to bring up the bill. And Democrats were threatening to force roll-call votes on unrelated bills, as a delaying action, to pressure Lott to bring up campaign finance reform.

In late September 1997, McConnell, sensing that the proponents of the McCain-Feingold bill weren't ready—they were still lopping off some provisions and changing others in order to garner as many votes as they could—entreated Lott to bring up the bill for debate. He urged him to get it over with.

So Lott took the bill's sponsors by surprise by suddenly announcing on Thursday afternoon, September 25 (the same day as Nicholson's worried meeting), that he would call up the McCain-Feingold bill the next day. (In another of his grandstand moves, Clinton on September 23 had sent a letter to Lott threatening to call the Congress into special session if it adjourned for the year without voting on campaign finance reform. His letter was dismissed as meaningless.)

When it came to this—to him—distasteful subject, Lott did the same thing he had done in the past. He brought up a bill without warning, not even telling its sponsors. This isn't done. But the whole idea was to catch the sponsors off-guard. Lott had no fears that the legislation would pass. He told the press, "I don't think it'll happen this year."

Ed Gillespie, the former Hill aide, now a lobbyist, called Lott's maneuver "a brilliant move by Lott to broadside them." Gillespie said, "The pressure was building, so the decision was to pull the plug."

In the meetings in McConnell's office of the interest groups opposed to reform, there was often some discussion of whether the Republicans should offer an alternative to the McCain-Feingold bill, but McConnell was firmly against that. Republicans never got credit for offering their own bills, he said, and the McCain-Feingold bill was "such an easy target, we should concentrate on that."

When word reached the coalition that one or another Republican was "shaky"—for example, Sam Brownback—one coalition member said, "Members of the coalition would come down hard on that person's office. Our local offices would call." When Tamara Somerville, McConnell's top aide, prized for her skill at "networking" to find out what was going on, learned of a Republican senator who might introduce a reform bill, that Republican was spoken to—by McConnell, by members of his coalition. This pressure was applied in at least three cases—and was successful in getting the senators to either back off or revise the bill to remove the offending sections (particularly if they proposed to reduce or eliminate PAC money).

On the Senate floor on the morning of Friday, September 26, when debate on the McCain-Feingold bill began, Lott was jubilant and sarcastic. He had put one over on his opponents, who were still drafting their bill. The version they finally offered to the Senate banned soft money and curbed the use of sham "issue ads." Using a partially true but essentially misleading argument he frequently employed, Lott told his colleagues, "Before you start changing the laws to try to see if you can fix problems, wouldn't it help if the laws on the books were obeyed and enforced?" (Congress had seen to it that the enforcement agency, the FEC, was inneffective.)

Lott also uttered on the Senate floor one of the themes Republicans spoke of among themselves. "There are a lot of people who don't want the people involved. They want the news media to dictate...who will be elected." That is, the presumed liberal media would control elections unless it was offset by Republican money.

LOTT'S ADMITTED strategy was to maneuver the Democrats into conducting a filibuster on the bill. He thought he had guaranteed this by offering his own amendment, originally sponsored by Don Nickles, to go at labor's strength harder than ever by proposing "paycheck protection." This would require that unions get the written permission of each member before spending a share of the member's dues on political activity. The proposal went much further than a 1998 Supreme Court decision *(Communications Workers of America et al. v. Beck et al.)*, which said that nonunion members had the right not to pay the portion of their dues that would go to political activity.

Labor was willing to accept the McCain-Feingold bill's proposal to enforce the *Beck* decision, but it strenuously opposed "paycheck protection." Though the proposal had a certain surface plausibility, it was clear to labor and their Democratic allies that the proposal was being made by conservatives whose purpose was to gut the unions' political strength.

The Lott-Nickles amendment was spoken of even among opponents of reform as a "poison pill"—an amendment that is aimed to kill a bill. Lott's cynical purpose, everyone understood, was to try to get his amendment attached to the McCain-Feingold bill, and thus force the Democrats to filibuster it to death. Using parliamentary devices at hand, Lott had made his and Nickles's "paycheck protection" amendment the pending business, and made it impossible for campaign finance supporters to offer amendments of their own. Such was the hypocrisy over Lott's proposal that a Republican strategist told me, "I think McConnell would oppose the bill even if it had 'paycheck' in it."

"Paycheck protection" had become conservative Republicans' new, useful totem. Republicans had been searching for years to come up with something that curbed labor and also would be appealing to the public. They thought they had done it this time. They felt that the "paycheck" proposal could break the power of the unions, divide the Democratic Party, and kill campaign reform. Some Democrats suggested, mainly for defensive and rhetorical purposes, that stockholders should be required to give permission for spending corporate funds for political contributions, but no one was serious about this argument.

That same Friday morning, John McCain rose to speak. In his customary earnest tone, he said, "Mr. President, the Senate now begins a debate that will determine whether or not we will take an action that most Americans are convinced we're utterly incapable of doing—reforming the way we are elected to office. Most Americans believe that all of us conspire to hold on to every single political advantage we have, lest we jeopardize our incumbency by a single lost vote....Mr. President, now is the moment when we can begin to persuade the people that they are wrong.

"The opponents will argue the people are content. I will argue that the people are alienated, and that this explains why fewer and fewer of them even bother to vote....And who can blame them when they are overwhelmed by the appearance that political representation in America is measured on a sliding scale. The more you give, the more effectively you can petition your government."

Drawing on illustrations produced by the Thompson hearings, McCain said, "If a Native American tribe wants to recover their ancestral lands—pay up, the government will hear you. If you want to build a pipeline across Central Asia—pay up, you get an audience with government purchasing agents. But if all you pay is your taxes, and you want your elected representative to help you seek redress for some wrong, send us a letter. We'll send you one back."

McConnell, pursuing his strategy of killing the bill over the First Amendment issue by focusing on the provision to curb phony "issue ads," rose and said: "An outside group seeking to criticize a member of Congress—they didn't like how he or she voted on day fifty-eight before an election—would then be prohibited by the federal government from expressing criticism of this incumbent during that period, would it not?" (No, not if a broadcast ad was paid for with hard money.)

McConnell continued raising another point on which Republicans reinforced each other: "We know darn good and well that all of this issue advocacy restriction in here is flat out unconstitutional....There is a lot of discussion going on all the time about public affairs in this country. The press is talking about it every day. Most objective studies would indicate that eighty-five to ninety percent of the people in that line of work are on the left. Hollywood is making statements all the time about what kind of society we have. Many of us feel about one hundred percent of them are on the left." (He overlooked, among others, Charlton Heston, Arnold Schwarzenegger, and Tom Selleck.)

At 12:40 P.M., Fred Thompson rose to address the Senate. Speaking more or less ex tempore from notes, Thompson, the trial lawyer, made the case for new legislation. "As I listen to this debate today," he said, "it is almost like under the current system we don't have regulation and that we are trying to impose regulation on an otherwise pristine system."

Thompson continued, "Under the current law, express advocacy is regulated now. It is regulated now. This idea that we are going to cut off someone from saying something or that we are going to shut people up and close people off is simply not true. That makes interesting rhetoric, but is not in this bill, it is not in this legislation."

In an exchange with Arlen Specter, also a sponsor of the bill, Thompson said, "What we have now is a system...that is becoming more and more isolated, more and more specialized....I have run as a challenger against a person who was a congressional incumbent, and then I have run as an incumbent. I have had the disadvantages and the advantages of both sides of it. But all I know is that all the PAC money goes to incumbents. It doesn't matter what anybody believes anymore; it is their likelihood of getting reelected."

Thompson was blunt about what he thought of Lott's using the antiunion provision as a "poison pill." He said, "I must say that I agree with the underlying intent of this legislation. I support the concept of this amendment. [But] I must say it makes it a little bit more difficult for me when it is openly expressed as an effort to kill the underlying legislation."

Thompson added, "I think the American people look at a system where we spend so much time with our hand out for so much money from so many people who do so much business with the federal government, who we are basically regulating and legislating on, and they look at the system and the amounts of money that are involved nowadays, and they don't have much confidence in it."

ON MONDAY, Carl Levin rose to challenge McConnell on his interpretation of the *Buckley* case. Levin was one of the very few senators who were smart enough and brave enough to be willing to take McConnell on, on this subject. Of medium height, slightly hunched, Levin obviously exerted great efforts each day to comb his hair from far over one side to the other to cover his balding head. Reading directly from the *Buckley* decision, Levin countered McConnell's interpretation and explained to his colleagues, "The Supreme Court explicitly held in *Buckley* that eliminating actual and apparent corruption of our electoral system—corruption which is 'inherent in a system permitting unlimited financial contributions'—was a compelling enough interest to justify Congress in imposing campaign contribution limits, although such limits collide with unfettered First Amendment rights of free expression and free association."

Levin was making an important contribution to a critical debate, but what he said received little attention.

AFTER A WEEK of only sometime debate, Tuesday, October 7, promised to be a day of high drama in the Senate. McCain-Feingold was to be voted on. Reporters filled the galleries, which was unusual.

That morning, Clinton held a little pep rally at the White House, at which he called on Republicans not to kill the legislation by filibuster. When a reporter asked about his credibility on the issue of campaign reform, Clinton replied testily—and irrelevantly—"I knew we would be outspent badly in 1996 but we weren't outspent as badly as we would have been if I had laid around and done nothing."

THERE WERE, at that moment, in effect two filibusters going simultaneously—Democrats against the Lott amendment and the Republicans against the underlying McCain-Feingold bill. Because of the filibuster rule, which had been abused by both parties in recent years, the sponsors of either proposal needed sixty votes to cut off a filibuster.

Actually, there aren't real filibusters anymore—no all-night sessions and cots in the Old Senate Chamber. Filibusters had often been used as a device to help Southerners stave off civil rights legislation and was justified as a means of protecting the minority from rash action. A capacity to shut them down wasn't devised until 1917, and in 1975 the number required to do so was reduced from sixty-seven to sixty. There had been many more filibuster threats in recent years as senators became more partisan and ornery. The practical result was that sixty votes were needed to accomplish almost anything in the Senate.

Now, the mere threat of a filibuster is enough to block action on something. And the filibuster is used on such trivial questions as whether a nominee to be general counsel of the National Labor Relations Board should be confirmed. In another example of how things have changed in the last twenty-five years, the average number of filibusters per year throughout the 1970s was five, and within the first four years of the 1990s that number had tripled.

TRENT LOTT had told John McCain, or so McCain thought, that he would first allow a vote to table, that is kill, without debate, his own amendment; such a tabling motion would require only fifty-one votes rather than the sixty to shut off a filibuster. At the time, the McCain-Feingold bill had forty-nine votes behind it—all forty-five Democrats, plus Thompson, Collins, and Specter, as well as McCain. Its supporters were hoping that two other moderate Republicans would join their side, giving them a majority to kill Lott's mischievous amendment. (Vice President Gore would be available to break a tie.) The critical difference would be made by about a half-dozen Republican moderates—including Olympia Snowe, of Maine, John Chafee, and James Jeffords, of Vermont—who had previously supported reforming campaign financing but were, in the new regime of the Republican Conference's enforcing party discipline, wary of crossing Lott. This group had begun worried discussions among themselves on what course to take.

But when Lott saw that his amendment was in jeopardy, he withdrew his offer of a straight vote on it—no straight votes if *he* might be defeated.

So now the question became whether the Democratic filibuster against Lott's "paycheck" proposal could be broken, with the Democrats taking the lead in trying to break it, which would then permit a vote to kill the amendment itself. The two parties' regular Tuesday lunches once again played a large role in the drama.

Fred Thompson and Susan Collins had agreed before the Tuesday lunch that they would question Lott's sincerity; they would ask whether, if Lott's amendment was adopted, the Republicans would support a ban on soft money.

At the lunch, Thompson rose and asked, "Is the Republican Party serious about having campaign reform or not?" Nickles replied that he was willing to consider a bill which placed a cap on soft money but didn't ban it. (This idea was circulating among Republican strategists worried about how the party would look if it obviously killed all campaign finance reform proposals.)

Susan Collins rose and said, "I need to know from Mitch, will you support a ban on soft money if the Lott amendment on union dues is approved?"

"No," McConnell replied.

"I just sat down," Collins recalled later. "To me it was very clear that there wasn't a sincere effort to get a bill."

At the same time, the Democrats decided at their lunch that if it appeared that there would be enough votes (fifty-one) to kill the

Lott amendment if their filibuster against it was stopped (sixty votes), they would throw their votes toward ending their own fili- buster. Then they would kill Lott's amendment. Everything hinged on whether Snowe would vote for or against Lott's amendment. It was thought that she would bring Jeffords along.

There was a lot of busyness on the Senate floor that afternoon. Snowe, who had helped rally moderate Republicans to support Lott as majority leader, at first said she'd vote for Lott's amend- ment, then that she was against it. (Snowe's position was particu- larly sensitive since she came from Maine, which in 1996 had adopted a system of public financing.)

In one corner, Lott was talking anxiously with three aides. Lott's press secretary, Susan Irby, looking worried, summoned McConnell to join them. Across the way, Daschle and other Democrats were urging Snowe—having virtually surrounded her— to vote with them to kill Lott's amendment. Thompson and Collins, sitting together in a back row, were laughing at all the scurrying around, and at the prospect of Lott being undone by other people's parliamentary tactics. It was a rare treat to see people pulling a fast one on Lott.

Vice President Gore was in his limousine on the way to the Capitol in case his vote was needed to break a tie on killing Lott's amendment.

But then Snowe let it be known that she wouldn't vote against the Lott amendment unless the Democrats would support a pro- posal she had ready regarding union dues, which they didn't want to do. So, the Democrats went back to their original strategy of voting against ending their filibuster against the Lott amendment. Thus, the McCain-Feingold bill would be buried.

There weren't enough votes to end either the Democrats' or the Republicans' filibuster.

The mini-coup against Lott had failed.

As they left the Senate floor, an obviously pleased Lott said to other senators, "Olympia saved the day."

Afterward, McConnell pronounced to the press "McCain-Fein- gold is dead." He called the Senate's inaction "a vote for free speech."

With a smirk, Lott had killed reform. A concerned Republican said, "Trent doesn't even try to have a façade of seriousness."

But the roll calls on shutting down the filibusters demonstrated that there were enough votes, fifty-two, in the Senate to pass the McCain-Feingold bill itself.

THOUGH CAMPAIGN finance reform legislation had been left for dead in the Senate, Daschle forced more roll-call votes on it. He saw the issue as advantageous to the Democrats and wanted to drive the point home that the Republicans were blocking reform. But some senators in the Democratic Caucus were becoming restive, because the bill being held up by the filibuster was the great pork bill of the year, if not all time—to spend $145 billion in federal grants for highways. Besides, it was now late October and members of Congress were bent on getting out of Washington.

IN THE LATE afternoon of Thursday, October 23, John McCain came running off the Senate floor to apologize for not being able to keep our appointment that afternoon. He and Lott and Daschle had been negotiating the terms of ending the filibuster on the highway bill and of bringing up campaign finance reform again in 1998. "We're that far apart," McCain said breathlessly, holding his thumb and forefinger less than an inch apart. "They'll bring up the bill in March and allow amendments."

Lott, who liked only his own clever maneuvers, was annoyed that Daschle was forcing more cloture votes, so he threatened to pull down the popular highway bill and blame campaign finance reform. "We know it's going to come back up," Lott said, "and maybe we'll stop trying to trump each other."

But the negotiations over bringing the bill back up dragged on, as Daschle and McCain sought from Lott a guarantee of a straight up-or-down vote on McCain-Feingold without having to round up sixty votes to end a filibuster. At a Republican policy lunch on October 28, McCain told his colleagues, "Every senator has a right to get a vote on his proposal," and he pledged that he wouldn't drag things out if the bill were brought up again. He pointed out that the House now seemed more likely to bring up a campaign finance bill, despite the resistance of its Republican leaders.

Finally, on October 30, an agreement was reached: On or before the close of business March 6, 1998, Lott or a designee would bring up a bill and McCain would be allowed to offer his bill as an amendment, and there would be a straight-out vote on it.

If the reformers won that vote, the opponents would still be able to filibuster. So, all the reformers got was a promise of a vote on some form of McCain-Feingold. It wasn't much.

IN AN INTERVIEW following the round of Senate votes on McCain-Feingold, Fred Thompson reflected on how hard it was to fix the campaign finance system. He said, "Anything that is potentially disruptive to a person's profession or professional ambition is threatening and therefore resisted. We've professionalized the political class; we're political professionals now. It gets to how we got here and how we stay here, and that's serious."

He continued, "Another aspect of the professionalism of the place is averting risk: which would be stating the truth about what needs to be done about entitlements, about Social Security. Campaign finance reform is the great unknown. You don't take chances with your medical license; you don't take chances with your legal license; you don't take chances with your election. Some people say reform would benefit incumbents. That's wrong. Incumbents have great advantages even without the money. In a revolutionary time you get a ten percent turnover. I think we're being very short-sighted. I think money is going to become more and more of an issue. I'm very satisfied that the genie's out of the bottle, but it's going to take a little while."

LOTT DIDN'T keep his word to McCain.

In early February of 1998, Lott tried to pull another surprise by bringing up the campaign finance reform bill well before the agreed-upon date of March 6. McCain and Feingold managed to stall him—but not for long. The bill was brought up later in February.

At a meeting in January in McConnell's office, McConnell's staff had given the assembled anti-campaign-finance-reform groups marching orders: Get your people working. McConnell had wanted the bill brought up as early as possible so that momentum couldn't be built behind it.

Lott didn't give McCain the straight-up-or-down vote on his bill that McCain believed he had been promised. And Lott once again resorted to parliamentary maneuvers to kill the bill. Even so, it became clear again in this round that there was a majority in the Senate for the McCain-Feingold bill. But not enough to surmount Lott's and McConnell's tactic of using a filibuster to kill it.

The institutional pressures—don't buck the majority leader and the main money man—and interest group pressures, and parliamentary tricks were sufficient to override the majority.

For the campaign finance reform bill to pass the Senate, eight more Republican supporters would have to be found, enough to end a filibuster, and no one thought that would happen within the year. That a majority supported reform was significant but irrelevant in the face of its opponents' use of an essentially antidemocratic Senate rule to kill it. But it's a rule that both parties wish to preserve as a weapon.

So, on February 26, 1998, the bill was pronounced dead.

BY THE TIME the bill came up the second time, national attention was elsewhere—to the extent that an essentially prosperous country focused on Washington at all. The two big subjects of interest were the recent revelations about the President's dalliance with the intern Monica Lewinsky, and what appeared to be an imminent showdown with Iraq over its blocking of U.N. inspections.

The decline in trust of Washington was now compounded, and collided with attempts to fix the political system. If, as several polls indicated, people didn't trust the politicians to fix that system, they had just been given confirmation of that view. And there was no folk memory of a campaign finance law having ever worked, as the 1974 act did for at least two presidential elections. And even had he cared to, Clinton was now in no position to sell political reform.

Fred Wertheimer, the former president of Common Cause and someone who has had as sustained a fighting spirit on this issue as anyone, said to me, "It looks like we're in a very defensive position and we have fifty-two votes in the Senate. They've been able to turn an obstructionist minority into the appearance that it's a majority view, and it isn't. We can't get across to audiences out there. The public is tuned out."

SPEAKING outside the Capitol on a bright afternoon, shortly after the bill was withdrawn for the second time, John McCain said, "I believe there will be more scandals, there will be more indictments and more people going to jail. There are probably scandals happening while we speak. The system is badly broken. We'll continue to try."

Under these circumstances, hardly anyone thought that the House of Representatives would pass a campaign finance bill.

11

———————■———————

"Seat-of-the-Pants Pique"

Christopher Shays, a moderate Republican representing Greenwich, Connecticut, and surrounding towns, was an unlikely-looking hero. A serious man with thinning blond hair who wore thick glasses, there was a slight nerdiness in his style—a squeakiness and nervousness in his speech, and often a worried look on his face. The nervousness stemmed in part from the fact that he was in a difficult position as a moderate in a party that had veered sharply right. Shays was essentially loyal to Gingrich—he tipped Gingrich off about the budding coup against him in 1997—but Shays sometimes took stands on issues that set him in opposition to Gingrich and the other Republican leaders. And the Republican leaders weren't patient with internal opposition.

Now Shays, who had backed other reforms of the political system, had taken on campaign finance reform, joining with Marty Meehan, a third-term Democrat from Massachusetts, to sponsor the McCain-Feingold bill in the House (where it became known as the Shays-Meehan bill). He was to come under strong pressures by the Republican leadership for this apostasy.

In a conversation we had in late October of 1997, Shays told me, "The real challenge of campaign finance reform is the leaders in both parties, not the rank and file. They're the ones who go around in corporate jets collecting large sums of money to solidify their position. This is about power and who has the power."

At times, like the other reform leaders, Shays had to argue with the reform groups, especially when he and his allies started lopping off sections of the bill in order to gain more support. "Marty and I felt that we were on a side rail and the train was going by," Shays told me. "I felt that periodic change was better than a perfect bill that never happens. We took key elements and exposed the opposition for what it was."

PRESSURES ON the House to act on campaign finance reform had been building, to the point that in November 1997, Gingrich was forced to promise that the House would vote on the matter in February or March of the following year. Gingrich, Majority Leader Dick Armey, and Majority Whip Tom DeLay were strong foes of reform and had tried to avoid the subject.

But, to put pressure on the Republican leadership to bring up campaign finance reform, some liberal Democrats—especially "Watergate baby" George Miller, of California—had been using guerrilla warfare. They forced time-consuming quorum calls and votes on motions to adjourn, thus tying up the House and making it more difficult for the leaders to get anything else done.

And by October 1997, at least twenty House Republicans had told the leadership that they couldn't go home without a vote on the subject. One hundred and five members threatened to hold up adjournment unless Gingrich promised a "fair, full, balanced, and bipartisan debate on meaningful reform." With a margin of only eleven votes, the Republican leadership was thus facing a conundrum. So, on November 12, Gingrich announced that the House would consider reform in February or March 1998, and he promised "a fair, bipartisan process."

At the time Gingrich made his announcement, Republicans feared that they might lose control of the House in 1998—and Gingrich was disinclined to put any of his members at risk. The struggle over control of the House was a blood war: with control came enormous power, the kind of power the Democrats had grown accustomed to over the forty years that they had been in the majority. They still thought of Gingrich as a usurper.

And Gingrich and his fellow leaders had made brazen use of

their newfound power to change many of Washington's arrangements. Despite their overreaching with the "Contract with America," and their setbacks, they had reshaped many of the country's laws, and forced the President to accept the concept of a balanced budget, so as to put the squeeze on domestic programs.

The Republicans were now enjoying the fruits of incumbency, a large portion of which came in the form of money. After they took power in 1994, the House Republicans set out to reap the financial benefits they believed they were owed after forty years in the minority—and reap they did. According to figures from the Federal Election Commission, Republican House members received a total of $28.1 million over the first six months of 1995, more than double what they took in during the same period two years before. Democrats, now in the minority, received only $17.4 million in the first six months of 1995—much less than they had raised in 1993. Republican fund-raising committees received a sharp increase, more than double their intake before they took over the House.

The Republicans wouldn't lightly let go of all these newfound advantages.

Fortunately for the Republican leaders, the House Democrats were deeply split on the subject of campaign finance reform. The Democratic Caucus was in disarray. Some liberals argued that the Shays-Meehan bill was pro-Republican in that it would cut off the soft money upon which they had become so dependent. Minority Leader Richard Gephardt, no fan of reform, felt that it would be a mistake for his party to support a ban on soft money.

Gephardt was also concerned, based on experience, that the reformers would move a bill, the Republicans would put something in it to hurt the Democrats—and Clinton would sign it. Vic Fazio, of California, the Democratic Caucus chairman, was also most unenthusiastic about reform. Both men were reluctant to give up anything that helped them fight the Republicans. Maybe they could take the House back.

Martin Frost, the chairman of the Democratic Congressional Campaign Committee for both the 1996 and 1998 elections, opposed changing the finance system, especially giving up soft money—and in this view he had the backing of the Black Caucus, whose members depended heavily on wealthy contributors from outside their districts. Both Fazio and Frost made it clear to reformers that they were concerned about the Democrats' fate if soft money was abolished.

The position of his leadership left Meehan somewhat isolated. Reformers aren't popular in their own parties, as Fred Thompson and John McCain learned.

One House reformer told me, "Individual members don't like reform. Nobody really wants reform, and those members who fight for reform get very unpopular. The leaders of both parties have mastered how to raise the money under the current rules. They don't want to change them. When you've worked on this issue for a while you get tired of pissing off the other members—it makes it harder to get other things done."

OVER BREAKFAST in the House Members' Dining Room in October, 1997, Marty Meehan, forty-two years old, youthful and apple-cheeked, with straight, salt-and-pepper hair and a broad Massachusetts accent, said, "I just don't see how a minority party positions itself on campaign finance and isn't for banning soft money."

Responding to the argument of his party leaders that the Republicans collect more money overall, so Democrats shouldn't give up soft money because only through collecting these unlimited funds could they stay in the game, Meehan replied, "That's nonsense. We should have learned a long time ago how to do grassroots collection and marketing. The Republicans have a small-donor base. Because we don't have the tenacity and the will to do the same thing it's an excuse that doesn't hold any water. It's a phony excuse. We should have had the will.

"I know they say we're closer in soft money. But it's absurd for Democrats to position themselves for campaign finance reform but against banning soft money. If we're not for banning soft money we'd might as well fold our tent."

But even the House reformers themselves were split, with each faction having such pride of authorship in its own approach, that Meehan despaired of getting the majority votes needed for passage.

FRESHMAN DEMOCRATS and Republicans had begun to meet early in 1997 to see if they could fashion a bipartisan bill.

At the same time, Republican leaders were telling the Republican freshmen, just as the Democratic leaders were telling the Democratic freshmen, that their party would be hurt if soft money was abolished. Soft money, the Republican leaders said, was essential in overcoming the Democrats' help from labor.

Bill Paxon, of New York, and a member of the leadership until Gingrich pushed him out for having participated in the aborted July 1997 coup attempt against him, told the Republican freshmen, "If you ban soft money, you might as well take your voting card and give it to the Democrats, because we'll lose control of the House."

At one point, a Republican freshman invited the Republican powers—including DeLay, Paxon, and McConnell—to one of their meetings. The message was clear: Don't do it. Chris Shays told me, "The leaders of both parties telling their freshmen that their parties would lose control says it all."

Tom Allen, a lanky, dark-haired man with deep-set dark eyes, a Democratic freshman from Maine, hadn't thought that if he was elected to Congress in 1996 campaign finance reform would be a big issue for him. He wanted to concentrate on what Minority Leader Dick Gephardt called "kitchen table issues"—jobs, education, health care, child care. Allen had raised money for former senators Edmund Muskie and George Mitchell, and he had run for governor in 1994. But in his run for the House, he had ended up having to raise far more money than he had expected.

The 1996 election was a new phenomenon for him. In an interview in early 1997, Allen told me that in 1996, "It was clear to me that political campaigns were more about money than they used to be." He explained the effect of this on the candidate: "The predominate fear is of getting blown out on television. You worry about it the whole campaign." Echoing what some senators had said about the new presence of "issue ads," he added, "What also was different about 'ninety-six was our role as candidates was diminished—because of all the other voices in the campaigns."

Once elected, Allen started having talks with some Republican freshmen. Asa Hutchinson, a freshman from Arkansas, suggested a bipartisan task force.*

But Allen had learned early in his House career how difficult it

---

*He was to do this again as a member of the House Judiciary Committee weighing the impeachment of President Clinton.

was to get agreement on an approach to reform. "Since every member is an expert and is wearing different spectacles, it's very difficult to get consensus. This goes right to the heart of everyone here, in a personal way. Because it's so close to home, it's very hard for members to sit back and look at the last three election cycles and say, "What does this mean to the system?'"

The bill that resulted from the freshmen's talks didn't go as far as the McCain-Feingold bill, now Shays-Meehan, did on banning soft money. (The hope was that this would mollify McConnell—as if anything would.) It also had a weaker provision on curbing phony "issue ads," but did call for disclosure of who was behind ads that mentioned candidates, and how much they were spending.

Despite the looser requirements in the freshman bill, the Christian Right and its allies still opposed it, because they oppose governmental regulation in this area, period. The Arkansas Right to Life Committee ran ads in November 1997 against Asa Hutchinson for supporting campaign reform. It also ran an ad against Asa's older brother, Senator Tim Hutchinson, when he cast one "wrong" vote on cloture in the Senate; Tim Hutchinson cast no more such votes. That both Hutchinsons were strong allies of the Christian Right gave them no immunity; on the contrary, it made them targets when they strayed. The Right to Life Committee ran ads also against Zach Wamp, a Tennessee conservative who had come in with the class of '94 and had a strong right-to-life record, but supported the Shays-Meehan bill.

Marty Meehan had been meeting with the various Democratic factions, and with the leadership, trying to get a consensus. "I've had hours and hours of meetings," he said wearily at our breakfast meeting. Shays was doing similar work on his side of the aisle. Shays and Meehan were frustrated by the fact that the freshmen wouldn't move toward their bill; but neither Allen nor Hutchinson could go beyond where their groups already stood.

Yet, despite the lack of consensus among reformers in the House, there was agreement that a bill must be brought to the floor.

IN LATE MARCH of 1998, Gingrich, who had promised a vote by the end of that month, called Shays and told him that there couldn't be a vote on his bill, because it would pass. In addition to its other sins, Gingrich said, the bill didn't include the antiunion "paycheck protection," and he couldn't let a bill leave the House without that. He told Shays that he was considering bringing campaign reform up under a special procedure—the "suspension" calendar, usually used for noncontroversial matters—that allowed no amendments, permitted only twenty minutes of debate to a side, and required a two-thirds vote for passage, which was out of the question for any real campaign finance bill. Like his Senate counterparts, Gingrich would use parliamentary tricks to kill campaign finance reform.

Shays responded to Gingrich, "You're going to be criticized for that, and I'll be one of them."

Shays also warned Gingrich, "I have to be up front with you. If our bill gets more than fifty percent, then you'll have a demonstration that it would have passed if it had been a fair vote."

On Tuesday, March 24, Gingrich gathered in one of his offices the other leaders and some of the reformers. Tom DeLay suggested that the reformers should consider "loyalty to the party."

Shays replied, "It would be hard for you to talk loyalty to me, when you tried to overthrow the Speaker."

Shays recognized that Gingrich was uncomfortable with this turn in the conversation. But, he told me, "I'd been looking for an opportunity to say that."

In other meetings, reformers got the sense that Gingrich was going to let the March deadline slide. He was floundering. Gingrich was furious with Shays for not supporting a set of meaningless reform bills the House leaders had drawn up. So, acting on what one knowing Republican described to me as "'seat-of-the-pants pique"—he added, "there's a lot of that"—Gingrich changed his mind and decided to bring up the bill under circumstances adverse to the reformers.

And then he did something that had become characteristic of his leadership—he overreached.

On Friday, Shays was tipped off by a reporter that on the coming Monday the Republican leaders were going to bring up four "reform" bills under the suspension rules and that the Shays-Meehan bill wouldn't be one of them. This strong-arm, partisan approach was becoming the order of the day in the Gingrich House.

Shays's response was unusual: He questioned Armey on the

House floor that afternoon as Armey made his customary announcement about the schedule for the coming week. (Among the other, more typical, bills scheduled to be brought up on the suspension calendar were the Rhinoceros and Tiger Conservation Reauthorization Act of 1998, and a bill "to consolidate certain mineral interests in North Dakota.")

By this time, most members, as also was customary, had fled to the airport. Shays would have been gone, too, but for the reporter who tipped him off. He wasn't even going to be given the courtesy of being officially informed of the leaders' plan. The House wasn't accustomed to hearing a member challenge a leader of his own party on the House floor. Armey, who is the heavy he appears to be, tried to muzzle Shays, who was able to question him only because the only-too-pleased Democrats gave him some of their time.

> ARMEY: Obviously, we have been receiving an enormous amount of requests, a sense of urgency, that would suggest that perhaps in order to respond to those people who have been so vocal on this matter that haste was more important to their concerns than the substance of the matter.
>
> SHAYS: ....Our distinguished majority leader says that haste is more important than substance, and I do not understand why he feels that way. Would he please explain to me why he thinks haste is more important than substance?...
>
> ARMEY: ....I am very pleased to have the opportunity to put this forward, and for those Members who felt so insistent that it ought to be done by the end of March, I would only suggest that obviously it is those Members that place the emphasis on haste as opposed to substance....
>
> SHAYS: With all due respect to the majority leader, I never stood in eleven years and questioned my majority leader, and I do not do this lightly, but I am having a difficult time understanding what is being said and what will happen, and I would like to have that clarified for me. Are you saying that we are moving in haste and that these bills are not substantive? Or that we are not moving in haste?....Our leadership, my leadership, said we would have a fair and open debate in February or March, and I am interested to know if this meets the leadership's definition of fair and open debate on campaign finance reform.

ARMEY: ....We believe that we are bringing to the floor next week, under suspension, all opportunities of merit...and we are very excited and proud for the opportunity to express their commitment to that by a yes vote.

SHAYS: Will you tell me who has decided that we brought all bills of merit? Who has made that decision?

ARMEY: This has been a decision that has been made through the entire leadership team in consultation with the committee of jurisdiction, and I appreciate my colleague's interest.

SHAYS: Mr. Leader, I asked a sincere question, and I would appreciate a sincere answer. And the question was: Was anyone in leadership on the other side of the aisle consulted before it was decided to bring out all four Republican bills?

ARMEY: ....[A]gain, I appreciate the gentleman from Connecticut for his interest, and the answer is no.

SHAYS: Then, Mr. Leader, how can that be a fair and open debate if we have not allowed people with differing views to present their bills and to make arguments before this Chamber? How does that meet the requirement of my leadership, who I like to believe is telling the truth.

ARMEY: Mr. Speaker, to my friend, the gentleman from Connecticut, let me just say, we are perfectly prepared to continue any further consideration of this subject as the year passes by....We are very excited about the opportunity we have afforded the body to vote on these next Monday, March 30.

SHAYS: Mr. Speaker....I would like to know if our leadership has made a determination to bring up the McCain-Feingold bill that was voted on in the Senate; and if so, when they intend to bring that up for a vote.

ARMEY: ....I appreciate again the interest of the gentleman from Connecticut. And these are the decisions that have been made with respect to what will be brought to the floor next week.

SHAYS: Mr. Speaker, has the leadership made any determination on whether or not they are going to bring McCain-Feingold to the floor of the House? [Time had expired, and Shays asked for unanimous consent that he be given more time to question Armey.]

ARMEY: ....If the Speaker is asking if the majority leader would be willing to ask unanimous consent to continue, the answer is no.

So, FOLLOWING the funeral of one of the members, the House of Representatives considered campaign finance reform on Monday, March 30, at 6:00 P.M. on the suspension calendar. It had to be done quickly, anyway, so that members could attend fund-raisers that night. The whole thing was a charade, and amounted to an abuse of power. Gephardt assailed the "outrage" and "travesty" of the "gag rule." His voice rose to a shout and his face turned red, as happened when he got, or appeared, agitated in debate. He came off as a serious reformer, which he wasn't—at least yet.

Matt Salmon, a flat-faced forty-year-old Republican from Arizona who came to Congress with the class of 1994, one of the leaders of the conservatives' rebellion against Gingrich, spoke quickly and nervously. "I'm ashamed, I really am ashamed to see how this is coming up tonight, that it is in the same manner as that of the leadership who ran the House for forty years under the Democrats. It is wrong." Looking unhappy, he added, "Let us stop telling lies to the American people. Everybody knows that the Republicans want to preserve the ability for big corporations to give bucks on the side through soft money to the ones in charge....[T]he Democrats do not want the unions to be restricted in any way."

"Shame on you," cried Marty Meehan, addressing the Republicans, as he tried but of course failed to get an instant change in the rules. The principal Republican bill, written by the leadership, lost by a vote of 74–337, with even some of the leadership abandoning it, and a separate bill providing "paycheck protection" lost fifty-two Republican votes—which should have been a signal to the leadership. Two inconsequential bills passed.

It was a low moment in the House.

It gave new strength to the forces for reform.

IN THE MEANTIME, a faction of the House Democrats called the "Blue Dogs," conservative Democrats mostly from southern or border-state districts and some of them in tough re-election fights, had started a "discharge petition," a rarely used device which can bring a bill to the floor if a majority signs a petition to do so. The Blue Dogs were conservatives on fiscal issues and conservative on some values issues, so they were often at some distance from the liberal Democratic leadership. As fiscal conservatives, they were concerned about the ability of special interest groups to spend a lot of money to protect their government subsidies. The Blue Dogs' main concern was to curb phony "issue ads," which had plagued some of them in the 1996 elections.

By the time of the "debate" on reform under the suspension calendar, the petition needed only thirty-one more signatures to prevail.

THE REPUBLICAN leadership's high-handed tactics in the House ignited the campaign reform issue. Over the Easter recess which followed shortly, the reform groups went to work. The League of Women Voters, Common Cause, Public Citizen, Public Campaign, and other reform groups used phone banks to call House members who might sign the petition, turned up at their town meetings, and asked why they hadn't signed it. They inspired newspaper editorials that focused on House members who might possibly support reform but hadn't signed, and gave their phone numbers. Campaign for America, a group founded by the prominent merchant banker Jerome Kohlberg, had helped Common Cause gather a million signatures on an earlier petition calling on the Congress to pass campaign finance reform, and helped Common Cause take radio ads during congressional debates on the matter. The new business constituency for reform was to grow over the next few years.

At that time, Ann McBride, the president of Common Cause, said, "We're finding it so easy to activate people." As for the polls that indicated that people didn't care about the issue, McBride said, "If you scratch beneath the cynicism, people want a government they can be proud of."

As THE EASTER recess approached, Senator Mitch McConnell sent "Dear Colleague" letters to House Republicans, urging them not to sign the discharge petition, and to oppose any reforms on the order of the Shays-Meehan (McCain-Feingold) bill. During the recess, Republican leaders called uncertain Republicans, pressing them not to sign the petition. Gingrich made calls from the road.

Shortly after Congress returned from the Easter recess, the discharge petition had two hundred and four signatures of a needed two hundred eighteen—enough to put a great fright into the Republican leadership. Ten Republicans had signed—at that point the margin of difference between the two parties—and then two more signed, and another was ready to do so. Some Democrats who had been reluctant to sign had been driven into doing so by the Republican leaders' tactics.

If the discharge petition actually worked, it would present the Republican leadership with the worst of all possible worlds: The Democrats would take control of the floor debate. On April 22, after an emotion-filled Republican Conference meeting, at which the twelve Republican signers were denounced, a panicked Gingrich scheduled another debate on campaign finance reform, to begin before the Memorial Day recess. But the leaders put the Shays-Meehan bill at a parliamentary disadvantage and sought to pit the reformers—backers of the freshman bill and backers of Shays-Meehan—against each other. Meehan, who had a close relationship with Allen, also from New England, tried once more to convince the Democratic freshmen to support the Shays-Meehan bill.

SHAYS ACCEPTED the flawed deal offered by his own leadership because he thought he now had at least a commitment to bring the issue to the floor. He took his name off the discharge petition, with some other Republicans following him, so as to remove that threat to the leaders. This episode showed that, as in the case of the last days of the 1996 elections, when the public was given something specific about campaign finance reform to focus on—in this case the discharge petition—rather than the amorphous form the issue usually took, it acted.

BY THIS TIME, Gephardt had become an outspoken advocate for reform. His reform-minded colleagues didn't know whether he now believed in it or had concluded it was good politics. But even if Gephardt had decided that it was good politics, that was a positive sign to reformers. The reform groups had worked him over, and some of his lieutenants already favored backing the Shays-Meehan bill. Gephardt had hesitated backing it because a Republican's name was on it. He told colleagues that it would be a good thing if the Republicans killed the reform bill, which does suggest at least a tincture of cynicism in his thinking.

In fact, the Democratic leaders' new thinking, according to a leadership source, was based in some part on cool calculation: that while Trent Lott and others might be right that the issue wasn't important in most congressional districts, it was significant in about ten percent of the districts.

"That's forty to forty-five districts," a House Democrat said, "and there's only an eleven-vote difference between the parties." He went on, "It's important in enough districts—especially suburban districts—to make it worthwhile. People against reform say it's not in the top ten lists, but it's top in some suburban districts, especially in Washington, Oregon, California, Massachusetts, and Maine—good government states."

THE ACTIONS of the House Republican leaders reflected something beyond their sometimes-thuggish style: It reflected the takeover of the Republican Party by the Christian Right. A prominent Republican, who, for obvious reasons, didn't want to be named, said, "All these people are catering to James Dobson [a radio show host and head of a Colorado-based organization called Focus on the Family], and Gary Bauer [the head of the Family Research Council]. They believe they have to. There's some fear that Dobson et al. will walk away from the party, taking ten percent of its supporters. They're the reason the DeLay-Armey faction is in charge of the Party."

Dobson had been critical of the Republicans for running on a "pro-family, pro-life, pro-moral agenda" and then not doing anything about those issues. He threatened to desert the Republican Party and take his five million listeners with him. In the early spring of 1998, House Republicans scheduled a meeting with Dobson and encouraged him to tone down his criticisms, which he did.

Gingrich, in turn, had to keep constant vigil over his place in the hierarchy. He wasn't a free man. Both Armey and DeLay had participated in the 1997 coup attempt against him, but it was actually driven by younger members, Gingrich's Red Guards, who faulted him for compromising with the President too much, for being insufficiently zealous about the social issues, such as abortion.

Thus, there had already been a coup within the Republican Party as a whole. This was to have implications for Clinton as the sex scandal unfolded.

IN A FURTHER cynical ploy, the House leaders made it clear that they intended to sink any campaign finance reform legislation through offering a multitude of amendments. Twelve different reform bills were made in order—or eligible for consideration—along with an unlimited number of amendments, whether or not they were germane. This made hundreds of amendments in order, which was quite unusual.

DeLay said, in his signature sly way, usually accompanied by a smile that broadcast his enjoyment of his own mischief, "The proponents of eliminating free speech want an open and fair debate," and he added, "and they're going to get it."

Steve Stockmeyer, the National Association of Business PACs lobbyist remarked, "Their idea of a 'fair and open process' is one that goes on for a long, long, time."

The leadership assumed that the whole thing would get so messy, so bogged down, that a reform bill wouldn't pass the House, or that whatever bill passed would be such a mishmash that the Senate wouldn't want to consider it, or that the House action would take so long that there wouldn't be time to enact a bill before Congress adjourned early in October for the 1998 elections.

A Republican lobbyist said, "Part of it's tongue-in-cheek, part of it's partisan politics, part of it's saying to Republican moderates, 'Okay, you screwed us, we're going to give you some pain.'"

The coalition of opponents to the legislation was transferred from McConnell's office to DeLay's office in the Capitol. Tamara Somerville, of McConnell's staff, organized the meetings in DeLay's office. Now the National Association of Realtors joined the group, invited in because they could add significant grass-roots strength.

At a meeting of the coalition on a late April afternoon, some twenty-five people crowded into DeLay's office. The meeting was significant enough that McConnell himself attended.

McConnell's message was the same as that he had delivered when the Senate bill was pending: "You can defeat this on First Amendment grounds."

McConnell added that he didn't want to see any bill come back from the House to the Senate.

DeLay told McConnell, "I think we can drag this out all summer."

"Does that mean nothing will come over before the August recess?" McConnell asked.

DeLay told him that's what he meant.

"I can handle that," said McConnell. "We can keep it bottled up until adjournment."

THE FLOOR DEBATE, which began on June 17, was an extended contest of wits and will: the antireformers led by DeLay using whatever was within reach, mainly amendments that had been designed by McConnell's office for the Senate debate in case a filibuster was broken, to beat down or wear down the reformers, and the reformers gradually molding themselves into an effective team.

Night after night—the debates usually occurred at night, since the campaign finance reform debate was considered a "filler" in the House's more urgent business—and week after week (but in the end it was considered in nine sessions), the opponents hurled trick amendments, amendments that had a surface plausibility but would kill the legislation. The supporters of reform fended off almost all of them. The teamwork that developed among the key supporters of reform—Shays and Meehan and Tom Campbell, a curly-haired, forty-six-year-old moderate Republican and former Stanford law school professor; Sander Levin, like his younger brother Carl, balding and smart, who with the help of little brother's material took on the "issue ad" arguments—came to resemble that of a champion basketball team whose members instinctively knew each others' moves, and whom to toss the ball to and when.

Each day, the reformers met in Shays's office, with officials of Common Cause and the League of Women Voters in attendance; Don Simon, the executive vice president of Common Cause, a man with bright red hair and usually looking worried, frantically drafted amendments and counteramendments. In so doing, he pulled the bill back from danger several times. Barney Frank, Democrat of Massachusetts and one of the smartest members of the House, attended the meetings of the reform leaders at their invitation because they felt that he understood the House rules better than anyone.

To offset the efforts of the opponents, reform groups set up a major phone-bank effort, to make calls to targeted districts on days when a dangerous amendment was to be offered. The reformers managed to get roughly four hundred editorials in nearly two hundred newspapers in the course of four months of debate.

THE REFORMERS' first real scare came on an amendment offered by Bill Thomas, Republican of California, who was close to the leadership, to negate all of the Shays-Meehan bill if any part of it was struck down by the courts—as some thought its issue ad provision might be. Very few bills passed by Congress contained such a provision. But it was defeated rather easily, with sixty-five Republicans voting with the Democrats—another omen for the Republican leadership. Despite the leadership's attempt to divide the freshmen reformers from the backers of the Shays-Meehan bill, Tom Allen consistently voted with the Shays-Meehan proponents to protect their bill, and Asa Hutchinson did so occasionally.

The long series of amendments offered by opponents of the Shays-Meehan bill led reformers to worry that the House leaders wouldn't keep their pledge to finish the consideration of the legislation by the time of the coming recess, to begin August 7. The reformers weren't aware that the August 7 deadline was just fine with McConnell. Moreover, when Senate Majority Leader Trent Lott was asked what he would do if the House passed a bill, he replied, "Nothing."

The supporters of Shays-Meehan—Shays, a gentleman, referred to it as "Meehan-Shays"—continued to beat back amendments, pointing out that some of them were "poison pills" designed to defeat the legislation.

On Tuesday night, Representative John Doolittle, the forty-five-year-old Republican from California who had been trying to kill campaign finance reform, offered a proposal that was ostensibly about voter guides put out by such groups as the Christian Coalition and the ACLU but which would have had the effect of gutting the provision to curb phony "issue ads" paid for with soft money.

This alarmed reformers: Only the day before, fifty-three Christian Right and other conservative groups, including one supporting development of an anti-missile system, had sent a letter to Members of Congress urging them to defeat Shays-Meehan and distorting the issue ad provision. The letter said that only the news media would be left free to criticize or endorse candidates at election time. But in the end, forty Republicans voted against this amendment—a sign to the reformers that they had more strength than was commonly thought.

ON THE EVENING of July 14, Majority Whip Tom DeLay, grinning, his dark hair slicked back as usual, offered another amendment which would have had the effect of gutting the issue advocacy provision of the Shays-Meehan bill. DeLay used a second line of attack, marching it right up alongside the First Amendment argument, and apparently thinking it at least as useful: that "federal bureaucrats" would judge what were proper "issue ads" and voter guides.

Tom Campbell, speaking in his gentle, calm way, backed DeLay into an embarrassing position.

CAMPBELL: Mr. Chairman, I thank the distinguished whip. I really have two brief points and I would appreciate his response to them. First, does the distinguished gentleman have an objection to requiring that a group that puts out a guide, such as the one by his side, that we know who contributed the money that paid for it?

DELAY: Yes, I have an objection.

CAMPBELL: Let me understand the gentleman. He does not believe the citizens of this country have the right to know who pays for an advertisement in a campaign of that nature?

DELAY: No, because we have experience—if we believe in the Constitution and the right of people to petition their government, whether it be by writing a petition or talking about my voting record or however they do it, the point is that if we believe in the Constitution and the people having a right to petition their government, then we do not want the government to be able to go and punish these people....

CAMPBELL: If the gentleman will continue to yield. As I understand the logic of the gentleman's position, then, he would never require any disclosure of who is behind funding campaigns?

DELAY: Not at all.

CAMPBELL: Not at all?

DELAY: Absolutely not. Not at all.

On occasion DeLay got so excited that he virtually jumped up and down as he addressed the House. At one point, he went so far as to exclaim, "I am really excited about this debate. I think the American people are really starting to understand what this is all about. This is incumbent protection....This is basically about people's freedom of speech." And on occasion his true nature came through.

When the House was debating a poorly worded and ill-considered amendment that would place the burden of proof on those who receive funds from foreign nationals, an obviously anxious DeLay rose to speak in the well of the House. Dressed in a charcoal-gray suit with blue shirt and a red and white print tie, DeLay grinned as he reeled off some of the names in the Clinton case, making fun of several of them. "If you gotta friend by the name of *Johnny Chien Chuen Chung*," DeLay said, emphasizing the name, "a Taiwanese American from Torrance, California, and his company does business with foreign nationals and comes up with $366,000 for the Democrat Party, then it is a high probability that when you receive that along with all the other stuff you have received, that you probably, in high probabilities, know that it came from foreign nationals....If you have a friend by the name of Arief and Soraya [pronouncing it wrong], and I can't even pronounce the last name, Wiriadinata [pronouncing Wiriadinata wrong], something like that, who donated $450,000 to the DNC and was friends with *Johnny Huang*, and later returned it because Wiriadinata could not explain where it came from, then probably there is a high probability that it is money from foreign nationals."

At this point, Shays tried to intervene, "Will the gentleman yield?"

DeLay gestured by holding up one hand that he would not stop, and continued: "And I could go on with *John Lee* and *Cheong Am, Yogesh Gandhi, In-Ga* [meaning Ng] *Lap Seng, Supreme Master Suma Ching Hai*, and George Psaltis [he stumbled over this]. These are American names, I know, and a lot of them are Americans and American citizens, but many of them did business with foreign nationals and brought money to the DNC and others."

Shays continued to try to interrupt, "Will the gentleman yield?"

When DeLay finally yielded, Shays said, "I know you did not mean it to sound this way but when I listened to it, it sounded this way: It sounded like if you have a foreign name, there was a high probability they were foreigners."

DeLay quickly responded, "I knew you would try to do that."

"That is what it sounded like."

"That is not my point. My point is that the administration and the DNC knew exactly who these people were, had known them for many, many long years, knew their contacts and I guarantee the gentleman, knew where this money came from." On this, DeLay had a valid point, but it was lost amid his nastiness.

DeLay's comments set off a storm, and six days later he apologized on the House floor.

ON JULY 14, one troublesome amendment got through the reform team's strong defense. It was sponsored by Vito Fossella, a Republican, who was elected to Congress in a special election in November 1997 to fill the seat of Susan Molinari, who had left Congress for what turned out to be a short-lived television career. The Republicans spent $800,000 in soft money for an "issue ad" blitz in this special election, which frightened the Democrats. Fossella's amendment said that candidates for federal office couldn't accept contributions from foreign, legal permanent residents, that is, green card holders. Given all the recent attention to foreign contributions, reformers knew that they couldn't defeat the amendment. Members of Congress simply couldn't be seen to be voting for accepting the contributions of noncitizens of any kind. So, as the reformers made the argument against it, they beseeched others to not let it become a "killer amendment."

Meehan said the amendment "may well be an unconstitutional provision," and he yielded to Patsy Mink, a longtime liberal from Hawaii, who usually wasn't much listened to, but at this moment she was.

"Just take a good look at me," Mink told a silent House. "If I were to hand over a campaign contribution to a federal candidate, what would be the first thing that the recipient would do? It would be to ask me whether I was a citizen of the United States. I am a third-generation American, but they would be forced to ask me that question because of my appearance."

Shays, despite his gentle demeanor, knew how to throw a fastball.

Shays said, "Mr. Chairman, this is one of those difficult moments in the process of bringing forth a comprehensive bill with many supporters. We tried to identify amendments as killer amendments, harmful amendments, benign or helpful amendments, and essential amendments to help the bill pass...I have to be candid with my colleagues, those who support Meehan-Shays, we are going to lose some supporters in the end if this amendment passes. It is likely to pass. But one of the things I find extraordinarily ironic is I hear a member say there is agreement this amendment has to be part of Meehan-Shays. Yet the people who are saying it are not going to be voting for Meehan-Shays. So this is not particularly a friendly amendment....I encourage my colleagues to realize that we cannot allow this amendment, if it passes, to be a killer amendment because they will have won."

Xavier Becerra, a forty-year-old, third-term Democratic congressman representing an Hispanic district in California, tried to shame the House as Mink had done. "Please, members," Becerra said, "do not confuse the term *foreign national* with what this bill really does, and that is it goes after lawful permanent citizens." He added, "This bill is a sweeping indictment of the eight or ten million people who are lawful permanent residents....We tax lawful permanent residents. We expect them to defend this country in times of war."

Addressing his fellow Hispanic members, whose support of a final bill could be crucial, Becerra said, "I encourage my colleagues who feel strongly against this amendment, do not let them win in the end. If they succeed in attaching this amendment, do not walk away, because that is the real reason why they are presenting this amendment...And I encourage my colleagues to realize that we cannot allow this amendment. If it passes...they will have won."

But the House adopted the amendment by a lopsided vote of 282 to 126, with several liberals who favored reform voting for it.

The amendment set off the expected reverberations in the Hispanic Caucus. To members of that caucus, who numbered seventeen, the amendment was an insult. So it put in question passage of a reform bill by the House.

DeLay was actually excited about the debate. In a meeting of his Free Speech Coalition on July 15, DeLay was on a high.

"I think we've got them on the run here," DeLay said. "I think we're accomplishing our objectives."

He felt that the strategy of offering loads of amendments was working. He was highly pleased that the Fossella amendment had been added to the bill, putting it in jeopardy.

McConnell, who attended the meeting, expressed some puzzlement about the House rules. He and some of the allied groups complained that they never knew what was coming up when, making it harder to mobilize behind a given amendment. In trying to confuse the proponents of campaign finance reform, DeLay was also confusing his own allies.

McConnell reminded the group that the Shays-Meehan bill was the ultimate target. And it was a good target, McConnell said, because of its constitutional problem. Once it was exposed, McConnell said, people would oppose it.

Toward the end of the House debate, the ACLU sent a letter to House members urging defeat of the bill because of the Fossella amendment barring legal permanent residents from making campaign contributions. The ACLU, of course, opposed the bill anyway, but the letter, signed by sixty-five ethnic groups, alarmed supporters of Shays-Meehan.

On the last two days of debate, at the end of July, opponents threw more "poison pill" amendments at the bill, but by now the supporters had coalesced, and fended them off with relative ease. In fact, DeLay and his band had given up. The supporters' defenses had held.

But there remained the question of which of the proposals—which the Republican leadership had pitted against each other—would prevail in the final voting in the week to come.

Over the first weekend in August, preceding the week when campaign reform would come to a final vote in the House, Shays and Meehan tried to talk the freshmen out of pursuing their own bill and to consolidate around their measure. Though Tom Allen was willing, Asa Hutchinson was not: The Republicans wouldn't release him to do so. The Christian Coalition opposed curbs on "issue ads."

Also over that weekend, Mitch McConnell was quoted in the *New York Times* saying, "You're more likely to see Elvis again than to see this bill pass the Senate."

In the late afternoon on Monday, August 3, when the critical votes were to be cast, Shays and Meehan were conferring on the floor. Elsewhere Democratic leaders were meeting with members of the Hispanic Caucus. Republican leaders were considering throwing their weight behind the freshman bill in order to kill off Shays-Meehan, which they (and the Christian Right) considered far worse.

Gephardt, addressing the House, paid tribute to Shays and Meehan. They had been more foresighted than he had, and they and their allies had put on a remarkable display of resilience and teamwork.

"I believe in all my heart that Shays-Meehan is the real solution," Gephardt said. It took him a while to get there, but once he did, he worked hard on rebellious factions to make sure it passed. "There's only one more obstacle," Gephardt said. That was to make sure that the Shays-Meehan bill got the most votes in the end.

Toward the end, DeLay rose to speak. "As everyone knows, I am opposed to this Shays-Meehan fiasco," he began. "This is just another example of big government picking winners and losers....What you are talking about is limiting the speech of our constituents and hiding behind the name 'reform.' The bill itself bans voter guides and score cards [it did not] and it bans these so-called sham ads that members hate to see run against them because it makes them uncomfortable when their voting report is brought before the American people....To my Republican colleagues let me just simply say that this is not reform. This is not good government. This is political disarmament."

DeLay concluded, "You do not have a free pass to violate our Constitution. Support free speech and vote down Shays-Meehan."

In reply, Shays said, "This is not disarmament, and it would be an absurd thing to suggest unilateral disarmament. How could it be unilateral disarmament to ban soft money to both political parties? Is the inference that Republicans benefit more from soft money than Democrats? Why would it be unilateral disarmament when we call sham issue ads what they truly are, campaign ads? It is not a freedom of speech issue. We do not say you cannot advertise. We do not say people cannot say whatever they want. They are just campaign ads, and you call them campaign ads. When you call them campaign ads, two interesting things happen; you cannot use corporate money and you cannot use union dues. The bottom line to this bill, it is about restoring integrity to the political system. Both parties, individuals, corporations, labor unions— everybody has to play by the same rules."

Meehan, the third-termer who had turned his seniors around, spoke for the Democratic side. "There comes a time in a legislator's life when he or she has to be held accountable for his or her vote. That day has arrived for the Members of the 105th Congress. Once in a generation Members of Congress take it upon themselves to change our campaign finance laws."

Meehan went on, "This is indeed an historic opportunity that only comes once in a generation, because it is not usual when members of the House have a bill with bipartisan support, a bicameral bill, so when we send this bill to the other body they have already spent time, with the majority members supporting it."

When he concluded, he received a standing ovation from his side; Tom Campbell joined the applause.

Zach Wamp, the conservative Tennessee Republican from the class of 1994, speaking in a broad southern accent, closed the debate for the Republican supporters of Shays-Meehan. He was Shays's choice. "Tonight really is the moment of truth," Wamp said in a ringing voice. He addressed his side of the aisle, "I say to my colleagues in the majority, this is the moment of truth. I ask members, Will they please put the public interest above their personal interest? Will they please put the good of government above their political party? Will members please do the right thing for the American people, and send the signal that we have gone the distance on reform?"

When Wamp finished, he was strongly applauded by the bill's supporters on both sides of the aisle.

Members were starting to file into the House for the vote. I encountered Meehan in the lobby behind the House chamber; he didn't look as jubilant as he might have. "I'm a little worried," he said, grimacing, as other members pushed past him to get to the floor. "But I think we're going to be okay." He was worried that Hispanics would defect because of the amendment banning contributions by legal resident aliens.

"I've got Bob Menendez [from New Jersey] at the door, working them," Meehan said.

Newt Gingrich, standing on the House floor, watched the green and red lights on one wall of the chamber as members cast their votes by electronic cards. He seemed isolated and irrelevant—even though he had inadvertently helped bring this moment about. Members stood on the floor in their clusters, and the place grew increasingly rowdy. It was a moment of high excitement. As a sign, several Hispanics voted yes early. Shays, the earnest WASP from Greenwich, stood with his arm around Levin, the brainy Jew from Detroit. They'd been through a war together.

Big cheers arose from the Democratic side when the tally board on another wall of the chamber showed that the Shays-

Meehan bill had reached 220 votes, more than a majority. But it still had to outstrip the freshman bill to prevail.

More applause broke out when the final vote was announced: 237-186—a lopsided vote for such a divisive issue. All of fifty-one Republicans voted for Shays-Meehan. Gingrich was proven right in his belief that if he allowed a straight vote on Shays-Meehan, he would lose. But to lose fifty-one Republicans was a humiliation.

AFTERWARD, Shays, asked in the hallway by a reporter whether he expected "any more games here," replied dryly, "I expect games every day."

Tom DeLay told a *Wall Street Journal* reporter, "The timing kills 'em. The DeLay strategy worked. Delay, delay, delay."

SHAYS DID FACE one more "game." DeLay decided to try to round up enough Republican votes for the freshman bill to make it overtake Shays-Meehan—and then kill the whole thing. He assigned Asa Hutchinson to find out if they could get forty votes from the Democratic side.

But the Democratic leaders, having got wind of the Republican leaders' latest gambit, worked to persuade Democrats to vote no, or be absent, on the vote on the freshman bill. (Shays worked to make sure that the fifty-one Republicans who had voted for his bill stayed put.)

After a short while, Hutchinson reported to DeLay, "I can't do it."

ON THE NIGHT of Wednesday, August 5, two nights after the House had voted strongly for the Shays-Meehan campaign reform bill, President Clinton attended a Democratic congressional campaign dinner in Washington, at the Mayflower Hotel. The guests were people who had agreed to contribute or raise a $100,000 check for the committee. First they were given a briefing on the status of the House races, and then they dined on summer vegetables, duck, Maryland crab cakes, fillet of beef, fillet of salmon, whipped potatoes, and green apple sorbet.

The President, looking pale and speaking in a flat tone, recited his priority issues—"save Social Security, pass a patients' bill of rights, improve the public schools, clean up the environment, and improve the economy." He also had the audacity to say, "The happiest citizen in the United States was me when the Shays-Meehan campaign finance reform bill passed the House last week." The toll that the sex scandal was taking on Clinton had become increasingly evident. In a little more than a week's time, he would appear before a grand jury.

ON THURSDAY afternoon, Doolittle's proposal to abandon all limits and have more and quicker disclosure of donations went down ignominiously (131–299). Asa Hutchinson then brought up the freshman bill, the last hurdle for the Shays-Meehan bill. "Let us pass something that will get through the United States Senate," Hutchinson said. Praise was poured on the freshmen for their fine effort, and then their bill was defeated 147–222.

The vote for final passage of the Shays-Meehan seemed almost routine. The House passed it 252–179. Sixty-one Republicans joined the Democrats in supporting it.

Something had happened that almost no one had thought possible.

12

———·———

Burial

When the campaign finance reform bill was killed in a Senate filibuster in late February 1998, John McCain told the Republican leaders that he wouldn't try to bring the bill up again. But because of the surprising action by the House, and the subsequent pressures by the reform groups on certain senators, McCain decided to bring the bill up once more.

Yet, by Wednesday, September 9, 1998, when the reform bill was scheduled to come up again, Washington was consumed with the Clinton sex scandal, the senators distracted. Senate Democrats, several of them in a panic that Clinton's behavior would cost their party seats in the November elections, or even beyond that, had been meeting in the caucus to figure out what to do. Tom Daschle was trying to stave off open defections from the President.

Trent Lott allowed the campaign finance bill to come up because he didn't want to split his party, and he knew that a reform bill wasn't going to be approved by the end of that Congress, which was expected to be in session only another month. The remaining steps were simply too high and difficult to navigate: passage by the Senate, somehow turning around eight Republicans to vote to end another filibuster; conferees representing the Senate and the House working out the differences between the bills passed by the two chambers, if by any wild chance the Senate passed a bill; and both chambers adopting the final bill.

During the August recess, reformers tried to get certain Republican senators up for re-election to change their position: Alfonse D'Amato; Ben Nighthorse Campbell, of Colorado; Christopher Bond, of Missouri; Judd Gregg, of New Hampshire. But whatever hopes, or illusions, the reformers entertained after the House passed its campaign finance bill faded quickly enough. Though D'Amato hinted that he might now support the bill—he was prone to election-year conversions—he wrapped his hint in enough conditions as to make it meaningless. The others showed no sign of changing their position.

Also during the recess, the antireform interests who had been working with McConnell and Delay met in McConnell's office on August 12 (McConnell wasn't there), and agreed that they should get letters from their members to the senators, urging them to hold firm, by August 31. McConnell's aide, Tamara Somerville, who had been checking around, reported that she didn't see any deterioration in their side's strength. She also said that when the Senate reconvened after Labor Day McConnell would talk face-to-face with every senator who had voted with him before.

ON THE DAY before the bill was to be brought back up, the other Clinton scandal, always in the background, made a reappearance. It was reported in the press that Attorney General Reno announced that she had initiated the ninety-day process of determining whether Clinton had violated the campaign finance laws by using "issue ads," paid for with soft money—Clinton himself had supervised the work on the ads—to help his own campaign rather than his party. This could lead to yet another Independent Counsel. Reno's action was based on recent information the Justice Department had received from the Federal Election Commission that the money spent on these ads should have been counted under the limited amount the Clinton campaign could spend once he accepted federal funding. Justice's action also followed a thirty-day preliminary investigation of whether there was sufficient cause to go further.

For months, Common Cause, Fred Thompson and other Republicans, and FBI director Louis Freeh had been pressing Reno to start such an inquiry. They also argued that Reno had a built-in conflict of interest in allowing the Justice Department to conduct an inquiry into the President's activities. When the federal prosecutor, Charles La Bella, who had been brought in in September 1997 to take over the campaign finance investigation from career Justice Department officials, was leaving his job in July 1998, he too recommended an Independent Counsel. Reno was under pressure from House Oversight Committee Chairman Dan Burton to turn over the La Bella and Freeh memos.[*]

In the internal arguments in the Justice Department, Freeh and La Bella maintained that it was hard to accept that the President, and perhaps others covered by the Independent Counsel statute, hadn't been involved in directing the effort to raise soft money in a way that destroyed the campaign finance law. Others in the Justice Department argued that there wasn't enough "specific information from a credible source" that a crime had been committed, as required by the statute, to warrant a criminal investigation. As for the part of the statute that gave the attorney general discretionary authority to trigger the act if she felt that it would be a conflict of interest for the Justice Department to conduct the investigation, this was harder to resolve internally. Ultimately, Justice Department officials prevailed, saying that there wasn't enough "specific and credible" information of criminal activity to trigger the act in this instance, either. Thompson and others were incredulous that the Department could come to such a conclusion, with good reason. ("We found that one harder to get rid of," was how a Justice Department official put it to me.)

AND SUDDENLY, on that same Wednesday morning that the campaign finance bill was to be brought up in the Senate, word spread that the report of the Independent Counsel, Kenneth Starr, who had begun in 1994 by investigating the Whitewater land deal but was now focused on the sex scandal, was on its way to Capitol Hill. It hadn't been expected so soon, and the prospect of its arrival set off a frenzy. A few hours later, two black vans, carrying both the 453-page report and masses of supplemental material, in thirty-six boxes, eighteen for each party, ominously drove up to the House side of the Capitol.

AT MID-MORNING Wednesday, aware of the odds, under the circumstances, against getting any attention to his cause, John McCain took to the Senate floor. Talking in his quiet, earnest way, McCain said, "This is not a happy time for America. It is not a happy time for the institution of government, especially the presidency, but also

---

[*] After he returned to San Diego, La Bella was passed over for the job as U.S. Attorney—at the behest of Barbara Boxer, liberal California senator and Clinton in-law, it was reported—and, in early February 1999, he resigned from the U.S. Attorney's office there.

the Congress. We are going through a very wrenching and difficult episode which already, I think, most of us would agree, ranks in the first order of crises that affect this country."

McCain continued, "When twenty-two percent of the American people say they believe that restoring values is the number-one issue they want Congress to focus on, I don't believe they are just referring to the problems concerning the presidency and that crisis. I think they are talking about the fact that they don't believe that they, as individual citizens, are represented here in the Congress in the legislative process. I think they believe that special interests rule. I believe that they are concerned that no longer are their concerns paramount, but only those of major contributors."

Referring to the House's action a month before, McCain said, "I appeal to all members of the Senate to listen to the majority of our colleagues in the other body, and to the majority of senators, and seize this historic opportunity to give the nation a campaign finance system that is worthy of the world's greatest democracy."

But McCain knew what was going to happen.

SHORTLY BEFORE NOON the next day, Fred Thompson rose to address the Senate. He stood behind a desk with a lectern atop it. As was his style, Thompson spoke ex tempore from notes, his hands in his pockets, the huge man with the big voice filling the nearly empty chamber. Thompson didn't declaim; he spoke in a conversational tone, but his voice and his size gave power to what he was saying. Only Russell Feingold, cosponsor with McCain of the pending bill, was on the floor to listen to him. Thompson had been speaking around the country about the problem with the campaign finance laws—he was in great demand, especially from fellow senators.

But that day, as he had on the road, Thompson spoke about the campaign finance problem in the broader context of the state of America, foreign and domestic.

"We have very much of a troubled presidency," Thompson said. "We have seen for some time now that while nobody has been paying much attention to a lot of these things, the level of cynicism continues to go up in this country."

He continued, "Now that we see the need for strong leadership, after we have done so much to destroy the confidence that the American people ought to be having in the leadership of this country, who is going to listen to our leaders?"

If the peace and prosperity the country was enjoying were to fade, Thompson said, "Who is going to follow the leadership of those of us in Washington who stand up and say here is the way; here is what we need to do; this is the way out of this problem....Who is going to follow us?"

And then he connected this larger question to the issue then before the Senate. "That is why this issue that we are discussing today is doubly important. It has to do with the very fundamentals of our government. It has to do with the way we finance campaigns in this country, the way we elect the elected leaders who in turn are supposed to lead us when we need that leadership. I must say, in my opinion we now have the worst campaign finance system that we have ever had in this country. In fact, you cannot call it a campaign finance system at all. It is a situation that is an open invitation to abuse. It is an open invitation to corruption. It is an open invitation to cynicism. And after the scandal of the 1996 campaign, if we do not do something about it, the level of cynicism is going to be even higher."

Thompson added, "We are spending more and more and more time going after more money from fewer and fewer people who have the millions of dollars that is fueling our system, the same people who come back before us wanting us to either pass or defeat legislation. Mr. President, I have said ever since I have been in the Senate, I say here again today, that it is a system that cannot last."

Thompson was still going when the twenty minutes allowed him by the reform side had expired. He asked for more time.

McConnell, who had just entered the chamber to check on what was going on, prevented Thompson from being allowed to continue. It was his final revenge on Thompson for the year.

Thompson, obviously not happy, gathered his yellow sheets from the lectern and strode out of the Chamber.

SHORTLY AFTERWARD, the Senate voted not to cut off a filibuster—by the same eight-vote margin as it had in late February. No votes changed. Campaign finance reform was effectively buried for the year. The fact that it now commanded a majority of the votes in both the House and the Senate was irrelevant.

With the Starr report having so recently arrived on Capitol Hill, hardly anyone noticed.

13

—■—

Impeachments

The impeachment and trial of President Clinton were testament to the changes that had taken place in our politics over the past twenty-five years.

The proceedings against Clinton reflected the rise of partisanship in the Congress, and the loss of a center there, the shift to the right within the Republican Party and the power of the right over Republicans in both chambers, the decline in civility, and even the decline in the quality of the politicians. Money also played a role, in particular in enforcing Republican discipline in the House of Representatives, but it was also a factor in the Senate.

The differences between the impeachment proceedings against Richard Nixon in 1974 and against Clinton in 1998 and 1999 were emblematic of these changes. (Nixon's case, of course, never reached the Senate.)

Certainly partisanship played a part in the Democratic Congress's actions against Nixon, as did sheer hatred of the man. But the partisanship and zealotry invested in the impeachment of Clinton was of a different order than that against Nixon, and had its roots in the changes in the current political climate and the new sense that "anything goes." Boundaries that used to be respected disappeared.

"Impeachment" used to be an awe-inspiring word. Before the Nixon case, the Congress had seriously considered such a drastic action against a president only once. And the impeachment of Andrew Johnson in 1868 had gone down in history as an illegitimate, partisan exercise, fueled by the passions that followed the Civil War. (Johnson escaped removal by one vote in the Senate.) When the word "impeachment" began to be used in connection with Nixon, it was a startling and even frightening development. Impeach a president and remove him from office? It had never happened.

The bipartisan chairman and vice chairman of Iran-Contra hearings had decided not to put the country through another impeachment. But by 1998, numerous House Republicans were treating impeachment as an almost casual matter. Bob Barr, of Georgia, also of the class of 1994, a mustachioed former prosecutor with a rabid manner, had been advocating Clinton's impeachment since November of 1997, over the Whitewater land deal in Arkansas and other scandals.

As soon as it seemed possible—in the summer of 1998—that the Monica Lewinsky scandal might lead to a serious impeachment effort, several members of the House Judiciary Committee jumped right out and declared that if the President had committed perjury, he should be impeached. Sober deliberations—of the sort that had gone on in the House Judiciary Committee in 1974—of what should constitute an impeachable offense didn't occur in the House committee in 1998.

THE POLITICAL CONTEXTS for the Nixon and Clinton impeachments were strikingly different. The Founding Fathers had predicted "factions," but even in the mid-seventies, interest-group politics were nowhere nearly as developed and sophisticated as they later became. The Christian Right movement didn't exist until the late seventies. Partisanship, at times of a very raw sort, had of course existed, but not with the regularity and on the order of the partisanship of the more recent period.

Between 1974 and 1998, the House Judiciary Committee itself, where both the Nixon and Clinton impeachment proceedings began, had undergone a vast change.

Through the seventies, people joined the House Judiciary Committee because they were interested in such issues as criminal law, copyright, patents, constitutional law. By the early 1980s the new assortment of inflammatory social issues—abortion, flag burning, crime, gun control—had developed as intense grass-roots issues, and they came under the committee's jurisdiction. Given these issues' lightning nature, House leaders of both parties recruited and assigned to the committee people who came from safe districts and who they were confident could stand up to public opinion on these issues. The result was that by the time the question of whether to impeach Bill Clinton arose, the Judiciary Committee was made up of members who represented and were supported by the extremes of both parties. Nearly all the members came from safe districts. These were people who wouldn't be threatened by public opinion. This turned out to be a crucial factor in the impeachment of Bill Clinton.

But the defining factor in what happened both in the House Judiciary Committee and in the House as a whole, and to a lesser but still significant extent in the Senate, was the role played by the fairly new and highly energized Republican base, with the Christian Right at its core. But the base also included donors (mostly of small amounts), small-business people, and the Party activists. (The "New Right" had pioneered raising small donations through direct mail, a legacy to the Republican Party.) By the nineties, the Christian Coalition itself dominated about twenty state parties, as well as the Republican base in most of the Republican House members' districts. The Christian Right was a power even in districts that it didn't dominate, as was the base as a whole. All of this developed in the years following Nixon's near-impeachment in 1974.

So, by the late nineties, in the House of Representatives itself, the base constituted what one Republican House member described to me as "a minority within a minority that dominates Republican primaries in most of our districts." And, significantly, the base was made up of the people who financed the Republican campaigns. It had to be paid attention. Some Republican House members were warned by the base that if they didn't vote to impeach Clinton they could expect a primary challenger from the right in the next election. This was a serious threat. Even if such a challenge was unlikely to succeed, it could absorb the time and resources of the incumbent and divide his or her support in the general election. There had been fresh examples in 1998 of candidates of the right taking on moderate Republicans in primaries.

The House Republican leadership's decision to go all out for the impeachment of President Clinton—the Democratic leaders in 1974 were more restrained—reflected the power of the base. It also put many of their members in a painful situation. Peter King, the iconoclastic Republican from the Long Island suburbs, who opposed impeachment, told me, "If the hard core of Clinton haters comes out in the primary, it's difficult for Republicans who were against impeachment to survive that."

King spelled out the dilemma posed to numerous Republicans: "If you vote against impeachment, it's hard to survive in a Republican primary, and if you vote for impeachment it's hard to survive in the general election."

The House Republicans talked a lot publicly about how Clinton's actions required his impeachment, but something else important, something that they didn't talk about publicly, was also going on. In moving against Clinton the Republican Party was pursuing a long-term, and parochial, goal that had nothing whatever to do with Clinton's alleged misdeeds. The party was using the impeachment of the President to strengthen its base. But that strategy carried its own danger.

Peter King told me, "The Republican Party is firming up its base in one hundred and eighty to one hundred eighty-five districts. People elected in those districts will stay in office a long time. In more moderate districts, it's going to make it harder for moderate Republicans to get elected. It will be hard for the Republicans to make a national governing party."

CERTAINLY THERE WERE Nixon haters, lots of them, who were furious with him for his prominent role in the 1949 Alger Hiss–Whittaker Chambers case (in which Nixon has apparently turned out to be correct about Hiss's guilt, even if his personal exploitation of the case was off-putting), as well as his exercises in red-baiting during his early political campaigns, and on the plain fact that he was hard to like. But—as a sign of how our political climate had changed—the Clinton haters were if anything more virulent and more organized: their tactics included constant attack by right-wing talk-show hosts, a new political force beginning in the 1980s; peddling of tapes by the Rev. Jerry Falwell, who had founded the Moral Majority and had his own television program, *The Old Time Gospel Hour,* on which he accused Clinton of numerous nefarious deeds.

The list of attacks on Clinton by the far right and their organs included accusations about murders of people who had been connected to him; charges that at a minimum he condoned drug-running through the Mena Airport, in Arkansas, while he was governor; insistence (despite the findings of two Independent Counsels) that former deputy White House counsel Vince Foster hadn't committed suicide, even that his body had been transferred from a safe-house kept somewhere by Mrs. Clinton to Fort Marcy Park, on the Virginia side of the Potomac River, where it was found; a series of lawsuits against Clinton and his aides by a conservative legal organization. One organization, Citizens United, published a newsletter called *Clinton Watch,* which included Whitewater investigation updates, recent rumors, and right-wing critiques of the Clinton agenda.

Moreover, the Clinton-hating had a strong cultural component and an aspect that was different from the Nixon-hating. The Clinton-haters saw the Clintons, however inaccurately, as representing the despised "hippies" of the sixties. There were the famous picture of the bearded Clinton at Oxford in the late sixties, his opposition to the Vietnam War (though he didn't participate in demonstrations against it), and his draft-dodging. Hillary Clinton represented to many the pushy, threatening, liberated woman.

The new aspect was the attitude of Clinton's strongest opponents toward his presidency itself. King, who came to the Congress the same year that Clinton assumed the presidency, told me, "There's been a mind-set since 1993 that he's an illegitimate President. I was struck by the absolute intensity of the hatred of Clinton. A specter of illegitimacy was hovering over him, and it got worse after 1994."

The power of the base, especially its Christian Right component, explained what many people found so puzzling about the actions of the House Republicans in Clinton's case: that they pursued impeachment in the face of overwhelming opposition to it in the national polls. They were far more concerned about the view of the base than about the national polls. The donors couldn't be offended. Turnout by the Christian Right was crucial to the party's fortunes in elections, in particular to its ability to hold on to control of the House.

REPUBLICANS ON the House Judiciary Committee were immune to arguments from other Republicans, a few of them in the House itself, that what they were about to do would hurt the party, and that the removal of a popular President wouldn't be good for the country. A major Republican figure I know, a man with excellent conservative credentials, trolled among the committee Republicans in December, trying to persuade them that, though he probably agreed with them that Clinton's behavior constituted impeachable offenses, they should use their prosecutorial discretion and decide that impeaching Clinton and trying to remove him from office was in neither the country's, nor the Republican Party's, interest. He failed utterly.

Referring to the committee's considerations, which included an entire day of hearings on the subject of perjury, I said to this person, "They're hearing perjury, perjury, perjury."

He replied, "They're hearing primary, primary, primary."

THE COMMITTEE CHAIRMEN in the two impeachments were markedly different. The strong contrast wasn't just in their personalities, but also in how they reflected the different political context in which each was functioning. Peter Rodino, an until-then obscure New Jersey congressman, about whom rumors of Mafia ties circulated (nothing came of them), was underestimated when he took on the role of guiding his committee through the treacherous waters. Henry Hyde, the Illinois congressman best known for his opposition to government support for abortions, was overestimated. An accessible, jovial, and usually gracious man, the big, rotund, silver-haired Hyde was popular with the press. (A friend of mine commented, "Joviality will get you everywhere in Washington.")

Rodino was a modest, quiet, gray man. The eloquence he reached toward the end of his committee's deliberations came from his simplicity and the intensity of the awe he had, as an Italian-born immigrant, for the American constitutional system. Hyde was a bigger, more colorful figure, in several senses, a coloratura speaker. When he engaged in House debate, one couldn't help noticing him.

Hyde, unlike several of his Republican colleagues on the committee, hadn't come across as a zealous ideologue. He had successfully opposed term limits, one of the tenets of Newt Gingrich's 1994 campaign agenda, the "Contract with America," and he had tried to temper the platform statement pushed by even more vehement antiabortionists at the 1996 Republican Convention.

But even though Hyde had said early on that any impeachment would have to be bipartisan, as the committee's deliberations went forward, he openly pushed for impeaching Clinton and pursued it even though it was a partisan effort. However, had Hyde reached to his left on the dais to the committee Democrats, it was most unlikely that they would have been receptive. The dug-in Democrats were engaging in their party's by-now highly developed specialty of branding Republican-led, dangerous committee proceedings "partisan" by being partisan themselves—just as they had done to the Thompson committee hearings.

Over time, Hyde's open determination to impeach Clinton revealed a certain zealotry beneath the joviality. Its most stunning display came when, at the conclusion of Independent Counsel Kenneth Starr's day-long, inappropriately prosecutorial testimony before the committee on November 19—his job was to report to the Congress evidence that might constitute an impeachable offense, but instead his report and his testimony argued the case for Clinton's impeachment—Hyde and almost all of the other Republicans gave him a standing ovation.

There were profound differences in how the two House Judiciary Committees proceeded. The Judiciary Committee of 1974 contained at least six members—two Democrats and four Republicans—who were genuinely undecided, painfully so, about whether to vote to impeach Nixon. The two Democrats—James Mann, of Virginia, and Walter Flowers, of Alabama—were quite conservative; these days, with the South no longer a one-party region, they might well be Republicans. (Flowers, a supporter of George Wallace, kept a small Confederate flag on his desk.) When these undecided members spoke, people sat on the edge of their chairs to try to determine which way they were leaning. In my own interviews with them as they were trying to decide, the strain on them was evident. Nixon was unpopular at that point, but he still had support within the Republican Party. The Rodino committee members, on both sides, had an obvious sense of the gravity of impeaching a president.

Such a sense was not conveyed by the Hyde committee's deliberations. The Hyde committee was a partisan combat zone—each side trying to score points off the other for the benefit of the House as a whole, which would have to vote on whatever articles the committee approved, and of the public. The outcome was clear weeks before the committee voted.

IN THE CASE of Clinton's impeachment, though a few Republican committee members suggested that they didn't know how they were going to vote—which guaranteed them television exposure—their claimed "agony" had a false ring. After talking privately and at length with some of them, listening to them describe their angst, it was clear how they were going to vote.

In the Rodino committee, the counsels for the two sides, John Doar for the Democrats and Albert Jenner for the Republicans—worked together and presented the evidence to the committee jointly. Their Hyde committee counterparts—for the Democrats Abbe Lowell, an experienced and combative Washington attorney, for the Republicans David Schippers, an old friend of Hyde's from Chicago—presented the evidence adversarially. Schippers appeared to desire some Clarence Darrow moments, and on occasion went over the top—telling the controversial Starr, for example, "It's an honor to be in the same room with you."

In 1974, the evidence presented to the Rodino committee by Special Prosecutor Leon Jaworski, in what came to be called "the bulging briefcase," remained secret. In 1998 the House Republicans spewed the evidence to the public—Starr's report, the videotape of Clinton's testimony before the grand jury—in the hopes of damaging Clinton, but the tactic backfired, and, when the videotape was shown, people reacted against the hidden-from-view prosecutors.

Rodino strove successfully to build a bipartisan coalition and in the end, as many as seven Republicans supported one of the Articles of Impeachment, and the other two were supported by six and two Republicans respectively. There was a seriousness of purpose and a dignity to their proceedings, as well as a bipartisanship, that legitimized them in the country's eyes.

The Hyde committee failed this test. Dignity, a sense of the occasion, was essentially absent from their deliberations. Some of the Republicans conveyed the sense that they were having a bang-up time in their pursuit of Clinton, like the gleeful horse-borne hunters in the movie *Tom Jones*. (Of course, Clinton had brought it on himself and the stag in the movie hadn't.) This was the party-led vendetta taken to a new level.

THE CHANGES IN our politics during the period between the two impeachment proceedings also accounted for the fact that the substance of the issues raised against Clinton as grounds for impeachment bore no resemblance, in seriousness or proportion, to the grounds for the near-impeachment of Nixon. Before Nixon left office, the House committee voted three Articles of Impeachment. They derived from the Nixon White House's having run a criminal conspiracy—involving a campaign-financed goon squad—right out of the Oval Office. Their activities included the famous break-in at the Democratic National Committee headquarters in the Watergate, but the gravest and most frightening offense was their raiding the office of Daniel Ellsberg's psychiatrist to search for goods to use against Ellsberg for having leaked the Pentagon Papers. This was a direct assault on people's Fourth Amendment right to "to be secure in their persons, houses, papers, and effects, against unreasonable searches and seizures."

Nixon used the most sensitive and potentially intrusive government agencies—the CIA, the FBI, the Internal Revenue Service—to cover up his crimes and to harass his political "enemies." Some "enemies" were wiretapped. Thus, fundamental freedoms and the Constitution itself were at stake, and it was a scary time. (That Clinton's attorneys and allies retained private investigators was cause for unease, but what these people did remained largely unknown by the time Congress completed the impeachment process.)

In the Nixon case, the impeachment process was used as intended, as a means of protecting the country from a President who was a threat to it—not simply as punishment for bad behavior. True "high crimes and misdemeanors" were involved. The charges against Clinton were more serious than his strongest supporters allowed, but they weren't in a league with the ones against Nixon.

In order to buttress his own position, Hyde invited Charles Wiggins, at the time of the Nixon impeachment a Republican congressman from California and the last holdout on the House Judiciary Committee against voting for the articles, and now a federal judge appointed by Ronald Reagan, to testify before his committee. But Hyde couldn't conceal his own shock when Wiggins said that though in the Clinton case he might vote for Articles of Impeachment in committee, he didn't think the House should vote to impeach. "I am presently of the opinion that the misconduct admittedly occurring by the President is not of the gravity to remove him from office," Wiggins said.

In the case of Clinton, the charges grew, of course, out of his having tried to cover up his reckless and pathetic affair with Monica Lewinsky. That his behavior was offensive went without saying. That, as he later admitted, he had been "misleading" to the nation was serious. But to remove him from office would be a radical, country-wrenching event. It was far less clear than in Nixon's case that the charges against Clinton rose to the level of "high crimes and misdemeanors" as the framers of the Constitution seem to have envisioned them.

And the Framers clearly intended that public opinion be taken into account—not dominate, but be taken into account. That's why the impeachment process was placed in the Congress, the people's house, and not in the courts. If a clever, highly popular demagogue committed more serious offenses, at some point the popularity would have to be discounted.

In strict legal terms, whether Clinton actually committed perjury was questionable because much of the case rested on the behavior and word of two people, himself and Monica Lewinsky, with no witnesses. Many prosecutors said they would never have brought such a case. The charges of "obstruction of justice" rested heavily on inferences and circumstantial evidence. In fact, because the House Judiciary Committee Republicans considered the obstruction case the weaker one, and because they worried about appearing to base their Articles of Impeachment only on a sexual relationship, they cast about for other issues and pressed Hyde to call witnesses. "My stomach was knotted at the idea of the Starr Report being only about Monica Lewinsky," a Republican committee member said to me at the time.

Starr's report, arguing for the President's impeachment, undermined his purpose through its near-obsession with the alleged details of Clinton's and Monica Lewinsky's sexual activities. There was, in fact, throughout Clinton's ordeal a pattern of zealots undermining themselves through their own zeal. Starr also refrained from telling the public, before the election, that he had found no evidence of impeachable offenses in the cases of the White House travel office or the FBI files.

For a short while, the Republicans considered including the financing of the 1996 Clinton campaign in the impeachment proceedings, but their interest had been based apparently on a misconception on Schippers's part of what was in Louis Freeh's and

Charles La Bella's reports. Some committee Republicans wanted to call other women Clinton had allegedly been involved with sexually, including one or two who had not yet come to light, to see if there had been a pattern of intimidating them to keep them from talking.

Asa Hutchinson, of Arkansas, concerned that the obstruction-of-justice case wasn't strong enough, was particularly keen to have the committee hear from Monica Lewinsky and Betty Currie, Clinton's secretary, among others. But Hyde resisted witnesses, mainly because, under public and White House pressure to "get it over with," he was determined to conclude the House deliberations by Christmas.

During the course of House debate on impeachment, Hyde said, "We had sixty thousand pages of testimony from the grand jury, from depositions, from statements under oath. That is testimony that we can believe and accept. We chose to believe it and accept it. Why reinterview Betty Currie to take another statement when we already had her statement? Why Monica Lewinsky, when we had had her statement under oath, and with a grant of immunity?" Hyde said in an earlier speech, "We don't need to reinvent the wheel."

So the House Committee—and later the House itself—in an abdication of responsibility, proceeded solely on the evidence of the Starr Report.

The perjury case was a hard one for the members to discuss publicly, having to do as it did with where the President touched Monica Lewinsky and whether he did it "with an intent to arouse or gratify"—arouse or gratify *whom* was not spelled out in the definition of "sexual relations" in the Paula Jones sexual harassment case against him, where this whole thing began. It was the President's word against Lewinsky's, as laid out in Starr's report. So the impeachment of the President went forward in the House with little discussion of what, exactly, he was being impeached for.

THEN-SPEAKER Gingrich was determined to see Clinton impeached. Gingrich brought to the impeachment proceedings the partisan zeal that had characterized his House career. His motivation was part personal revenge against Clinton, who had bested him in their great showdown following the 1994 elections—particularly on the Republican blunder of shutting the government down over a budget fight—part bitterness over his having been reprimanded by the House in 1997 over ethics charges, and fined $300,000, and part the effort to build his party's base. Gingrich pushed Hyde (not that he needed much pushing) and influenced some of the early decisions.

Hyde himself became increasingly offended by the White House tactics against his committee—which he should have expected. But, however irrelevant to the grave question at hand, personal feelings, in particular animus toward Clinton, and over how he handled the inquiry, entered into the impeachment process. Hyde's increasing hostility toward Clinton and intent to see him impeached was described by aides and allies as originating in what he saw as the President's and the White House's insulting treatment of him and the Congress. The Republicans took particular umbrage at Clinton's (or his lawyers') cheekiness in responding to the eighty-one-question questionnaire the Judiciary Committee Republicans had sent him on November 5. (Did they really expect him to admit crimes he had been thus far unwilling to admit? The questionnaire was a deliberate setup, so that Clinton's answers would annoy undecided moderate Republicans.) There was a great deal of talk about how contrite Clinton did or didn't seem—in his serial, embarrassing, and, to many, unconvincing apologies—as if not being sorry enough was an impeachable offense.

THE HOUSE FRESHMEN of 1994, now sophomores, who had done so much to change the temperament in the House, continued to believe that they had a unique insight into the American polity. In party conferences in September and October of 1998, they expressed their conviction that the American people wanted Clinton out, that the polls indicating otherwise were being rigged by the unions, and that the phone calls to their offices in defense of Clinton were phony. Peter King said to me, "There was a lot of hooting and hollering in the Republican Conference. I said to myself, 'I've been here before. This is exactly what it was like just before the government shutdown.'"

The fates of Clinton and of Newt Gingrich were strangely entwined. Paradoxically, Gingrich in 1994 had restored his party to power in the House on a grand ideological platform. But when the question of impeaching Clinton arose, he reverted to his instinctive combativeness and partisanship, and committed the ultimate blunder of turning the 1998 elections into a referendum on the Clinton scandal. At the same time, he and the other Republican leaders provided their party with little in legislative accomplishments or Republican goals to take to the voters. Gingrich was vulnerable also because he had once again lost out to Clinton in the final budget negotiations in the fall of 1998.

The loss of five Republican House seats in the 1998 election, on top of what the conservative ideologues in the House saw as his other failures, led to Gingrich's undoing as Speaker—when he saw what was coming, on November 6, three days after the election, he abruptly announced his resignation from the Speakership and the House. The result, oddly enough, was that the Republican drive for impeachment intensified.

Gingrich was undone from his right—by the same forces, which included a number of members of the class of 1994, that had almost deposed him as Speaker in the rebellion of July 1997. These were the same forces that felt most strongly that Clinton should be impeached.

In the upheaval that followed the 1998 elections, only Majority Leader Dick Armey, who had led in making donations to the Republican House members' campaigns, and Tom DeLay, who since 1994 had been the party enforcer, the one who held the whip organization in his hands, who had worked to refashion K Street in the Republican image, and who also donated generously to House candidates, held on to their posts. Such was DeLay's power that he was the only House Republican leader who wasn't even challenged.

So DeLay took over. He lent his whip organization to install Bob Livingston, the Appropriations Committee chairman, to help him become Gingrich's successor. And, contrary to many published reports—and his own display of grief on the House floor—DeLay withdrew his support when Livingston, about to be exposed in Larry Flynt's *Hustler* magazine as having had several affairs in recent years, owned up to the Republican Conference, on the eve of the House's voting on the Articles of Impeachment. Like Gingrich's, Livingston's resignation was pictured by some as a noble act, but, like Gingrich, Livingston had no choice. Other members told him that he had to go.* (And later it was DeLay who pushed

---

*Inevitably, after Livingston left Congress, he opened his own lobbying firm in Washington.

for the installation as Speaker of Dennis Hastert, his own deputy whip, whose office was next to his.)

DeLay readily stepped into the leadership vacuum on impeachment. Livingston, not yet officially Speaker, was loath to make the impeachment question his first official business, and Gingrich was busy lining up corporate board memberships and speaking fees ($50,000 a speech) for his postcongressional life and didn't want impeachment to be his last official business. This left DeLay, who had the will and the tools to enforce discipline, in charge.

The first thing DeLay did was major, and of historical importance. He announced publicly and firmly on Sunday, December 6, on *Fox News Sunday,* that he wouldn't permit a vote by the House to censure Clinton rather than impeach him. This put the squeeze on the Republican members, most of them moderates, who were leaning against impeachment but didn't feel they could vote against it without also voting to condemn in some form Clinton's actions.

And the Republican base applied pressure as well: Right-wing talk-show hosts ginned up their listeners to lean on uncertain House Republicans—and angry calls flowed into those members' offices. Michael Forbes, a sophomore from New York who in 1996 was the first House Republican to call for Gingrich's ouster as Speaker, and who strongly opposed impeachment, was warned privately by Livingston, who had become his patron, that he couldn't vote against impeachment.

Even a few *conservative* Republicans who were considering voting against impeachment were told by their county chairmen that they might face a primary opponent, and received threats from Christian Right groups in their district that their personal lives might be exposed. What came to be called "the politics of personal destruction" was being waged on both sides.

Mark Souder, a second-term congressman from Indiana and a true social conservative, had done daily commentary on a Christian radio program, had been involved in the coup attempt against Gingrich, and was one of the original group that had signed Bob Barr's impeachment motion. But he had serious questions about whether what Clinton was now being charged with constituted impeachable offenses.

"I'm a big history buff," Souder told me later. "I'd read about Clay and Webster and presidents since I was a kid. While I found Clinton's behavior abhorrent, I questioned whether they constituted impeachable offenses."

After Starr's report was made public in September, Souder said publicly that Clinton's behavior was horrible and he should resign, but that he didn't think his actions were impeachable offenses. After the 1998 election, Souder was quoted in the *New York Times* as saying, "It's important to send a signal to Chairman Hyde and the Republican leadership, they don't have the votes. The public doesn't want impeachment, but our base can't stomach his behavior. So it puts Republicans in a very difficult position."

Souder told me, "That went back to the district." He added that radio talk-show host and sometime presidential candidate Alan Keyes "attacked me." (Keyes also attacked Peter King.) Christian Right groups in the district went after Souder. He was visited with threats that he would face a primary opponent in the next election.

PETER KING argued that a true conservative position would be to oppose the impeachment of Clinton on the existing grounds, as Charles Wiggins did. King, more conservative than the moderates—he had a ninety-three percent positive rating from the Christian Coalition—argued that conservatives, after all, believe in traditions and institutions and a strong presidency. This had been a guiding principle for many of them during the Nixon impeachment proceedings.

But more than two decades later, many conservative Republicans saw things differently, or thought they did. They had opposed the Independent Counsel law but apparently weren't perturbed by Kenneth Starr's prosecutorial overreach. And Republicans who had never been strong supporters of the sexual harassment law, in expressing their indignation at Clinton's attempts to evade the truth in and perhaps obstruct the Paula Jones case, spoke of his trying to deny Jones's "rights in a civil rights case." (Jones's grounds in bringing a suit for sexual harassment, three years after Clinton apparently made a lewd approach to her in a Little Rock Hotel room, were held without basis by a federal judge who dismissed the case in April 1998.)

THE FORCES behind impeaching Clinton were unstoppable. And so, on Friday, December 11, and the following day, the House Judiciary Committee voted on the proposed articles, and approved four. The first charged Clinton with perjury before the grand jury; the second with perjury in the Paula Jones case; the third with obstruction of justice; and the fourth with abuse of power for having answered impertinently the questionnaire. The articles drafted by the House Committee went further than those against Nixon: They called not only for Clinton's impeachment, trial, and removal from office, but also barred him from holding any federal office in the future. This last sanction, provided in the Constitution, had never been involved before.

No Democrats voted for any of the articles. The committee Democrats decided not to offer amendments to "improve" the Republican-drafted articles so as to make them more palatable to Members of the House. In the "consideration" of the articles the Democrats needled the Republicans about the vagueness of the charge of perjury in Clinton's grand jury testimony, knowing that the Republicans didn't want to get into such detail as where the President allegedly touched Monica Lewinsky and for what purpose. Barney Frank, the sharpest of the Democratic needles, said "The majority doesn't want to talk about the specifics, 'Did the President touch her here or not touch her here,'" because the American people wouldn't accept the impeachment of the President on those specific grounds.

When Asa Hutchinson heatedly listed the grounds for the article charging perjury before the grand jury, he included some that hadn't been contained in the Starr report. Taking note of this, Frank called the proceeding "a shell game—under which pea is the impeachment?"

WHAT HAPPENED NEXT in the whole House signified the loss of numbers and of strength of the center. (Its strength on campaign finance reform was an exception, wrought by the usually underestimated strength of its constituency.) As the voting on impeachment approached, as many as forty votes—mostly of moderate Republicans—were believed to be up for grabs. But the moderates turned out to be a wobbly group. Before the House was to vote, King was prepared to come out for a censure proposal, and he was told by one moderate that about a dozen others were ready to join him. But when King was about to announce this to the press, he found himself alone. King went ahead anyway.

Christopher Shays, who had stood up to the Republican leaders on campaign finance reform, had taken the position even before the election that the President's transgressions didn't amount to impeachable offenses. Under great pressure, and, toward the end, with most of his moderate colleagues going over to the side of impeachment, Shays wobbled slightly.

On Thursday night, December 17, two days before the House was to vote, Shays told a well-attended, evening town meeting in Norwalk, Connecticut, that he had planned to vote against impeachment, but that now he was "totally reexamining my position." On Friday morning, at DeLay's urging, Shays, like numerous other Republicans, went to the Ford House Office Building, on Capitol Hill, where the documents relating to the question of impeachment were held, to view some secret evidence. The main feature of that evidence was the deposition (in the Paula Jones case) of "Jane Doe No. 5," which stated that Clinton, while the Attorney General of Arkansas, had sexually assaulted her. (The story hadn't been satisfactorily corroborated.)*

Shays felt, he told me later, that "it was a very ugly story," which made him consider voting for the pending article, charging Clinton with obstruction of justice. Shays didn't think that Clinton had committed perjury. And then he started wondering how this new story amounted to obstruction. Still, Shays told me later, "I was almost looking for a reason to vote for impeachment."

On Friday, Shays, at his own request, had a meeting with Clinton. "Mr. President," Shays told him, "my constituents want you impeached. And, Mr. President, my constituents don't want you impeached." Shays, who had decided not to ask the President questions about the case since he didn't think he could believe the answers, offered Clinton some suggestions about what to say and do to help him out of his difficulty.

"I don't feel that I had much impact," Shays remarked to me later.

The strength of DeLay and his outside allies was on display in the days leading up to the vote, as, one by one, Republican moderates announced their position for impeachment, giving as the reason the poll-tested mantra, that the President had "lied under oath."

---

*In late February, 1999, Jane Doe No. 5, Juanita Broaddrick, went public, and gave a long interview to NBC and other news outlets. Her story, in which she claimed the Clinton had raped her, was neither provable nor disprovable. But Clinton's denial, made through his attorney David Kendall, didn't convince a great many people that something along the lines of Broaddrick's story didn't happen. It had come to that.

UNTIL THIS tormenting dribbling out of Republican moderates, who said they would vote for impeachment, the White House had believed that enough of them would vote against impeachment that the President would escape the humiliation of being the second president in American history to have been impeached by the House. It had been confident from the time of the November congressional election, in which the Republicans lost five House seats, that there weren't enough votes to impeach the President. For that reason, it had urged that the proceedings move expeditiously, that the House "get it over with."

So, after about the first week of December, when the White House began to realize that the votes weren't going their way, it started to consider means of calling for a delay, but decided that it couldn't get away with that tactic politically. Yet it had a very strong ground for doing so: the President was being impeached by a lame-duck Congress. But now, having urged swift-conclusion to the impeachment proceedings, it was too late to make such a case. Such a move would have been seen as a brazen turnabout, and it could have involved lengthy court proceedings. (Later, Senate Democrats told the White House not to pursue the lame-duck issue, arguing that they had the votes to block Clinton's being thrown out of office, so don't drag things out.) As a result, a very important constitutional issue, or at least one of principle, was left unaddressed.

In the voting on Saturday, December 19, the House's rejection of two of the four Articles of Impeachment that the Judiciary Committee had approved—on perjury in Clinton's deposition in the Paula Jones case, and his handling of the questionnaire sent by the Judiciary Committee Republicans—suggested that even the House Republicans had some sense of the egregious. Besides, Lindsey Graham, the second-term South Carolinian who had made himself instantly interesting ("Is this Watergate or Peyton Place?") and had perfect Christian Right credentials, had let his colleagues off the hook by opposing Article II, charging the President with perjury in the Paula Jones case. Graham's reasoning was that the Jones case had been dismissed. Article IV, based on the President's impertinence on the questionnaire, was defeated by a nearly two-to-one vote.

The result of the House voting was a mishmash of weakly grounded and vague charges of perjury by the President in his grand jury appearance on August 17, which looped back to include his Paula Jones deposition. But the perjury charge was weakened by the House's rejection of the article on perjury in the Jones case. The other remaining article charged Clinton with obstruction of justice, most of which involved the Paula Jones case.

Only five Republicans (Christopher Shays, Peter King, and Mark Souder among them) voted against Article I, covering perjury; the margin on Article III, covering obstruction of justice, which passed by nine votes (with Shays and Souder voting for it) indicated that it might not have passed if the new Congress, just-elected in November, had been handling this momentous matter rather than the lame-duck Congress—which included Republicans who had been defeated at least in part over the pursuit of the President. Five Democrats voted for each of three Articles of Impeachment, and only one—the highly conservative Gene Taylor of Mississippi—voted for the article involving the questionnaire.

Only two Republicans were willing to support an appeal of the ruling of the chair that a censure motion was out of order. (The parliamentarian is highly influenced by whoever controls the House, and for a member of that party to appeal such a ruling is considered highly disloyal.) "I think a lot of them just lost their nerve," Peter King said later.

Within two days after the House vote, four moderates who had voted for impeachment wrote to Senate Majority Leader Lott urging censure. This wasn't exactly a portrait of courage.

To ensure their success, the leaders of the House impeachment drive told wavering colleagues that a vote for impeachment should be considered just a censure vote (though impeachment is impeachment)—that there was no chance the Senate would vote to convict Clinton, which would require a two-thirds vote. Hyde staved off talk of any deals before the House voted by stating that such a thing could take place after the Articles of Impeachment reached the Senate.

Impeachment of a president was treated as if it were a highway bill, or any other legislation that the House passes in the expectation that the Senate will fix it, or simply bury it.

Hyde told the House, "We suggest that censuring the President is not a function permitted in this chamber. Maybe across the rotunda, where the sanctions of an impeached person are imposed, that is another situation." (But Hyde was to change his mind.)

DURING THE HOUSE debate Hyde said, "The rule of law stands in the line of fire today." And as was his wont, seeking to inflate the importance of the moment, he reeled off a long list of historical allusions: the Magna Carta, the Constitutional Convention, Bunker Hill, the Civil War, and more.

Charles Schumer, Democrat of New York, who had just been elected to the Senate, summed up much of what had brought the House of Representatives and the country "to this day." He said, "What began twenty-five years ago with Watergate as a solemn and necessary process to force a president to adhere to the rule of law has grown beyond our control, so that now we are routinely using criminal accusations and scandal to win the political battles and ideological differences we cannot settle at the ballot box.

"It has been used with reckless abandon by both Parties....We cannot disagree, it seems. We cannot forcefully advocate for our positions without trying to criminalize or at least dishonor our adversaries over matters having nothing to do with public trust. It is hurting our country. And it is marginalizing and polarizing this Congress."

THE ANGRY House debate—replete with catcalls and hooting—and the partisan voting on a gloomy, cloudy, Saturday afternoon made for a profoundly sad day in Washington, and shook the country. The changes in our political life coupled with Clinton's inexcusable behavior, his putting his own interests above everyone else's, even the country's, had caught up with us. There was nothing in this whole business to feel good about.

But, given the Republicans' behavior and the buoyancy of the economy, and even, outwardly at least, of Clinton himself after the House acted, Clinton's rating went up—to an all-time high of 73 percent—and the Republican Party's sank to the low thirties—its lowest level ever.

14

———■———

Across the Marble Corridor

What next happened in the Senate also reflected the changes in our politics in the past twenty-five years and the forces that had been eroding that institution as well.

Over the Christmas break, Trent Lott, sensing danger for his party in the Senate's spending too much time on a trial of the President on the charges that had come over from the House, floated a plan that would dispense with the matter quickly. Lott's concerns were justified. The 1998 election hadn't gone at all well for the Republicans, in part because they had made the sex scandal an issue, and now the party was taking a beating in the polls over the House Republicans' behavior in adopting two Articles of Impeachment.

The plan, offered by Democrat Joseph Lieberman and Republican Slade Gorton, who was very close to Lott, proposed that the Senate, after briefly hearing the charges and the evidence, vote on whether, if the charges were true, the President should be removed from office. This was, after all, the ultimate question. Removal, which would require sixty-seven votes, was highly unlikely, the sponsors thought, so why have a long trial? By this shortcut, it could all be over in as little as three days, or at the outside two weeks.

Some of the Senate's most influential Republicans shared Lott's eagerness to get rid of the matter as quickly as possible. Mitch McConnell, whose job it was as head of the National Republican Senatorial Committee to keep the Senate in Republican hands, publicly backed Lott's plan, along with Gorton and Ted Stevens, of Alaska, the chairman of the Senate Appropriations Committee, a conservative who was highly influential among the Senate Republicans These were pragmatic people.

What Lott wanted above all else was that the Senate not look like the House.

But when the Senate returned to Washington in early January, Lott found, as he had before on other matters, that he couldn't control the centrifugal forces pulling within the Senate Republican Conference. Once again, Lott's job was being made difficult by the loss of the center in the Senate in the past few years. His Senate party had been pulled to the right, and former House members who had come to the Senate were more loath to compromise. So now Lott was under tremendous cross-pressures, and dealing with an issue with large consequences for his party.

STANDING IN THE WAY of Lott's speed-up plan were about twenty conservative Republicans who wanted to inflict as much punishment as possible on Clinton through a long proceeding, and even some less ideological people who felt that the Senate shouldn't simply dismiss the whole thing without the semblance of a serious inquiry. This last group included Fred Thompson and Susan Collins.

The very fact that the House's action was widely seen as lacking legitimacy led some Republicans to believe that they had a duty to straighten matters out for history.

FRED THOMPSON was sitting at home in Nashville over Christmas when he heard about Lott's plan. As he thought about it, Thompson became concerned that the process was being too abruptly short-circuited. He called Howard Baker, his sponsor during Watergate and still a mentor.

Baker told Thompson, "Fall back on the regular order. We have rules on impeachment. They've been there a long time."

"My own thinking evolved during that time," Thompson told me later. "I had time to think it through."

He said, "We could take care of short-term concerns and invite long-term problems. I'm concerned that one hundred years from now we'll have all kinds of theories—people saying that we should have looked at this or that." He also felt that if Clinton wasn't convicted (as just about everyone expected), convincing the Party base that the Senate had looked at the matter carefully was "a legitimate concern."

LOTT ENCOUNTERED particularly strong resistance from conservative senators highly respectful of the Republican right: preeminently Phil Gramm, of Texas; but also Mike DeWine, of Ohio; John Kyl, of Arizona; and Larry Craig, of Idaho.

Rick Santorum, the busybody freshman senator who, as we saw earlier, had imposed himself as an ideological enforcer among the Senate Republicans, had already interjected himself into the impeachment process. When, in mid-September of 1998, conservative Republican Senator Orrin Hatch, of Utah, the chairman of the Senate Judiciary Committee, floated the idea of a deal to circumvent impeachment with a censure of the President, Santorum suggested in Republican Senate meetings that Hatch should be stripped of his chairmanship. (This echoed Santorum's attempt to strip Mark Hatfield of his chairmanship.)

Now that the House had impeached Clinton, Santorum took the position in meetings of the Senate Republican Conference that the House managers of the trial in the Senate should be granted whatever they wished. But in his public appearances Santorum appeared thoughtful and uncertain about how he should vote; he was up for re-election in 2000 and his home state of Pennsylvania was by no means safely Republican. (In all, thirteen Republicans up for re-election in 2000 were from states that Clinton had carried in 1996, which put them in an awkward position. Six other Republicans were up for re-election.)

Though the Republican Party's base didn't have the same force in the Senate as it did in the House, more diffused as it was within a given state than in a congressional district, it still wielded great influence. A Republican senator told me, "The effect of the right is more on each individual Senator than on the Senate itself. It's a state-by-state matter."

WHAT VIRTUALLY no one, in or out of the Senate, had anticipated— but in retrospect should have—was that the forces behind the impeachment drive in the House, literally (in the form of Henry Hyde and the committee impeachment enthusiasts he had appointed to manage the case in the Senate) and figuratively (in the form of donors, the Christian Right, and other components of the Republican base) would betake themselves across the marble corridor of the Capitol and try to impose their will on the Senate.

"The Senate was in denial," a leading Republican strategist said later. "With the outcome of the election, there was an immediate and compelling understanding that impeachment was dead. The original reaction of the Senate to the fact they'd have to deal with impeachment was that they were totally shell-shocked. So they weren't as prepared as they should have been."

Suddenly, House Republicans were no longer saying it was now all up to the Senators and were no longer shrugging at, much less promoting, the idea that the Senate could bury impeachment through a deal. After meeting with Lott, Henry Hyde wrote him a stinging three-page letter protesting Lott's proposed shortcut, and he and his colleagues demanded that they be permitted to have a full-blown Senate trial, with witnesses. The House Republicans argued that if Clinton weren't removed from office no future President could be removed—which was of course ridiculous, but by now the ridiculous had become commonplace.

"They just want to vindicate themselves," a leading, and upset, conservative Republican said of Hyde and the other committee Republicans. He could scarcely believe that the Senate would actually proceed with a trial, or that the House Republicans were pushing for one. But, he said, "They feel they've been vilified, and when you talk to them about the polls they say, 'That's already happened.' They're almost fatalistic about it."

The renegade New York Republican Peter King gave me a slightly different assessment of what was propelling the House Republican managers. He said, "They're going to push as hard as they can. They want him out of there—that's what it is."

The House Republicans' effrontery in demanding a full trial wasn't appreciated by many of their Senate counterparts, but many also felt that they couldn't just brush them away. And the base was demanding that they not do so.

The most agitating question before the Senate was whether the House Republicans, the "managers" of the case before the Senate, should be allowed to call witnesses, as they were demanding. Their unstated reason for wanting to call witnesses was that they might turn up new evidence that would damage Clinton. The House Republicans wanted to bring into the Senate deliberations other women who hadn't been considered relevant to the House proceedings; Washington was filled with rumors about other "Jane Does." The House Republicans also wanted to be able to call witnesses who might strengthen the obstruction-of-justice charge—as some had wanted to do in the course of the House Judiciary considerations.

Out of fear that if they couldn't agree on how to proceed they might resemble the raucous and partisan House, Senate Democrats and Republicans, meeting on Friday, January 8—in the Old Senate Chamber where Mike Mansfield had addressed them almost eleven months before—reached a unanimous but fragile compromise on how to proceed. But they were able to accomplish this only by putting off the more difficult questions, such as whether to allow the House managers to call witnesses. After the meeting there was much self-congratulating all around, but the Republicans remained divided among themselves over the question of witnesses, and Republicans and Democrats had differing views about where to go from there.

THE REPETITIOUS presentation of the case to the Senate by the House managers, beginning on January 14 and lasting three days, bespoke the lack of discipline and the zealotry that had lain behind the House's action, and it also exposed Hyde's weakness. Rather than present a tight, focused case to the Senate, Hyde allowed thirteen Republican members of his committee (of twenty-one) to have their big moment. They threaded their presentations with arguments for calling witnesses—by making the contradictory arguments that they were presenting a clear-cut case against Clinton but needed witnesses to show that. They had shown scant reluctance to impeach the President without having called witnesses. But, maybe, somehow, a witness would change the equation in the Senate.

Despite the repetition and the more than occasional insult to their intelligence, to many senators' surprise, in totality, the House managers appeared to make an effective case. The repetition may even have helped. Given the highly negative reviews of the House impeachment proceedings, the senators, who hadn't paid close attention to the matter until now, had expected to behold a bunch of mean-spirited yahoos who didn't remotely have a case. But on the first day, Thursday, January 14, 1999, the sharp-featured and bright-eyed Asa Hutchinson, a former U.S. attorney in Arkansas, skillfully presented a seemingly strong case that Clinton had obstructed justice.

That same day, James Rogan, a former California municipal judge and deputy district attorney, his face pale and elongated, giving him a somewhat funereal aspect, attempted to make an extensive case that the President had committed perjury. But, Rogan actually undermined his argument by adding many alleged examples of perjury to the charges that Starr had mentioned in his report and to the ones that had been mentioned during the House deliberations, as well as the examples the House had cited in its trial brief submitted to the Senate, sometimes stretching to do so.

By the end of the first week of the Senate trial, the obstruction-of-justice charge was now widely considered the stronger one, and not just by Republicans. It had been considered the weaker one by the House, and was adopted by a much closer vote than the perjury charge. And the view was widely held—not just among Republicans—that obstruction of justice was far a more serious offense than perjury. Some Senate Democrats, White House aides, and allies of the President were shaken.

"I was surprised by their case," a Democratic senator whose vote was considered uncertain told me. "People thought they would come over and disgrace themselves. I think they made a very strong case."

A White House aide told me, "Some Democrats are a little concerned about the fact pattern, but they don't want to get bogged down in the fact pattern, because the facts aren't particularly good."

On the weekend that the House managers concluded their case, a close ally of the White House told me, "Democrats and the White House think they've been hurt. The House members, repetitions and all, showed that there's a case there." Safety, the White House was advised—if it needed such advice—lay in taking on the Republicans on "partisanship."

The White House ally said, "It's risky for us, but it's riskier for them. It makes them nervous."

IN THE COURSE of three days of presentations on Tuesday through Thursday of the following week, the President's attorneys poked holes, some of them large, in the House managers' case, particularly Hutchinson's—which was now the most important one to try to take apart. Relying on information supplied by David Schippers, the Hyde committee's majority counsel, Hutchinson had misplaced the time of a judge's order that Lewinsky should be a witness in the Paula Jones case, on which rested an important piece of the Republicans' charge that the President, through his friend Vernon Jordan, had tried to help Lewinsky get a job in exchange for her silence.

On Tuesday, January 19, Charles Ruff, the White House counsel, wheelchair bound (the result of an illness contracted while serving in the Peace Corps in Africa), with a gravel voice and a fierce ability to focus on the opposition's weak points, opened by demolishing Hutchinson's account of the relationship of the judge's order to other events. Ruff, using a pointer and the same chart that Hutchinson had used, showed that by the time, in the early evening, that the judge issued her order, Jordan was on a plane to Amsterdam.

But the President's attorneys didn't totally demolish the managers' case.

The main concern of some senators, on both sides, who weren't sure where they would come out, was over Clinton's alleged "coaching," through his assertions and questions to his secretary Betty Currie on the day after he gave his deposition in the Paula Jones case on January 17, 1998. ("Monica came on to me, and I never touched her, right?") Clinton had been surprised by the amount of information Paula Jones's attorneys had about his liaison with Monica Lewinsky—provided by the treacherous Linda Tripp in whom Lewinsky had made the mistake of confiding. (Tripp was also feeding the information to the Independent Counsel's office.) Clinton had suggested to the Jones lawyers at least six times that they ask Currie about something they had asked him. ("Betty will know"; "Betty should know.") This fueled suspicions that Clinton was setting up a witness and then coaching her.

The President's lawyers argued that Clinton couldn't have been engaged in witness tampering—a serious charge—as the House managers argued, because at the time Currie hadn't been called before the Jones inquiry, and never was. But the House managers brought out that Currie was in fact subpoenaed later on for the Jones case. (She didn't appear because Kenneth Starr asked that that process stop because now he himself was investigating the Lewinsky matter.)

The House managers also brought out for the first time that Clinton had actually gone through his assertions/questions exercise with Currie a second time, by which time Clinton had to know that Kenneth Starr had entered into the Monica Lewinsky case, and was likely to call Currie. The President's counsels' argument that these sessions were simply to prepare him for press inquiries wasn't entirely convincing.

Some senators, such as the moderate Republican Susan Collins, were also concerned about how gifts given by Clinton to Lewinsky ended up under Betty Currie's bed, and could imagine no sequence of events that didn't have the President suggesting to Currie that she retrieve them from Lewinsky. (Lewinsky had testified that Currie had called her and said, "I understand that you have something for me.") But this had to remain an inference.

On the other hand, Collins, among others, felt that the case that Clinton had committed perjury before the grand jury hadn't been made convincingly—and that White House attorney Gregory Craig was convincing in his argument before the Senate that the legal test for perjury hadn't been met by the House managers. Besides, the perjury charges were about sex—a subject most senators preferred to avoid. But while Collins was concerned about the obstruction of justice possibilities, she wasn't sure that, even if she became convinced that the President was guilty, he should be removed from office.

AT THE END of the President's defense, coming as it did on top of his politically successful State of the Union speech on Tuesday night, January 19, Trent Lott was bent once again on ending the Senate proceedings as quickly as possible. The weekend of January 23–24 produced a flurry of negotiations, rumors, and a growing sense that the trial would be over in a week. On the Sunday talk shows, enough Republicans said that they didn't favor hearing witnesses, that the White House was encouraged in the thought that the votes for witnesses weren't there. And so was Lott.

But Lott continued to find it harder to get out of the quagmire than he had expected, and there was near panic among the Republicans. A Democratic senator, watching Lott's difficulty in pulling his troops into any kind of formation, said, "I never thought I'd feel sorry for Trent Lott."

The House managers' desperate move over that weekend of calling on a willing Kenneth Starr to seek a court order to compel Monica Lewinsky to meet with some of them—which occurred at the Mayflower Hotel on Sunday—was a political blunder. (It was also another intervention of the Independent Counsel in the impeachment process.) It was an affront to even Republican senators since it violated the unanimous if tenuous understanding all one hundred senators had reached two weeks before. But it didn't help Lott and his allies end the trial. "It didn't backfire enough," said an ally of and advisor to the White House.

A Republican senator said to me then, "Right now it's 'Who gets blamed for the failure to convict Clinton?' Nobody wants to bell that cat. It's 'Why me, Lord?' A lot of us are keeping quiet. You've got a lot of people not saying a word."

LOTT'S EAGERNESS to get rid of the trial had to do with his own preoccupation with polls. On January 12, Linda DiVall, a respected Republican pollster, addressed the Senate Republican Conference. Her message was a grim one. Her postelection survey said that the number of people who turned out in November 1998 who called themselves moderates had increased by fifty percent, and that the Republicans lost that vote fifty-five percent to forty-five percent. Voters who listed their highest concerns as education, health care, the economy, and Social Security, voted Democratic in overwhelming numbers, DiVall said. Republicans ran ahead only on the subject of taxes and in the category of morals and ethics. If the Republicans were going to succeed they had to develop an agenda that met people's concerns.

"Make no mistake," DiVall warned the Republican senators, "impeachment politics are driving down the perceptions of the Party."

A Senate Republican said, "From the beginning, Trent's shown the greatest interest in getting it over. Though he was consistent in wanting to end the trial, he jumped from idea to idea about tactics, some of them not conducive to ending the trial."

Another Republican senator, referring to Clinton's former strategist, said, "It's the Dick Morris syndrome. Trent's just like Clinton in adhering to the polls on a daily basis." (Morris was in frequent contact with Lott, another former client, during the Senate trial.)

In one meeting of the Republicans, Lott said that the polls showed that people wanted to hear what the President would say as a witness, "So let's call him."

A Republican senator said of Lott, "It's about his place in public esteem, and he's also interested in the Party and the Senate. If he could get a majority of the Senate to write a letter to the President asking him to testify he'd do it. It might be the lead story, and he finds people wanting to know what the President will say."

On January 25, 1999, Lott and nine other Republican senators sent a letter to the President containing ten questions, some of them rudely put. Most Republican senators didn't see the questions before they were sent to the White House. The White House declined to respond.

Despite his desire to end the trial, a Republican senator said, "Trent wants to be able to throw the House members a bone. He was one of them once. And the letter to the President was for the right-wing zealots in the Senate. But he also wants to make an impression as a fair-minded majority leader."

Lott also had his own home-state political exigencies. Mississippi was sharply split on the impeachment question, and Lott was up for reelection in 2000. Jesse Jackson had turned up in Mississippi to help blacks register to vote. A colleague said, "It's a hot potato for Trent that he would like very much to drop. It elevates the risk for him."

LOTT HAD BEEN taken aback by the 1998 election result of zero Republican gains in the Senate, leaving the party ratio at 55–45. He and McConnell had hoped to garner sixty Republican seats, giving them near-absolute control since they would have enough votes to shut off a filibuster.

Following the election, there was in fact a move among some Senate Republicans to replace McConnell: the Senate Republican candidates had also run without a message, and as head of the campaign committee McConnell had made some ill-considered decisions about the allocation of funds, some of them out of pique over campaign finance reform. McConnell virtually denied funds to Linda Smith, a House Republican from Washington State who was running for the Senate and who had annoyed the party establishment by strongly advocating campaign finance reform, until it was too late: And at that McConnell gave Smith about a fifth of what she was eligible to receive. Smith lost.

And McConnell poured money into Wisconsin in an effort to defeat Russell Feingold, a leading backer of campaign finance reform. Feingold set a limit on his own spending and also rejected party "issue ads" on his behalf. (Outside groups—the AFL-CIO, environmental groups—did air ads attacking his opponents.) McConnell thought Feingold could be defeated. Feingold won.

Despite these errors in judgment, McConnell, who was in a position to grant and withhold campaign money, wasn't toppled.

THE SENATE TRIAL broke open long-standing tensions between the House and the Senate. A Senator who had served in the House told me, "House members think that senators are pompous people who are always getting themselves on television. They think, 'We do all the work. We know the issues and they don't.'" An individual House member has more time to focus in on a specific issue, while a senator has to deal with several of them concurrently.

And House members feel keenly, and not without reason, that senators look down on them.

That House members were now trying to tell the senators what to do, insisting that there had to be a full trial, that there had to be witnesses. Some of the House managers talked down to the senators (or so the senators thought), which led to nearly open hostilities. A Republican senator described the atmosphere at the time: "They're telling us 'You've got to handle it like we want you to or we'll trash you.' No one has actually said it, but it's the underlying threat."

The view of the House managers about their treatment by the Senate was given bitter expression by Hyde in the course of the argument over whether witnesses should be called.

Standing at a lectern in the well of the Senate, Hyde said, "I sort of feel that we have fallen short in the respect side because of the fact that we represent the House, the other body, kind of blue-collar people." He also played on class resentments by referring snidely to the "parade of professors" that the administration had sent to testify before his committee during an afternoon session on standards of impeachment. Hyde went on, "You know what an intellectual is? It is someone who is educated beyond their intelligence."

At another point, Hyde told the Senate, "I know. Oh, I know what a nuisance we are in the bosom of this body, but we are a *constitutional* nuisance." Hyde and his colleagues were preparing the way for a schism in the Republican Party that was quite likely to outlast the proceedings against Clinton, and reinforce the intensity of the right.

In the two days of questioning of the House managers by senators and the lawyers for the White House that followed the prepared presentations, Democrats and Republicans asked questions that would help their particular side, thus underlining the partisanship just beneath the surface of the dignified, even solemn, Senate proceedings. And the House managers, in their intensity about pushing their case as far as possible, started to come across as obsessed, even crazed.

The Democratic senator whose votes on the articles were thought to be in question, and who had been impressed by the House managers' case about obstruction of justice, said to me, as the House managers' presentation went on, "They're fanatics. And Hyde is the biggest fanatic of all."

And as some Republicans senators saw it, the House managers were receiving a stupendous and otherwise unobtainable amount of publicity and were loath to quit the field. A Republican senator said, during the third week of the trial, as the argument over whether to have witnesses went on, "They're still on stage while the trial goes on, and when it's over they're gone. They probably don't understand that themselves. This is quite a big thing for them."

Another Republican senator said of the House managers, "If they don't come up with anything, they've got safe districts back home, but if they keep on and on and on it's just going to make it worse for the rest of the party." (James Rogan, who argued the perjury case before the Senate, would be an exception to the safe-district point, having won his House seat from California by less than fifty-one percent in the last two elections.)

The Republican senator continued, "The House guys have a pretty narrow view of their role, and we have a broader view."

FOR HISTORY'S SAKE, if not for the convenience of the senators, there was, in fact, a valid argument for letting the trial go on for a while. It wasn't worth having a substantial segment of the population thinking, and saying intensely, that the trial of the President had been hijacked, that the House members hadn't been given a chance to make their case. It wasn't worth unloosing "grassy knoll" theories, which are still with us from the Kennedy assassination. Most Clinton-haters would never be satisfied unless he was driven from office. But there was a point to giving the House managers enough of a chance to make their case that it would not appear then or in the future that the Senate had put in the fix for its own convenience and out of panic over polls. As for the widespread complaints that the whole Lewinsky business was taking too long, people said they were "tired" of Watergate, too, and that process took more than two years. But the real problem was that the House managers could not be satisfied.

IN ANY EVENT, the impeachment and trial of President Clinton wasn't about legal arguments scored or challenged, or about the individual facts. It wasn't about crime. It was about punishment. It was about whether, even if Clinton had done everything he was being charged with doing, he should be removed from office. Whether or not he had technically committed perjury, and whether he had technically obstructed justice, it still got down to the magnitude of the offenses, and their context, and whether or not, as former Senator Dale Bumpers put it in his speech closing the President's defense on Thursday, January 21, "proportionality" was being observed.

Bumpers reluctantly made the speech at Clinton's urging; the two men weren't close. Clinton had almost made a run against Bumpers while he was in the Senate; Bumpers felt that he wouldn't have made many of the compromises Clinton had, and he was bothered by Clinton's character. (Bumpers himself had once seriously considered a run for the presidency.) But larger things were at stake here. Bumpers felt that the Constitution was being abused. He was disturbed by the number of Arkansans whose lives had been ruined by all the investigations. His speech, emotional, indignant, ringing, folksy, was a reminder of the rhetorical talents now gone from the Senate. But it didn't appear to convince anyone undecided about Clinton's fate.

CLINTON HAD DONE many sly things to hide his carryings-on with Monica Lewinsky, and he tried to stay this side of the legal line. He seemed quite cognizant of where the line was. To assess what happened, one had to back away from the details and see the whole, and visit common sense. Common sense said that Clinton did whatever he could to cover up the so-called affair and that in essence, if not technically, he had crossed the line. He asked for too many suspensions of disbelief.

For seven months, until he was trapped by a semen-stained dress, he lied, misled, put other people in legal jeopardy and cost them steep legal bills, trashed people who were inconvenient, and sought court protections that ended up weakening the presidency. Secret Service agents may have to testify about what they've seen while covering the President; the President can't talk with aides and friends with confidence they won't be subpoenaed; a president's communications with White House lawyers aren't privileged. Some of these changes were also the handiwork of the prosecutor, Kenneth Starr.

This was a disturbing picture. The zealousness of the House managers didn't cancel out Clinton's deeds. Many uncommitted people, and even some of those who defended him publicly, thought that whatever the details and tortured explanations, Clinton was guilty in the overall sense, but that ejecting him from office was a disproportionate response. This created a state of ambiguity, and, politically, ambiguity is hard to deal with. In this sense, Nixon's case was much easier.

One idea some senators toyed with for dealing with the ambiguity, and finding political safety, was to separate the question of whether the President was guilty (which would only require a majority vote) from that of whether he should be removed from office (which would require a two-thirds majority). This separation of the two questions had been done in only one instance, the impeachment of a judge, early in our history. The idea of dividing the vote on each of the articles against Clinton was first pushed by pro-impeachment forces while the trial was under way. Lindsey Graham, the baby-faced, soft-spoken South Carolinian who always tried to sound reasonable as he tried to push the President out of office, floated the suggestion just after he had made his low-keyed, folksy, and cleverly framed argument to the Senate that Clinton's deeds called for his removal from office.

But the idea, which also could give the House managers partial vindication, was mischievous and a trap. Senators who chose this route were setting themselves up for the charge that they had allowed a convicted felon to remain in office. It had the potential of setting off a civil war within the Republican Party. And the idea was constitutionally questionable.

After some debate among the Republicans, the thought of separate votes to convict and to remove was reduced to one by which there would be a "finding of fact" on each article, charging what Clinton had done. The advantage, said Susan Collins, one of its principal sponsors, was that "it would keep the President from gloating." But this approach was tricky, too, because it called for a verdict of sorts, yet it would require only fifty-one votes, as opposed to the sixty-seven votes needed to convict. In a Republican Conference meeting on the afternoon of February 3, Fred Thompson rose to speak against it.

"We have great flexibility," Thompson told his fellow Republicans, "but we shouldn't hamper future trials by setting a floor, by saying that a future President can get away with this—lying, a cover-up. That would become part of the impeachment process. It's never been done before.

"The lack of clarity of the Founding Fathers is not all bad," Thompson told his fellow Republicans. "It gives us the flexibility to come up with what we feel is impeachable.

"It might serve a very narrow purpose now"—provide safety for some who didn't want to vote to convict Clinton—"but it won't serve as a mark on him for future generations." Besides, he argued, the Democrats would probably oppose it, so "it would be just another 'partisan' vote." (Having had his own searing experience with the White House's setting Republicans up for "partisanship," Thompson was particularly sensitive to this point.) Thompson's words to his colleagues ended the discussion of "finding of fact" as a way to condemn Clinton without voting to oust him.

At the White House, the President—and his wife—were extremely close observers of what was happening on Capitol Hill. Mrs. Clinton, not inactive behind the scenes, was vehemently opposed to anything but straight votes on whether or not the President was guilty. The President, just as he had during the Thompson hearings, called certain Democrats late at night to complain of the treatment he was receiving at the hands of the Republicans. The main recipients of his calls were Torricelli, Daschle, Christopher Dodd, of Connecticut, and Tom Harkin, of Iowa. These were the Democrats most involved publicly in defending the President.

In these calls, Torricelli told me later, Clinton made it clear that he expected loyalty from the Democrats. He had made a real commitment of his time in getting Democratic senators elected, and they owed him, he said. He also told them, this was such an outrageous, partisan action by the Republicans that he had a right to expect loyalty.

Clinton was distressed when the senators reached a unanimous agreement on how to proceed with a trial. Why were the Democrats cooperating with the Republicans? Why weren't they pointing out what a "partisan" exercise the impeachment was?

"The President felt an enormous sense of injustice," one Democratic senator said. Also, as a lawyer, Clinton believed that certain rules should apply. "He didn't realize that this was a political process," a Democratic senator told me. "That was said to him, but he never accepted it."

MEANWHILE, in the week beginning January 25, Lott still had to resolve the witness problem. The White House didn't want witnesses for the same reason the House managers wanted witnesses: Something might turn up. The mere presence of Monica Lewinsky before the Senate might embarrass the President. The President was ahead; why take a chance? And it also might embarrass the senators.

LOTT DISPATCHED emissaries—John Kyl, a former House member and a hard-liner on having a trial, and Arlen Specter, a former prosecutor, who had also been for calling witnesses—to the House managers. They delivered Lott's message: They could have only three witnesses. And thus Lott eventually solved this difficult political problem. The House managers could take depositions from three witnesses, and the time remaining for the trial would be limited. The House managers had talked of wanting fifteen or eighteen witnesses, largely for negotiating purposes. If the House managers didn't agree to the Senate Republicans' terms, Lott's emissaries told them, the Senate wouldn't vote to have witnesses at all.

Lott's was a deft solution that kept Republican senators who opposed witnesses, and allies of the House managers, who did want them, within the corral. His use of ad hoc committees, usually made up of people with disparate points of view, to resolve some of the thorniest problems was imaginative and largely successful.

Now Lott was facing another Democratic attempt to label the Republicans "partisan." On January 27, to the great relief of the White House, which had worried about where he would end up, Robert Byrd, the elder statesman from West Virginia, the self-appointed guardian of the Constitution, moved to dismiss the trial. Allies of the President had reminded Byrd that he would have to run for reelection in 2000 and would need help in raising funds. And the question of whether to call witnesses was also pending before the Senate. The result was negotiations going on all over the place—in the hallways, in senators' hideaways—on what to do.

Though it took sixty-seven votes, or two-thirds, to convict the President, the rules could be set by majority vote, which gave the Republicans, with fifty-five senators, the advantage. But the Republicans wanted to avoid party-line votes so as to escape having their actions, like the House's, deemed "partisan." One much-discussed idea was that both votes—on dismissal and on witnesses—be set aside, so the Senate could move on to the final voting on the impeachment articles.

But under the rules the Senate had adopted it took only one objection to foil any plan, and this one was foiled. Anyway, "partisan" votes would be useful to the White House. Minority Leader Tom Daschle managed to look sorrowful on television at the prospect of party-line votes.

THE IDENTICAL party-line votes on Thursday, January 28, on whether to dismiss the case (no) and whether to call witnesses for deposition (yes)—with the exception of Russell Feingold who voted with the Republicans in each instance—gave the Democrats the material they wanted for charging that the Republicans were being "partisan." (That the Democrats were also being partisan didn't deter them.)

After the votes, inevitably, the Democrats pointed out that, with forty-four Democrats voting to dismiss, there wasn't a chance that Clinton would be convicted.

Lott's emissaries to the House managers had an impact on the witness list itself. John Kyl, among others, was strongly opposed to summoning Betty Currie to appear in the well of the Senate. The gentle and loyal Currie was a sympathetic figure, and, a Republican senator said, "They didn't like the idea of white southern males beating up on a middle-aged, loyal, black woman." And there was some concern among the House managers that if Betty Currie remained loyal to the President on the stand—and there was no reason to think she wouldn't—she could, Asa Hutchinson told me, "hurt us in several elements of obstruction." So the key person on the most serious obstruction charge, "witness tampering," was eliminated from the witness list.

The House managers already knew that Vernon Jordan wouldn't be helpful, but that could hurt only the part of the obstruction of justice charge that accused Jordan of helping Lewinsky find a job in order to keep her silent about her relationship with the President. But calling Vernon Jordan, the President's close friend who was woven throughout the House's obstruction case—but not charged by Starr with anything—was a given.

James Rogan told me, "I don't think our obligation is to present anything new. Our obligation is to present the case. The question is what kind of precedent you set. The point is to have a fair trial."

As for the House managers' struggles with the Senate, Rogan said, "They keep shooting the corpse but the corpse keeps wriggling."

The desire of others to call Currie assumed, of course, that she—or anyone else close to the President—would for some reason change testimony already given numerous times. Monica Lewinsky would of course be called. To assuage the many senators, of both parties, who were horrified by the thought of Lewinsky appearing in the well of the Senate, not to mention her being asked about the sexual details of her relationship with Clinton, the House managers pledged that they wouldn't ask her about "salacious" matters.

The senators' opposition to calling Currie set the House managers off in various directions in search of a third witness. They considered calling Kathleen Willey, who had accused the President of groping her when she went to him for help in finding a job, and about whom Clinton had given some questionable testimony to the grand jury, and who had said that she'd been harrassed by strangers. It was known by then that the attorney for the big Democratic contributor Nathan Landow (whose daughter was a friend of Willey's), but who had taken the Fifth Amendment rather than testify about his possible role in trying to keep Willey quiet, had hired a private investigator for the Willey case.

So the issue about Willey was whether there was obstruction of justice in the case; whether, in fact, there was a pattern of obstruction—intimidation of potential witnesses—where Clinton's alleged sexual adventures were concerned. (In one of the more unnerving episodes, for nearly a week the White House put out all sorts of negative information and allegations about Willey after she talked about her encounter with Clinton on *60 Minutes* on March 15, 1998.) But some of the managers were stopped by the thought that calling Willey would turn the whole thing into the "sex case" the Democrats were trying to charge it was.

So, they decided on Sidney Blumenthal, a senior aide to the Clintons. The House managers' interest in Blumenthal stemmed from their belief that Clinton had told Blumenthal that Lewinsky was a "stalker" who had "come on to me," with the intent of tarnishing her in the press. Such stories did appear in the papers. They also hoped that women would be outraged by Clinton's trying to trash Lewinsky (and other women he had been involved with as well). The managers deemed Clinton's comments to Blumenthal "obstruction of justice." But the idea, which had started with Starr, that Clinton had lied to his aides in order to get them to repeat the lies to the grand jury was a stretch. Clinton lied to everyone.

IT WAS MORE in Lott's interest to reach a bipartisan agreement than it was in Daschle's, but Lott, after days of negotiations, couldn't get bipartisan agreement. After it was resolved in the Senate that three witnesses would be deposed by the House managers, there remained the issue of whether the depositions of the witnesses could be videotaped. The Democrats strongly opposed videotaping, knowing that videotapes have a way of turning up in public. So the Republicans had to put their own proposal before the Senate. There would be videotaping, but whether the videotapes would be shown in the Senate was left for later.

An unhappy Hyde remarked of the Senate Republicans' limitations on witnesses, "I'm glad those people weren't at Valley Forge or the Alamo." He and the other House managers had long since begun to look like whiners, but this remark by Hyde breached the tense protocol between the House and the Senate.

Such was the whining by the House managers that Senator Edward M. Kennedy was moved to remark to reporters, "We took an oath to preserve and protect the Constitution, not the House managers."

A NUMBER OF Republican senators were motivated by Clinton's looking too celebratory when the Paula Jones case was dismissed while he was traveling in Africa. (He was seen through a window, a big cigar in his mouth, jubilantly banging on bongo drums.) His holding a little rally in the Rose Garden, surrounded by House Democrats, just after the House voted to impeach him, had gone down badly, and not just with Republicans. The Senate Republicans didn't want Clinton to gloat if they voted not to remove him from office. To some extent this was a genuine feeling; but it was also being used by anti-Clinton people to wring the strongest condemnation of Clinton possible out of the Senate. Like the House Republicans, the Senate Republicans were letting their personal feelings, or Clinton's attitude, affect decisions on the most solemn, constitutionally sensitive, question that could come before them.

FRED THOMPSON, no pal of Lott's, served on three of his task forces to try to work out problems. Thompson's history as a trial lawyer and his moderate mind were of value to Lott at this point. Thompson took part in the negotiations on what to do about witnesses.

"We're trying to get out of Dodge City on the one hand, and not give the House the brush-off on the other," he told me at the time.

And, once again, as in the case of his hearings on campaign financing, Fred Thompson found himself up against New Jersey Democrat Bob Torricelli, who now was forcefully and frequently arguing on television that what the Senate was doing was illegitimate.

Thompson was trying to establish some legitimacy to the Senate trial. "We have to consider how history will look at it," he said. "It's not a matter of holding the line to hold the line. A lot of people want to avoid the Andrew Johnson thing, that this is a bunch of radical Republicans that got out of hand. That's where we stand now. The people up here have to avoid going down in history as radical Republicans, but we also shouldn't go down as saps." Thompson was aware that the Clinton scandals, writ large—even beyond the Lewinsky scandal—had a number of loose ends remaining. Something could happen that mocked those who had wanted to dispose of the trial and let Clinton off quickly.

The Republicans' inclusion in their resolution of videotaping the depositions was a clear signal that there wouldn't be what were constantly referred to as "live" witnesses. The resolution provided that senators could view the videotapes privately. Even Republican senators didn't buy the House managers' arguments that it was crucial to behold the witnesses' demeanor, see "the look in their eyes." (Not many senators would be able to do this in the large Senate Chamber.) And Lott gave Daschle a veto on calling any further witnesses—which meant there wouldn't be any more—and set February 12, just before the Presidents Day recess, as the end-date for the Senate trial. Lott seemed to have finally gotten the thing under control.

The essentially party-line votes on January 28, on which the Republicans prevailed on whether witnesses could be called, and on motions by Daschle to prohibit the videotaping of their depositions, and to move immediately to votes on the articles themselves, gave the White House an opportunity, as one lobbyist close to it said, to "dial up" the rhetoric on "partisanship." The Democrats lost the votes—but the White House achieved its real goal.

Naturally, the Democrats charged that the Republicans were being "partisan," and that the Senate votes showed that the sixty-seven votes to convict weren't there, and that the Republicans were "dragging things out."

Clinton aides instinctively returned to their "war room" tactics, first developed in the 1992 campaign. White House press secretary Joe Lockhart said, "The fact that the Senate continues to be diverted from its business is the responsibility of the Republican majority."

But what the White House spokesmen or Democratic senators were saying was only a part of the exercise of trying to make these charges take hold in the country. The White House faxes out "talking points" to the allied lobbyists and political advisors around town who are likely to get a call from a reporter. (There were also regular strategy meetings at the White House of former aides and other close advisors.) For the impeachment crisis, there was a daily conference call at 11 A.M. of key White House aides and the political advisors around town. The word went out less formally to Democratic officeholders and party activists around the country.

A well-connected Democratic lobbyist in Washington explained to me: "Public officials, state party chairmen, and party activists around the country follow what they hear from Washington. They hear it's okay to piss in Republicans' boots. That's what Democrats do." (The Republicans have a similar, if not more sophisticated, message system.)

THE FINAL STAGES of the Senate drama had the feeling of inevitability. Most of the senators knew by then how they were going to vote. They had heard the arguments and also public opinion. The prevailing view among Republicans was that it should be got over with.

"We've already dug ourselves six feet down," a Republican senator said to me. "No point in going any further." He added, "The House guys won't give up."

About ten Republicans were believed to be uncertain on at least one of the articles, but the Democrats who had been considered possible bolters—Byrd, Dianne Feinstein, of California, Daniel Patrick Moynihan—appeared to be in place. But though most senators had known all along how they were going to vote, the trial did have an effect on the thinking of many of them. "The Democrats have learned more about the facts, the Republicans have learned more about the law," a Republican senator said. The facts were more serious than many Democrats had thought; a number of Republicans focused more closely on what it would mean to convict the President, and on whether the constitutional standards had been met. Some Republicans studied the Federalist Papers, in which the Founding Fathers discussed the standards for impeachment and conviction. Senators, being very busy people, hadn't really focused on these things before the Articles of Impeachment reached the Senate—which they hadn't figured on happening.

Inevitably the taped depositions were shown to the Senate, but they, too, made little difference. Monica, the practiced child-woman, stayed with her—and, largely, the President's—story. A few of the things the witnesses said seemed somewhat improbable. For example, Lewinsky's insistence in her testimony that, when the President called her at 2:30 A.M. to talk about the fact that she was going to be named a witness and suggested that she file an affidavit so that she wouldn't have to appear, he hadn't tried to affect what she said in her affidavit, wasn't convincing.

But the witnesses had their stories and they were sticking to them; Kenneth Starr hadn't been able to shake them, and the House managers who questioned them for the Senate trial got no further. There was a certain amount of Republican dismay at Edward Bryant, of Tennessee, for his hapless questioning of Lewinsky—"I wnat to refer you to the first so-called salacious occasion"—but Lewinsky, no dope, and heavily coached by her attorneys, wasn't going to give out any more information than she absolutely had to. The calling of witnesses proved as useless as most people thought it would be.

The denouement in the Senate was governed by the fact that everyone knew that the President wouldn't be convicted of the charges and removed from office. For some senators, this provided a "free vote"—they could vote to convict the President without assuming responsibility for the consequences. "Free votes" (of the sort that used to be cast routinely for campaign finance bills that people knew wouldn't pass) provide a haven for hypocrisy. It seemed that Article I, covering perjury, wouldn't even win a majority vote. At the same time, some Republicans were pressing for a majority, at least fifty-one votes, on Article II, obstruction of justice, so that the House managers would feel better, their efforts redeemed. This was perhaps the worst rationale for voting to convict a president that had ever been put forward. Besides, the House managers had been indulged for almost five weeks.

"Free vote" or no, a vote to convict a president is a serious, historic matter; it shouldn't be too much to ask that senators cast such a vote out of firm belief. But the habit of positioning, of playing it cute, was now so deeply ingrained in the politicians that some of them couldn't even shake it when it came to probably the most historic vote they would ever cast.

In meetings of the Republican Conference, Lott, the former cheerleader, would say things like "We should all stick together," but, according to several accounts, Lott didn't put pressure on his Republican colleagues to vote to uphold the House. Even the partisan Lott understood that pressuring colleagues on such a grave constitutional matter was inappropriate. But this wasn't true of others.

On Wednesday, February 10, the senators, in closed session (according to antiquated Senate rules on trials), began to make their final, fifteen-minute statements. By Thursday, February 11, the day before the final voting was to take place, it wasn't at all certain that there would be a majority for either charge. By then, four moderate Republicans had announced that they would vote against both articles: James Jeffords, of Vermont; John Chafee, of Rhode Island; Olympia Snowe, of Maine; and Arlen Specter, of Pennsylvania. (Specter, who likes to stand apart, offered the "Scottish verdict" of "not proven.") That left Susan Collins, who was known to be troubled about the obstruction-of-justice evidence. If she voted in favor of Article II, there would be a majority for it; if she voted against, there would be a tie.

On Thursday, Collins was pressured, on the Senate floor, by five Republican senators to cast the fifty-first vote for Article II. Collins would not name those who pressured her (in a closed session), but I learned that one of them was Rick Santorum. She was told that there should be a majority on at least one of the articles. She was told that if there wasn't, it would amount to a repudiation of the House managers. Collins even went to Lott to complain about the pressure she was receiving, and Lott said that he was not treating the votes on the articles as tests of party loyalty, that he wouldn't even order a whip count of who would vote how, as is ordinarily done.

Collins had decided sometime before that though the President lied under oath, he didn't commit perjury. On the obstruction question, she consulted with a friend at the Harvard Law School; she did a lot of reading. And she made up her mind on Tuesday night. She was convinced by the evidence that Clinton did obstruct justice, but not convinced that the offense was sufficiently serious that the President should be removed from office. She felt that it wasn't an offense against the state, which a number of people argued was the criterion the Founders had in mind for removing a president from office. In this view, impeachment and removal were remedies intended to protect the people from a president, not to punish him. If the President had used the FBI to cover up his activities (as Nixon had), in Collins's mind that would be a different matter.

Collins spent a sleepless night Tuesday night, getting up and writing and rewriting drafts of her statement. And on Wednesday, when she told those pressuring her that her vote wasn't "in play," they finally left her alone. The group of five Republican moderates who now said they would oppose both articles illustrated what a small bloc the Senate moderates were now reduced to. And all were from the Northeast—mainly New England—which used to dominate the Republican Party.

JUST BEFORE THE final voting on Friday, Lott introduced a resolution that the Independent Counsel should investigate whether there was, in fact, a telephone-taping system within the White House. A number of observers thought that Lott was on some sort of attention-getting lark, but in fact there was real seriousness behind his move. What one senator described to me as "a credible source," a government employee, had told a senator that there was such a system, possibly for calls related to national security, and then the matter was discussed among other senators. The fact of Clinton's supreme recklessness in talking to Monica Lewinsky—including "phone sex"—on unsecure telephone lines was paid little attention throughout the whole uproar over his acts.

But to some people—including former Senator Sam Nunn, who had headed the Armed Services Committee, and who talked about it on CNN in late January, it was a highly serious matter.

Nunn said that "For people to say that the President of the United States having—allegedly—telephone sex is strictly private, and has nothing to do with official duties, means they've never been acquainted with the world of espionage and the world of blackmail." Nunn also asked, "What if a foreign agent heard a young woman carrying on discussions, and then tapped her telephone?"

In his speech just before he cast his votes, Republican Senator Richard Lugar, of Indiana and a respected figure on foreign policy issues, said, "Even in this post–Cold War era, foreign intelligence agents constantly look for opportunities for deception, propaganda, and blackmail. No higher targets exist than the President and the White House. The President even acknowledged in a phone call with Ms. Lewinsky that foreign agents could be monitoring their conversations....With premeditation, he chose his own gratification above the security of his country and the success of his presidency."

Fred Thompson reflected on the "supreme irony" that this story—like the Ervin hearings, where he brought out the existence of the Nixon White House tapes, through his questioning of Alexander Butterfield—could also end up involving tapes.

DESPITE THE inevitability of the result, the final voting on whether the President should be convicted on either article was dramatic.

Nothing like it had happened in more than a hundred years. The senators took their role seriously, standing as their names were called and saying "guilty" or "not guilty."

The fact that ten Republican senators, Fred Thompson among them, voted against Article I, the perjury article, showed the weakness of the House managers' case. Thompson was one of five Republicans who split their votes on the two articles. (The others were John Warner, of Virginia, Ted Stevens, of Alaska, Slade Gorton, of Washington, and Richard Shelby, of Alabama.) Thompson had prepared a fifty-one-page brief outlining his views. (A Democratic operative was impressed that Thompson, who might have national ambitions, would go against the party base on either article.) The vote on Article I was 45–55, and on Article II it was 50–50. Despite his possibly shaky position in Pennsylvania, Santorum voted for both articles. So did Lott, who as a member of the House Judiciary Committee in 1974 had voted against impeaching Nixon for far more serious offenses.

No Democrat broke ranks. Moynihan, who had been considered an uncertain vote at first, impressed several of his colleagues with the argument, which he first made in December 1998, that in removing the President from office, "you could very readily destabilize the presidency." Moynihan repeated the stability theme in his statement in the Senate before the voting: "Impeachment is a power singularly lacking any of the checks and balances on which the Framers depended. It is solely a power of the Congress. Do not doubt that it could bring radical instability to American government."

Republicans charged that the Democrats were being "partisan," but no Democrat thought that Clinton should be removed from office. The Democrats were also put off by the House managers' excesses. "They made a big mistake," a Democratic senator told me, "in charging that the President had committed crimes, and resting their case on that. That meant that they had to prove him guilty of the crime 'beyond a reasonable doubt'—and they couldn't do that." The arguments of a few law professors on cable television notwithstanding, the prevailing, and only sensible, view was that impeachment didn't have to be based on a crime, nor would any old crime require impeachment.

And despite the seeming effectiveness of their opening arguments to the Senate, the House managers had done a sloppy job of
preparation, which was based in turn on inadequate work in the
House. As Nicole Seligman, one of the President's private attorneys, put it in her argument to the Senate in support of the motion
to dismiss, "The House had a constitutional duty to gather and
assess evidence and testimony and come to a judgment as to
whether it believed the President should be removed from office—
not to casually and passively serve as a conveyor belt between Ken
Starr and the U.S. Senate, not to ask this body to do the work the
House failed to do."

After the votes on the articles, a tough resolution to censure
the President which had been drafted by Dianne Feinstein, and
Robert Bennett, Republican of Utah, and had thirty-eight sponsors, was blocked by the highly partisan Phil Gramm, of Texas. A
test of the issue, which required the assent of two-thirds of the
Senate, received only fifty-six votes. (Some senators treated this as
a "free vote" as well.) Like their House counterparts, the Senate
Republicans weren't eager to let Democrats, through voting for a
censure resolution, slide off the hook of having supported Clinton
on the votes to convict.

IT ALSO ENDED on an ominous note. The impeachment and removal
of Clinton had already become the glorious cause for the Republican right. And as Peter King had revealed to me, it had begun by
being as much about building the base of the party as it was about
getting rid of Clinton. But the venomous feelings about Clinton
had grown and deepened.

Rather than just accept that they had lost, the House managers
continued to complain that they hadn't been given a fair chance,
with a full trial. The day after the final Senate voting, Lindsey
Graham said in a television interview, "I think, looking back in history, it's going to be looked at as a trial that was truncated, that we
were trying to meet a political deadline that was more artificial, I
think, than real."

In his closing statement before the Senate, Hyde revealed the
depth of his feelings, showing that for him the issue of impeaching
and convicting Clinton was every bit as important a cultural matter

as abortion was. After floridly citing the words of Henry V before the Battle of Agincourt, Hyde said, "I wonder if, after this culture war is over, this one we are engaged in, an America will survive that is worth fighting for to defend."

So, with Hyde at the forefront, the Republican right, even though—in fact, because—they had lost, established a new martyrdom, and a new cause.

15

——•——

Reason for Hope?

The cumulative impact of the downward spiral of our politics over the past twenty-five years was enough to cause widespread despair on the part of the public. We saw the inability, or unwillingness, of the politicians to deal with our broken, corrupt campaign finance system—our most serious problem—and the brutal, and ultimately successful, attempts to stymie those who tried, whether it was Fred Thompson with his hearings on the finance scandals of the 1996 election, or the majorities for reform legislation in the Senate and the House. We saw the hypocrisy on the subject on the part of many of the politicians, including the President. We saw the series of nasty partisan fights over nominations; the retaliatory, almost predatory, instincts of the politicians; the clear evidence of the decline in the quality of the politicians and the rise in their pettiness; and then the Götterdämmerung of the impeachment and trial of President Clinton, in which an unworthy man overmatched zealous foes who showed no sense of boundaries or proportion. Clinton prevailed, but with his stature greatly diminished. He was simply the guy who got by.

Any credibility Clinton might have had remaining to him was now completely shattered. The damage was particularly serious when it came to foreign policy. His commencing the bombing of

Iraq the day before his impeachment was to be taken up on the House floor raised questions as to whether this was coincidental. Trent Lott said, "I cannot support this military action....Both the timing and the policy are subject to question." This was a most unusual thing for a congressional leader to say.

In retrospect, Clinton's ordering, three days after he testified before the grand jury in August, the bombing of targets in Afghanistan and the Sudan looked more and more dubious. (They also led one administration official to remark privately that the President's foreign policy consisted of "policy by raid." This was before the bombing of Yugoslavia began in late March.) The sad reality that now the President couldn't be trusted at all presented a dangerous situation for the country.

THE IMPEACHMENT and trial of President Clinton provided clear evidence of the political corrosion of Washington in the twenty-five years since Watergate and the eviction of Richard Nixon from the presidency, which was deemed, at the time, to have cleansed our political system.

It was unrealistic to think of Clinton's impeachment and trial as having cleansed our system. Too much bitterness remained among the Republicans on the right and their allies who had sought the President's impeachment and removal—and among the President and his associates, who had strong, virtually automatic, retaliatory instincts. Whatever his outward demeanor, Clinton had spent most of the impeachment and trial in a rage, and he was a master of resentment.

Despite the much-discussed "bonding" that was said to have taken place among senators of both parties, who had spent twenty-four days together on the Senate floor—some senators did start to slip out after a while—it was not to be long before political realities swept such romantic notions aside.

Shortly after the final voting on Friday, February 12, Trent Lott, meeting with reporters, let loose his bitterness over the President's victory. "I fear this saga is not over," Lott said. He made it clear that he could no longer trust Clinton on any subject, and threatened to exclude administration officials from future budget negotiations.

Edward M. Kennedy said, "The Radical Republicans at the end of the twentieth century will be condemned even more severely by history for their partisan vendetta."

Other instances showed that partisan bitterness, even in the Senate, which had behaved better than the House, ran deep. Only six senators showed up at a "reconciliation" gathering on February 25, called by Joseph Lieberman, the Democrat from Connecticut, and Sam Brownback, the Republican from Kansas.

Though Clinton had a new opportunity to get things done— the big ones, like preserving Social Security and Medicare—typically, he proposed easy courses, using some of the budget "surplus" to meet the rising costs, especially with the advent of the "baby boomer" generation, rather than undertake a more politically difficult restructuring. And there was a strong sense among some of the President's advisors—one perhaps shared by the President himself—that it was more advantageous politically to not achieve these things, so that the Republican Congress could be blamed for inaction and Clinton's passionate desire to see Gore and a Democratic House elected in 2000 could be fulfilled.

AND NOT LONG after the impeachment and trial, the President found himself embroiled in yet another scandal involving China—this one set off by a *New York Times* report on March 6, which said that China had stolen nuclear secrets from a government weapons lab in Los Alamos, New Mexico, and as a result was able to advance its nuclear technology by a substantial leap. Though the theft was believed to have occurred in the mid-1980s during Republican presidencies, the report said, it wasn't detected until 1995 and the Clinton White House wasn't notified until April 1996. But the White House apparently did nothing about this until 1997 and Congress wasn't told about it until 1998, when it was conducting its own inquiry into the transfer of satellite technology.

China was Clinton's Circe. The lure of political "engagement" (for which candidate Clinton had criticized President Bush), of more trade with China, and thus more business for American corporations—and of campaign funds, whatever the source—caused smash-ups that were, at a minimum, embarrassing. What made them more suspect was that they all occurred in the same period of time from 1995 to 1996: The FBI briefing of National Security Council staff members about possible Chinese involvement in our elections (information that supposedly wasn't passed up the line), making it easier to transfer sensitive technology, such as satellites, to the Chinese, and the seemingly laid-back reaction by the Clinton White House to its learning about the theft of nuclear secrets.

And at that same time, the administration was intent on improving its relationship with China. Clinton's trip to China in 1998, despite his expressed optimism, if not naiveté, yielded nothing in the area of human rights. The nuclear nonproliferation and nuclear test–ban agreements China had signed were now suspect. Taiwan was under new threat from the mainland.

Though others asserted one, Fred Thompson told me after the nuclear-secrets scandal broke that he didn't think there was a direct connection between the fund-raising that could be traced back to Chinese sources and the administration's handling of the spy scandal. But he did see a pattern: "The connection I see is the way the Clinton Administration handles all these things in relation to China: putting the best interpretation on these activities, seemingly inept investigations, and a lack of candor with the Congress.

"Whether you're talking about campaign finance, whether you're talking about missile transfers, whether you're talking about espionage," Thompson said, "it all has a familiar ring.

"You can weave any web you want—it depends on what your standard of proof is—but if you use common sense, there's a pattern." The pattern, he said was of coverup, of determination not to disturb the new policy of "engagement" with China, of resisting attempts by the Congress to find out what was going on.

THE SEX SCANDAL left a great deal of damage. In the end, Clinton left a stain not only on a blue Gap dress but on the Oval Office itself. People thought about it in a new way. Whatever his aides' denials and side steps, Clinton planned to go all out to defeat any vulnerable House managers (there were few), and was determined to return the House to Democratic hands. (Labor made a two-year commitment toward that effort, with plans to repeat its 1996 and 1998 efforts, which featured "issue ads," as well as turnout drives.) And groups on the right were determined to punish Republicans who voted against the Articles of Impeachment, and also go after some Democrats who voted against them. Their expectation was that some of the "loose ends" still lying about would give them new ammunition.

In fact, just as conservatives reveled in the revelation of Juanita Broaddrick's claim that Clinton had raped her twenty years before, Democrats on Capitol Hill were shaken, and wondered aloud whether "this will ever end." They had a sinking feeling that it would not—not so long as Clinton was president. And now even some of those on Capitol Hill who had been his strongest defenders throughout the impeachment and trial didn't come to his defense. No one—not a Cabinet officer or even a White House aide—said flat-out that they believed him. Clinton had made believing him impossible and defending him an embarrassment. (In April, the judge in the Paula Jones case cited Clinton for contempt for giving "false, misleading, and evasive answers that were designed to obstruct process.")

So the bitterness engendered by the impeachment and trial of Clinton wasn't likely to disappear soon. Notwithstanding some clucking in the press and elsewhere about "retaliation," revenge was the natural order of things. Our political dialog became coarser as a result of the sex scandal, as did the nature of a wide swath of the media coverage, bent as it has been increasingly toward entertainment and *faux* combat. And the forces opposed to reforming the corrupt system of financing our elections remained in place.

AMERICAN POLITICS goes in cycles: cycles of hope and despair, optimism and pessimism, anger and contentment. The Clinton presidency has been an almost disorienting series of highs and lows. But the momentary status of a given presidency or of the economy—however key to the national mood of the moment—does not displace the endemic problems in the political system.

The 1998 election saw an acceleration of what's gone wrong in the way our elections are bought and paid for. More than twice as much soft money—over $162 million more—was raised by the two political parties in the 1998 election as in the previous nonpresidential elections, according to figures reported to the Federal Election Commission and compiled by Common Cause. As usual, the Republicans outraised the Democrats in soft money, $96.1 million to $66.2 million. The amounts, of course, don't include the in-kind contributions by the interest groups on both sides.

The most generous contributors of soft money in the 1997–1998 election cycle were several labor unions; tobacco (Philip Morris) and communications companies. As for individuals, the biggest donors over the years, through themselves or through their Amway Corporation, were longtime Republican contributors Mr. and Mrs. Richard DeVos, who donated a million dollars to the

Republicans. The runner-up in individual contributions was Bernard Schwartz, chairman of the Loral Corporation, who, as we saw earlier, was already Clinton's biggest contributor and who in February 1998, received a controversial waiver to use Chinese rockets to launch his company's satellites; Schwartz contributed $871,000 to the Democrats for the 1998 election.

According to *Broadcasting and Cable* magazine, more money was spent on television ads in the 1998 election than in the 1996 *presidential* election. The amount, $531.9 million, "shatters the previous record set in 1996, when total political TV spending totaled $405 million," the magazine reported. (These amounts didn't include the fees that go to the people who make the ads.) In the last midterm election, the magazine said, "a then-record $356 million" was spent on ads. It's no wonder that the broadcast industry opposes free air time for campaign ads.

The 1998 election produced another onslaught of "issue ads"— most of them attack ads—by the parties, with the Republicans spending far more on them, and by outside groups.

In a switch of strategy from 1996, labor spent far less on ads in 1998 than it had then, this time concentrating on turnout. But despite the efforts on both sides to get their allies to the polls, what actually happened was that the Democrats' *decline* in turnout from 1994, when it was quite low because of Democratic anger at Clinton, was smaller than that of the Republicans. Overall turnout was an abysmal thirty-six percent—lower than for any midterm elections since 1942.

Because of labor's change in strategy in 1998, less money was spent by candidates to combat their ads—and by other candidates to combat corporate ads—and overall spending by congressional candidates dropped slightly from 1996. But, taken together, spending by candidates and the parties and "independent" groups is believed to have amounted—for the first time—to over one billion dollars.

And more House candidates than ever—one out of every six— spent more than one million dollars on their races. According to a study by Common Cause, seventy-eight percent of those who spent at least that amount won. But what matters is not the amount spent, but what candidates had to do to raise it—in terms of spending time soliciting donors as well as giving special attention to donors—and perhaps returning their favors.

On February 17, 1999, Senator Frank Lautenberg, Democrat of New Jersey, stepped before reporters gathered in his Newark office and announced that he wouldn't run for a fourth term. He said, "A powerful factor in my decision was the searing reality that I would have to spend half of every day between now and the next election fund-raising...I would have to ask literally thousands of people for money. I would have had to raise $125,000 a week, or $25,000 every working day. That's about $3,000 an hour."

Nevertheless, such are the benefits of incumbency that ninety-eight percent of House incumbents who sought re-election, and ninety percent of Senate incumbents, were re-elected in 1998. House incumbents enjoyed a nearly five-to-one advantage over their challengers in overall contributions, and nearly a ten-to-one advantage in PAC money. Senate incumbents raised more than twice what their competitors did, and enjoyed a nearly nine-to-one advantage in PAC money.

After new House Speaker Dennis Hastert took office in early 1999, he offered industry lobbyists audiences—in exchange for contributions to his own PAC. In another innovation, in March of 1999 Tom DeLay instructed his sixty-five deputy whips to raise money for endangered Republicans, including two who had been managers of the Senate trial of the President. And, despite the misgivings of some on the right who now questioned whether it was feasible to pursue their moral and cultural goals through politics, the Republican Party was working to make the impeachment and trial of Clinton a fund-raising tool, even as it tried to reposition itself away from being the party of impeachment.

If the political status quo is to be changed, the advantages of incumbency have to be reduced. This was the purpose of some of the McCain-Feingold bill's provisions that were dropped even before the bill reached the Senate floor: providing free or reduced-cost airtime for candidates who voluntarily limit their spending, and placing limits on overall PAC receipts.

And in a new departure, candidates for the presidential nomination in 2000 have found still another way to evade the limits on contributions to their races ($1,000 for individuals and $5,000 for PACs) by setting up their own PACs and "nonprofit organizations" for which they themselves raised soft money—otherwise banned direct contributions by corporations and labor and unlimited contributions by individuals. These new committees were established in states with lenient laws on soft money. Before, soft money was raised only by the parties. Under the new ploy, the soft money could go directly to the candidates, and could be used for bogus "issue ads."*

So now the laws governing *contributions* to candidates for the presidential nomination, like those covering contributions to the eventual nominees, have been rendered meaningless. On top of that, some presidential candidates considered forgoing the federal funds so as to be free of the *spending* limits that accompany the receipt of federal funds. That would free the candidates to spend an unlimited amount of hard money—needed to pay for the direct costs of campaigning in addition to a portion of the television ads. If this were done, if a major-party frontrunner decided to go that route, shucking off all limits, that would complete the cycle of going back to the Watergate days, and before—when there were no limits at all.

THE FEDERAL ELECTION COMMISSION once again proved its fecklessness when December 10, 1998, it rejected unanimously the report of its auditors which said that the Clinton and Dole campaigns had improperly benefited from "issue ads" paid for by their political parties, largely in soft money. They also rejected the auditors' recommendation that the campaigns repay the government millions of dollars. The six commissioners made this major decision after viewing only one such ad, one of the mildest ones, on behalf of Clinton in 1995. (The fewer ads they looked at, the easier it was to reach to the conclusion they wanted to come to.)

Fred Thompson and Common Cause had been arguing for some time that such ads undermined the federal election laws by effectively allowing the presidential candidates to accept public funding, signing an agreement not to raise any more funds for their campaigns, and then to benefit directly from ads paid for by soft money that they helped raise. (And in Clinton's case helping to design the ads).

If the FEC wouldn't act on this ruinous circumvention of the law, that left Attorney General Reno. But, within days of the FEC's action Reno announced that she wouldn't appoint an Independent Counsel to investigate possible violations by the Clinton campaign and the Democratic National Committee.

*Lamar Alexander and Steve Forbes began doing this as early as 1998.

Thompson was sufficiently worried about the collapse of the campaign finance laws that as the new Congress got underway in 1999 he was planning to introduce legislation to reestablish the principle that candidates couldn't take public funds and then raise unlimited soft money contributions. "We should say," he told me, "'Hey, we didn't intend this.'"

Another way of salvaging the presidential system would, of course, be for the Congress to pass a law abolishing soft money—a proposal that majorities in both chambers approved in 1998 as part of the reform bills that were ultimately blocked. (The McCain-Feingold and Shays-Meehan bills were reintroduced in mid-January 1999. House Democrats were readying another discharge petition to force action in the House on a reluctant leadership.)

DESPITE THE ADVERSE trends in our political system, overall, there are in fact grounds for hope, and actions that people can take to improve it.

The history of great reforms—be they women's suffrage, civil rights legislation, the minimum wage, the lobbying laws—is that they take a long time, and require stamina. The late Arthur Vanderbilt, dean of New York University Law School and Chief Justice of the Supreme Court of New Jersey, said, "Judicial reform is no sport for the short-winded."

Reform of our campaign finance system to get at the worst, most corrosive problem in our political system isn't a lost cause. The argument that "people don't care" doesn't stand up to scrutiny; it's a convenient ruse used by opponents of reform. Public support for campaign money reform has been growing. Again and again, polls show that when people are asked about it directly, they are strongly in favor of it, even if they do not list it as one of their top priorities. In a survey conducted in August 1998, voters in eight states were asked if they preferred major changes, minor changes, or no changes in the campaign finance system. In all eight states—including New York, North Carolina, Ohio, and even Mississippi (home of Trent Lott)—pluralities called for changes. Majorities did so in New Hampshire and Indiana.

When the public is given a chance to focus on campaign finance reform, to react to it per se, they react in its favor. They did this toward the close of the 1996 elections when the Clinton fundraising scandals broke, and also when, after the House Republican leaders arrogantly played a bone-headed trick on reformers, the spotlight was turned on the discharge petition, which worked, confounding the Republican leadership.

Majorities in the Senate and the House voted for significant reform in 1998. Had the leaders of each chamber not resorted to parliamentary tricks, a new law might well have resulted. We can never know, short of applying lie-detector tests (which are faulty, of course), how many people voted for campaign reform in the House because they considered it a "free vote": They knew there wouldn't be time for a bill make its way through the congressional maze, so they could vote for reform without having to worry about being forced to rearrange their ways of raising money and staying in power.

But by 1998, even if members of the House and Senate thought that their votes actually might lead to passage of a new campaign finance law, it's doubtful that they would have voted differently. There are fewer places to hide. There's more public interest than ever in reforming the campaign system; the monitoring groups are more sophisticated; more editorial pages than before are engaged. The hypocrisy-detectors are more sensitive. If there were secret ballots in the Congress, that might be a different story. But there aren't.

So what can be done?

One of the strongest motivations for politicians is embarrassment. The more attention paid to their corrupt or even questionable transactions—the more exposure that there is of them—the more pressed they are likely to feel to change the rules. Even apparent linkage between contributions and votes (or deliberate inactivity) is enough to cause trouble for a politician.

Fear can also have a galvanizing effect on politicians. Several who went through the 1996 election found themselves losing control of their own campaigns, and emerged with changed minds about reform. Some had a similar experience in 1998. Glenn Ivey, the shrewd Democratic strategist, thinks that once the politicians have gone through three election cycles—thus affecting the entire Senate—their interest in reform will increase dramatically.

Another powerful motivator is public opinion. The strong positive response with which people respond to the specific question of reform needs to be better understood by policy makers and citizens alike.

The movement in the states for public financing of state elections, led by public campaign, is valuable in itself, but it also gets reflected back in Washington. The people who represent states that have adopted such reform take that into account. And the idea is spreading. In 1998, voters in Massachusetts and Arizona, the two places where reform was on the ballot, approved referendums calling for the adoption of such a system. (Maine and Vermont already had adopted a public financing system.)

There needs to be more education, of politicians, journalists, and interested citizens, on the bogus arguments that some of the reforms under consideration—such as curbs on phony "issue ads," or abolition of soft money—would violate the First Amendment's protection of free speech. These arguments rest on false if convenient interpretations of the *Buckley* decision. Perhaps more Senators, taking a leaf from the House, can be motivated to do more homework and to show more courage in responding to this argument. It isn't all that hard, as some House members showed in the 1998 debate.

As for specific reforms, abolition of or caps on soft money, and curbing fraudulent "issue ads" remain high priorities. (An "issue-ad" provision should be drafted in such a way as to get maximum bipartisan support and so that it can be clearly explained.) A strong argument can be made for public financing of congressional campaigns—along the lines of the original voluntary presidential system before the soft money destroyed it—and more people should be making the case. That's the only way to get it on the agenda over time.

Reformers should overcome their resistance to raising the limit on individual contributions, set at $1,000 in 1974, to at least partially index it to take into account inflation since then. (Today's equivalent of $1,000 would be $3,000.) This is not only reasonable—it would represent no change in real dollars, and it would reduce the amount of time that candidates have to spend raising money—but it might also be useful in trying to reach an overall compromise.

The nexus between campaign finance reform and issues the public says it cares more about should be made clearer. There's an obvious case to be made that the current finance system works against many of these things, and it can also be shown more clearly and dramatically that the current system is quite costly to the individual citizen. The relative power of money in congressional decisions can lead to policy that rewards contributors at the expense of everyone else: certain tax cuts, unwarranted subsidies, special holes in the regulatory system. Among the things that can get squeezed out are money for education and improvements in medical care. This, too, shouldn't be a hard argument to make.

A lot of people who aren't intrinsically opposed to campaign reform—who have nothing to lose from it—brush it off on the grounds, drummed into them by anti-reformers, `that no reform exists for long. The 1974 reforms lasted through at least two Presidential elections. Reformers should make clear that they do not think any particular set of changes will create a perfect world, or will last forever.

Inevitably, the political operatives will figure out new ways around at least some them. Reformers need to show that they understand that reform has to be seen as a continuous process, constantly watched for what new development needs fixing—and it can be presented that way. This is done in all sorts of other areas, especially in regulatory fields (such as communications, drugs); tax policy is always undergoing change. So, why not in this area as well?

Obviously, the beneficiaries of a broken system will be resistant to fixing that system. The proprietors of the system have their hands on its gears. The only people who can force them to let go are the citizens. In 1998, they went farther toward achieving that than almost anyone had thought possible.

As FOR THE BROADER, and well-founded, complaints about the political system, as well as campaign finance reform, citizens can have a greater impact on the politicians and government policies than they realize. Politicians are a responsive lot. They do keep their ear to the ground—or to the e-mails, faxes, and phone calls their offices receive on a given issue. They do this even when they know that they are hearing only from the most intensely interested citizens. In a panel discussion in early 1998 about campaign finance reform, two Senators said that there were "few" subjects a year on which they received two hundred to five hundred calls. One of the Senators, Joseph Lieberman, said, "Three hundred calls—that's a lot of calls."

The politicians listen to what is said at town meetings, and they talk about it with their colleagues when they return to Washington. They know in that case, too, that they're hearing from their most intense constituents, but they also are aware that these citizens are the opinion-spreaders, the village communicators, so they pay attention.

To fail to vote out of disgust is to waste an opportunity. Morally, one forfeits one's right to complain.

If people are unhappy with the quality or political bent of their congressman, or feel that the parties' nominees don't really represent their district or state, but simply an organized faction, the answer is to mobilize behind an alternative, get out there and vote and persuade others to vote. This can offset the power of any organized group behind the "unrepresentative" candidate. Primaries for congressional office are notable for low turnout, and candidates can get on the final ballot by default. The next step, of course, is to vote in the final election and mobilize others to do so. Many of these races are turnout fights, and such efforts can determine the outcome.

To dismiss Washington as "irrelevant"—and therefore unworthy of one's attention or efforts—is to overlook the fact that that's where law and policy are made on taxes, medical care, the quality of our air and water, Social Security, the national defense, foreign involvements, the safety of airplanes, abortion, securities regulations, the release of new drugs, gun control, the soundness of our banks, disaster relief, continuing education and training, to name just some. And it's where the state of our schools, housing, transportation, and the overall economy are heavily affected. It's where our national priorities and the tone of our national discourse are set.

Only if the citizens hold their government to account, demand that their politicians meet a higher standard, and that they fix the most fundamental problem in our political system today, might Americans have a government they can feel better about.

INDEX